BUILDING BLOCKS
in Life Science

FROM GENES & GENESIS
TO SCIENCE & SCRIPTURE

GARY PARKER

First printing: April 2011
Second printing: August 2017

Master Books®, P.O. Box 726, Green Forest, AR 72638

Master Books® is a division of the New Leaf Publishing Group, Inc.

ISBN: 978-0-89051-589-1
ISBN: 978-1-61458-545-9 (digital)
Library of Congress Number: 2010943139

Cover by Diana Bogardus

Unless otherwise noted, Scripture quotations are from the New King James Version of the Bible.

Please consider requesting that a copy of this volume be purchased by your local library system.

Printed in the United States of America

Please visit our website for other great titles:
www.masterbooks.com

For information regarding author interviews,
please contact the publicity department at (870) 438-5288

Master
Books®
A Division of New Leaf Publishing Group
www.masterbooks.com

Dedication

To Dr. Jan (Mrs. Andy) Mercer

Students, colleagues, and textbook salesmen remember Dr. Jan as a stalwart advocate for critical thinking and fair treatment of creation in discussions of origin in the college science classroom. Tourists remember Jan as a gracious leader, opening up the wonders of God's creation on tours worldwide. Children and grandchildren remember her as a blessing. For Mary and me, Jan and Andy are dear friends and models of Christian hospitality and service.

Photo Credits:

A=All, T=Top, M=Middle, B=Bottom, L=Left, R=Right

Photos: iStock.com: 93BR
Wiki Commons: 33TR, 50TR, 141T
Dr. Gary and Mary Parker: 7TL, 10, 23, 48B, 50BR, 51BR, 54BR, 55TR, 57BR, 64, 70BR, 71TR, 82BR, 87, 88T, 89B, 90T, 92BL, 95, 96, 99, 101, 102R, 108R, 109TR, 110, 112BL, 113, 116, 120, 124BR, 126TR, 127, 128, 129, 133, 134, 135, 144BR, 145TL, 147, 148
Debbie Werner: Audio Visusal Consultants Inc.:142TR
Other photos: shutterstock.com

Table of Contents

Introduction to the Creation Foundation Series: War of the Worldviews

This Creation Foundation Series gives young people ANSWERS — answers from science and answers from Scripture — ANSWERS that show how SCIENCE and the BIBLE fit together to give answers we all need for all of life!

According to the evolutionist's worldview, each life form, including each human life, is the result of time, chance, and millions of years of struggle and death — what Darwin called the "war of nature." It must be depressing for students to hear over and over again that they are just products of time and chance caught up in a grim and ceaseless "struggle for survival" that ends for them (and the whole universe!) only when death finally wins.

The Bible has a much happier ending: life wins, new life in Christ! According to the biblical creationist's worldview, God created living things with plan and purpose, all working together in harmony. "Darwin's war" is real enough today, but it brought struggle, death, disease, decline, and disaster (Noah's Flood) into the world only after man's sin and selfishness ruined God's perfect creation. Christ's sacrificial love conquered sin and death, and His return brings new life — rich, abundant, and eternal.

When young people know what they believe and WHY THEY BELIEVE IT, they can stand firm on their own faith, even defend it to scoffers, and encourage all with reasons for hope in Christ and new life in Him (1 Pet. 3:15).

Unit 1: Biological Change: Darwin vs. Design

CREATION

CORRUPTI

CATASTROPHE

The scientific "war of the worldviews" began as a *battle over biology*. The foundations for biology as a science had been laid in the 1600s and 1700s, primarily by Christians freely using the Bible as the basis for understanding the world of living things. The definition of *species* as an interbreeding group of organisms was based on the biblical record that God had created living things to "multiply after kind" (Gen. 1), each with a special role to play for the good of the whole. Patterns of trait distribution among different kinds, the basis for biological classification, were seen to reflect "theme and variation." Theme and variation in music, for example, are used today to identify a master composer (theme) and the extent of his/her creative genius (variation). Similarly, variations within and among different species proclaim the creative genius of the Composer of Life, and the unified theme points back to one God with a *common plan* uniting all living things.

Those early creationists were well aware that the peace and harmony of God's perfect creation had been tarnished by mankind's sin. "Pure science" was seen as "thinking God's thoughts after Him," but "applied science" (e.g., making eyeglasses, treating disease, waste removal, etc.) was devoted inpart to bringing healing and restoration to things gone wrong— until the final restoration would be accomplished by the coming again of the Great Healer, Jesus Christ.

All that changed in 1859. Evolutionists used Darwin's popular new book, *Origin of Species*, as the basis for both attacking the Bible and reinterpreting the scientific evidence supporting the creationist model. Variability within kind was replaced with change from one species to others; boundaries between kinds with missing links between species; ecological cooperation with competition; common plan with common ancestor; struggle and death as problems to overcome with *struggle and death as pathways to progress*. Finally, *evolutionists made Darwin's "war of nature" a substitute god*, an alternate religion, and the authority of God's Word was replaced with the supremacy of human opinion.

As we shall see, the study of genetics and the laws of heredity make it very hard to believe in evolution and very easy to accept the "4 Cs" of biblical history: *Creation, Corruption, Catastrophe*, and *Christ*: (1) God's perfect creation, (2) ruined by man's sin, (3) destroyed by Noah's Flood, (4) restored to new life in Christ.

4C theme	
1	Creation
2	Corruption
3	Catastrophe
4	Christ

Genes and Genesis

Modern evolution began as a theory of biological change, belief that limitless genetic change could produce all life ultimately from one common ancestor by "descent with modification." Ironically, this genetic theory was based on astonishing *ignorance and misunderstanding* of the laws of heredity. It wasn't just the evolutionists who didn't know how genetics worked; no one else did either. The basic laws of heredity we take for granted and teach in middle school today were first discovered by Gregor Mendel, an Austrian monk, and published in 1860, the year after Darwin's book — but Mendel's work was not discovered and made a part of science until over 50 years later.

We understand today that hereditary features (skin color, tongue-rolling ability, length of nose, blood type, etc.) are encoded in sections of DNA molecules called genes. Figure 1.1 is the "schematic diagram" of a DNA double helix with the open sections representing active genes. G, C, A, and T are *bases* in DNA that act like "letters" in a code that "tells" the cell how to make the proteins related to each hereditary trait. Most activities in living cells are controlled by proteins called enzymes.

The second gene shown, for example, "tells" the cell how to make the enzyme (tyrosinase) that produces *melanin*, the coloring agent for skin, hair, and eyes. If another genetic factor blocks this gene's function, lack of skin, hair, and eye color results, a condition called *albinism*. The third gene shown codes for production of a liver enzyme (parahydroxylase) that helps to process nutrients in milk. Babies born with a certain defect in this gene can develop brain damage from drinking milk (but this result, called PKU, can be avoided by putting the baby on milk without phenylalanine — which is a key ingredient also in the artificial sweetener aspartame).

The first gene diagrammed in Figure 1.1 "tells" the cell how to make *hemoglobin*, the protein that carries O_2 in red blood cells. Real genes average about 1,200 base "letters" in their genetic codes. A change from T to A in the sixth position of the coding sequence for the beta chain of hemoglobin causes blood-producing cells to make abnormal "sickle cell" hemoglobin. On a lighter note, there's even a gene that determines whether or not you can taste PTC (phenylthiocarbamide)! To "tasters," PTC is intensely bitter; to "non-tasters," it's tasteless. (Imagine the fun you could have at parties — but only imagine it!)

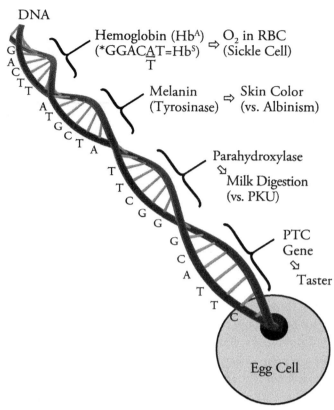

DNA

Hemoglobin (Hb^A) (*GGAC<u>A</u>T=Hb^S) ⇒ O$_2$ in RBC (Sickle Cell)

Melanin (Tyrosinase) ⇒ Skin Color (vs. Albinism)

Parahydroxylase ⇨ Milk Digestion (vs. PKU)

PTC Gene ⇨ Taster

Egg Cell

Figure 1.1. Sections of DNA called genes often direct production of proteins related to particular traits.

Cells of most adult plants, animals, and human beings usually have two genes for each trait, one inherited from the father and the other from the mother. Using letters to represent genes, we could use R to symbolize the gene found in people who can roll their tongues, for example, and r for the gene related to "non-rolling." A person with two R genes (RR) would be a tongue "roller," and a person with two r genes (rr) a "non-roller."

What about an Rr person with the mixed (*hybrid* or *heterozygous*) gene pair? If one gene produces enough product or influence to cause the whole trait to develop, it's called dominant. R is a dominant gene, so Rr individuals are tongue rollers, just like RR persons are. Since even one R gene makes a person a tongue roller, nonrollers must be rr. Genes that usually produce no direct effect are called recessive, and their trait (or lack of trait) is expressed only when there's no dominant gene present.

Genes that produce different effects on the same trait are called alleles; the R and r genes that affect tongue rolling are alleles. If one allele is dominant and the other recessive, two variations of a trait can be expressed, e.g., tongue rolling (RR or Rr) and non-rolling (rr). Variations increase if there is lack of dominance ("blending") between alleles. For example, crosses of pink-flowered four

o'clocks with genes Pp produce three variations of flower color: red (PP), pink (Pp), and white (pp).

Genetic results among the children or off spring of given parents can be shown in a Punnett square. The pair of alleles found in parent cells separate into single genes during the formation of sex cells (egg and sperm in people and most animals; spores in most plants). The sex cell genes of one parent are listed along the left side of a square; the sex cell genes of the other parent are along the top. Punnett squares for the tongue rolling and flower color examples described earlier are shown below.

	R	**r**
R	**RR** tongue roller	**Rr** tongue roller
r	**Rr** tongue roller	**rr** non-roller

	P	**p**
P	**PP** red	**Pp** pink
p	**Pp** pink	**pp** white

When sex cells come together at fertilization, alleles are reunited as pairs in all possible combinations, as shown in the boxes inside the big square. Th e results in the squares show that, on average, three children out of four of Rr tongue-rolling parents will also be tongue rollers (RR or Rr), but one in four on average will be non-rollers (rr), unlike either parent. Only one-half of the off spring of the pink-flowered plants (Pp) will be pink like their parents: one-fourth will be red (PP) and one-fourth white (pp).

Variety increases further when more than two allelic variations of a gene exist ("*multiple alleles*"). There are three alleles for ABO blood types, for example, which we can symbolize LA, LB, and l⁰. Any one person can have only two of these three alleles, *but our first parents, Adam and Eve, could have been created with a total of four alleles for a given kind of gene*, two alleles in Adam and two different alleles in Eve. Even the three ABO blood group alleles produce four different blood groups from six different gene pairs:

AB	L^AL^B, which are "co-dominant" genes, each producing a product
A	L^AL^A or $L^A l^O$, since l^O is recessive
B	L^BL^B or $L^B l^O$
O	$l^O l^O$, the recessive pair that makes no product

God is the Author of variety, and created in His image, we see "*variety is the spice of life.*" Genetic variation within each created kind seems to serve two purposes in God's plan. For people especially, genetic variation guarantees each person will be a *unique individual* with a special place in God's plan no one else can take. For plants and animals, genetic variation enables members of a created kind to "*multiply and fill*" *many different environments*, or meet changes in existing environments.

Certain flies, for example, have a gene for producing a key energy enzyme that exists, with lack of dominance, in two allelic forms, one that works best at high temperatures (T^H) and one at low (T^L). The fly population, then, includes individuals designed for high temperatures (T^HT^H), low temperatures (T^LT^L), and medium temperatures (T^HT^L). As the flies move through a forest, the flies designed for high temperatures stay in the sun, those for low temperatures stay deep in the shade, and the medium temperature flies move along the edge of the branches — *all three splendidly designed for their different environments*, and the population able to adjust should the temperature change drastically in either direction.

Using nothing more than one mixed pair of alleles and ordinary laws of heredity, God enabled the first of each kind to produce descendants that could "multiply and fill" dark, shady, and light environments; salt, brackish, and freshwater; and high, middle, and low altitudes, etc.

Variation within kind increases even further when two or more sets of alleles affect the same trait ("*multiple genes*" or "*polygenic inheritance*"). Human skin color provides an excellent, very important, and often misunderstood example.

<table>
<tr><td>Question</td><td>How many skin colors are there among people living today?</td></tr>
</table>

The answer may surprise you: one! You never met anyone with a skin color different from yours! Everyone has the same skin coloring substance, a protein called melanin. Certain skin cells (melanocytes) in some people make lots of melanin, so they have a very dark melanin color. Others make only a little melanin and appear very light. Most people make a "medium" amount of melanin that produces various brown skin tones. So everyone *has the same skin color, just different amounts of it* — NOT a big difference at all!

There are at least two different genetic sites (segments of DNA) that influence how much melanin a person produces. We can call the alleles at one gene site A and a, and alleles at the other site B and b. Persons inheriting all "capital letter" genes, AABB, would produce the most melanin and be *very dark*. Persons with aabb genes would produce the least melanin and be *very light*. Persons with two "capital letter" genes (AaBb, AAbb, or aaBB) would produce a medium amount of melanin and be some shade of brown. Persons with three "caps" (AABb or AaBB) would be a shade darker, and those with one "cap" (Aabb or aaBb) a shade lighter.

What skin tone, or what gene combination for producing melanin, was present in the first two human beings, Adam and Eve? The Bible doesn't tell us, so we can't be sure. But the Bible does say that Adam and Eve were designed to be the parents of all people, so it seems God would have enabled them to produce the rich variety of unique individuals we have today. To get the most variety in the least time genetically, the best place to start is in the middle. So if we assume our first parents were "medium brown" with genes AaBb, how long would it take to get all the variations in skin tone or amounts of melanin we see among people today?

The answer may surprise you. It's not a million years, a thousand years, or even a hundred years. Starting with AaBb genes, we could get ALL the different amounts of melanin and ALL the variations in melanin skin tone we see today in just ONE *generation*! Figure 1.2 shows the routine genetics involved. Each AaBb parent would produce egg or sperm with one gene of the Aa pair and one of the Bb pair equally in all possible combinations: AB, Ab, aB, and ab. The boxes show the 16 possible combinations resulting from union of egg and sperm cells. As Figure 1.2 shows, the likelihood is 1 in 16 (¹⁄₁₆) that a child of Adam and Eve would be *very dark*, with genes AABB producing the greatest amount of melanin. The probability is also ¹⁄₁₆ that Cain, Abel, Seth, or one of their brothers or sisters would be aabb and be very light. An average ⁶⁄₁₆ would be some medium shade of brown similar to their parents, 4 a shade lighter, and 4 a shade darker.

From two people with one melanin skin color to people with five different shades of melanin color in just one generation — wow!

When God commanded our first parents to "multiply and fill the earth" with a variety of uniquely special descendants, He did not have to wait for "*miracle mutations*" or "*millions of years*." The ordinary laws of heredity He established show us how we can go from two medium-brown people to people with all the different amounts of melanin and all the different skin tones from very lightest to very darkest in just one generation! And so far we're only talking about two gene sites out of over 30,000 in people, and sites that have only two alleles each when four are possible! Wow!

Without mutations (to be discussed later) the principles of skin color inheritance could produce most of the variation among people today in just one generation: straight to wavy to curly to "super curly" hair; round or oval "eyes": thick to thin lips; numerous variations in height and body build; etc.! Tremendous variability built into the first of each created kind would also allow plants and animals to "multiply and fill" the earth's ecologic and geographic diversity. It seems God did indeed make "variety the spice of life."

A couple with **melanin** control genes
AaBb (Adam and Eve?)
would have "**medium**" skin tone, and each
would make four kinds of reproductive cells,
as shown along top and side of this
"genetic square":

genes in mother's egg cells

		AB	Ab	aB	ab
genes in father's sperm cells	AB	AA BB	AA Bb	Aa BB	Aa Bb
	Ab	AA Bb	AA bb	Aa Bb	Aa bb
	aB	Aa BB	Aa Bb	aa BB	aa Bb
	ab	Aa Bb	Aa bb	aa Bb	aa bb

Each box in the larger "Punnett square" shows the gene combination possible in a child.

As shown in the pictures below, children of "medium" parents could have **most to least melanin** and **color darkest to lightest** with 4, 3, 2, 1, 0 "capital letter" genes indicated with each picture.

Figure 1.2. Inheritance of melanin skin color

AABB	AABb or AaBB	AAbb, AaBb, aaBB	Aabb or aaBb	aabb
(4 "capital letter" genes)	(any 3 "caps")	(any 2 "caps")	(any 1 "cap")	(0 "caps")

Like the condition we postulated for Adam and Eve in Figure 1.2, people in India today have all four versions of the melanin control genes: A, a, B, b. Some people from India are as dark as the darkest central African; some are as light as the lightest northern European; most are somewhere between. Our family once knew a family from India where the children of just one couple ranged from the very darkest to the very lightest found anywhere on earth today. Many biology textbooks today contain a news picture of twin boys. Why? One was as light as his English father; the other twin (fraternal) as dark as his Nigerian mother. What is really surprising in that story is that anyone would find it surprising in a so-called scientific age. The ordinary genetics involved requires a Punnett square with only four boxes (Figure 1.3). So, when people from different backgrounds get together, we're right back to *no more and no less* variation in amounts of our one skin color than God built into our first parents.

Dark Nigerian Mother
(AA Bb)

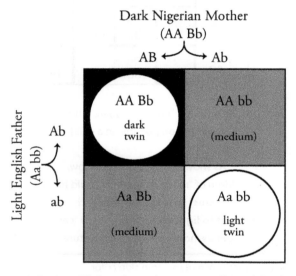

Figure 1.3. Dark and light twins today are as easily explained as Adam and Eve having children from darkest to lightest in one generation.

What would happen to variations in amounts of melanin skin color after God broke people up into different language groups at the Tower of Babel (Gen. 10:1–9)? If one migrating language group included only individuals with "cap" A and B genes (AABB), then all they could pass on to their children would be A's and B's, and individuals in that group would remain only very dark (AABB), generation after generation (like some populations in central Africa). An isolated language group moving away with only "little" a and b genes would be very light (aabb) through its generations (like some northern European populations). A group could even get "stuck in the middle" (like some Native American and

Oriental populations). If a group contained only cap A and little b genes, all its members would be "medium brown," with genes AAbb. Each AAbb parent would give their child 1A and 1b, so the children would all be medium-skinned, AAbb, through their generations. Similarly, aaBB parents would only produce medium aaBB children for endless generations. It's only medium-brown parents with one each of A, a, B, and b genes (AaBb) that can produce a generation with the full range of melanin amounts and skin tones.

Without all four melanin control genes, some language groups leaving Babel would produce generations with only one skin tone.

Only Dark	Only Medium	Only Light
AABB	aaBB or AAbb	aabb

Sad to say, we all know that different amounts of our one skin color (melanin) were once used to assign people to different so-called races. As late as the 1930s, evolutionists were even teaching that some races were "less evolved" or inferior to others. Scientists now agree with what the Bible said all along. As Paul preached in his "creation evangelism" message in Athens, "He has made from *one blood* every nation of men to dwell on all the face of the earth" (Acts 17:26; NKJV; emphasis added). There's only ONE "RACE," the HUMAN RACE, and we're all parts of it! Think how much trouble and heartache we could have been spared if only we had listened to God's Word, and not man's opinion, right from the beginning!

God endowed our first parents, and the first parents of each created kind, with the potential to produce tremendous variability among individuals, and God delights in our diversity. As if the above were not enough, additional factors introduce even more variability into human skin tone. Melanin itself actually comes in two different forms: eumelanin that grades *black to brown* in different amounts, and phaeomelanin that grades *red to yellow*. Thickness of skin, kind of fat under the skin, and amount of blood circulation through the skin all have effects that can, for example, make people with the same medium amount of melanin appear more yellow-brown, red-brown, or dusky-brown.

Many people "tan," up to their genetic maxima of course, only when and where they are exposed to sunlight, and they "fade" with less sun exposure. Oftentimes traits are expressed or repressed in accord with environmental cues, but only within genetic limits. Tanning illustrates the nature/nurture principle that both the genes we

Height and weight are two factors influenced by nature and nurture.

produce (mathematically, not physically!) would greatly exceed the number of *atoms* in the universe, estimated at 10^{80} — a 1 followed by 80 zeroes. A leading geneticist (an evolutionist) calculated the number of genetically different children a single couple could have at 10^{2017} — a number "zillions of times" larger than the number of atoms! And he said that staggeringly HUGE number is a *low* estimate!

Wow! YOU ARE SPECIAL! Nobody in the past ever had your combination of genes; nobody in the future will ever be just like you. You have an absolutely unique combination of genes that gives you a special place in God's plan that no one else can ever take! The next time you look in a mirror, think about how incredibly special you are — and remember that each of your friends and every other person has a unique place in God's plan, too!

What does this awesome variability mean? For one thing, it reflects God's creativity. God created the first man from the "dust of the ground" and the first woman from a portion of his side, and God rested from those kinds of creative acts at the end of the creation week. But we still see God's creativity unfolding before our eyes in a different way in the birth of each child. As they relate to the genetic potential God created in our first parents, we may not yet have seen the fastest runner or the greatest

inherit ("*nature*") and our surroundings ("*nurture*") influence the traits we manifest. *Height, weight, intelligence*, and *temperament*, for example, are complex traits influenced both by nature (many genes) and by nurture (family, cultural, and even nutritional conditions surrounding our upbringing).

Expression of genetic potential in plants is especially sensitive to environmental conditions. A scrubby willow bush on the Arctic tundra, for example, may grow as a luxuriant tree if transplanted to a temperate zone streamside. American men today average much taller than the medieval "knights in shining armor" who averaged only 5 feet, 4 inches (1.6 m) because of better health and nutrition, not because of any genetic changes or "evolution."

Think back over all the variability related to just two major gene pairs that influence melanin skin color. Now think about the fact that the full gene set (genome) in a human cell contains over 30,000 *different genes*! If only a fraction of these genes existed in simple allelic pairs like R and r, the number of unique, individual human beings a single couple could

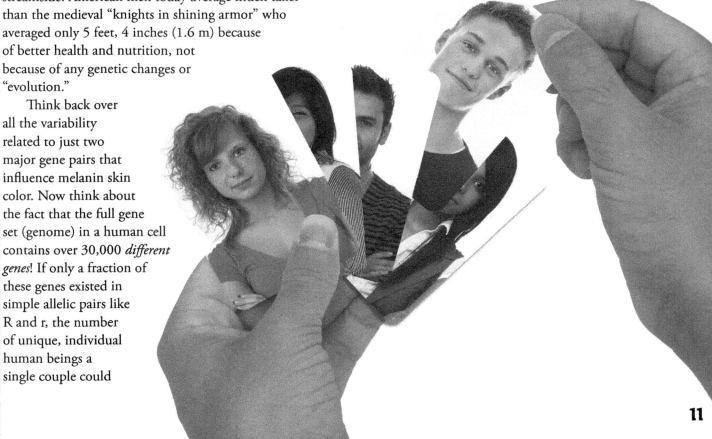

mathematical or musical genius. These genes were not produced one at a time by evolution — time, chance struggle, and death operating over millions of years. This *unfolding of genetic variability built in ahead of time* can be called entelechy, but NOT evolution.

As the descendants of each created kind multiplied to fill the earth, we see their genetic potentials unfolding (*entelechy*). God created "bear kind," for example. But as bears moved into different environments around the world, their in-built genetic variability came to visible expression in black bears, brown bears, grizzly bears, polar bears, etc. Entelechy diversified created "dog kind" into specialized sub-types: foxes, wolves, coyotes, etc. Just by shuffling pre-existing genes, animal breeders have brought out in domestic dogs an astonishing range of variation — in size, from Chihuahua to St. Bernard; in nose length, from bulldog to collie; in fur, from hairless to Pekingese; in speed, from basset hound to greyhound; in affection, from pit bull to Labrador; in intelligence, from sheep dog to _____ (you fill in the blank) — and all these in a dazzling variety of colors and markings! Think also about the tremendous genetic variability brought to visible expression (entelechy) in "cat kind," "rose kind," "tomato kind," etc.

Geneticists call the shuffling of pre-existing genes recombination. Perhaps you've played a game with the common deck of 52 cards that includes four groups (hearts, diamonds, clubs, and spades), each with 13 different numbers (2–10) or "faces" (J, Q, K, A). In one game called bridge, each of four players gets a "hand" of 13 cards. You can play bridge for 50 years (and some people do!) without ever getting the same group of 13 cards! The "hands" you are dealt are constantly changing, and each is unique — but the deck of cards remains always the same.

Although the comparison is not perfect, a deck of cards illustrates the concept of variation within created kind. The hands dealt are *unique*, *different*, and *constantly changing*, like the individual members of a population, but the deck of 52 cards remains *constant, never changing, always the same*, like the *created kind*. Ever-changing individuals in a never-changing group, or individual variation plus group constancy: that's variation within created kinds.

Though distinct, these two dog breeds represent variation within the created kinds.

Form your foundation.

Science and Scripture agree:
There's just one race, the human race.
All of us have the same skin coloring protein, melanin, and shuffling AaBb genes can produce all variations in melanin color in just one generation!

1. Complete the paragraph with these key words:

   DnA   dominant   hybrid   alleles   gene   recessive   blending

   Sections of a _____ molecule that aff ect particular traits are called _____. Genes in adults usually come in pairs called _____, like T and t for "tasters" and "non-tasters" of PTC. A "mixed pair." Tt, is called _____ (or heterozygous). If Tt is a taster, then T is a _____ gene, and only tt could express the _____ trait. If T and t represent tall and short and Tt were medium, the inheritance pattern would be called _____.

2. If both parents were hybrid tasters (Tt), what is the likelihood they could have a non-tasting child? (**0-none, ¼, ½ , ¾, 1-all**) _____. If Tt represented parents of medium height, what fraction of their off spring would be taller than parents? (**0, ¼, ½, ¾, 1**) _____. Shorter? _____. Medium like their parents?_____ .

3. Darwin's followers once taught that there were diff erent "races" of human beings with diff erent skin colors that were in diff erent stages of evolution. But science and Scripture agree: all people belong to only (how many?) _____ races(s), and human skin color depends primarily on only (how many?) _____ molecule(s), a protein called _____.

4. If two pairs of genes controlled the amount of melanin skin color and Adam and Eve were AaBb, they would be (**very dark, dark, medium, light, very light**)_____. How many of these fi ve shades of melanin skin color would be found among their children? (**1, 2, 3, 4, 5**)_____. So, how many generations would it take to go from two people with one skin color to people with all the various amounts of melanin color we see today? (**one, one thousand, one million**)_____. Evolutionists believe it takes lots of time to produce little variation; science and Scripture (see the chart on p. 9) show that it takes (**lots, little**) _____ time to produce _____ of variation.

5. God delights in diversity! Th e number of combinations among genes created in Adam and Eve is far (**greater/less**)_____ than the number of atoms in the cosmos – meaning YOU are SPECIAL with a UNIQUE place no one else can take in the whole (**country, planet, universe**) _____.

6. Why is it important for Christians to relate God's world and God's Word – science and Scripture?
   _____
   _____

7. Use the following words and phrases to fi ll blanks in the paragraph below:

   plan, purpose, and special creation   God   better   life (wins)
   time, chance, struggle, and death   Darwin   worse   death (wins)

   According to the biblical worldview that gave birth to science in the 1600s and 1700s, the fi rst of each created kind of life resulted from _____. But the Bible also records that man's disregard for God (sin) brought the processes of _____ into God's world, making things _____. In the 1800s, _____ argued that the processes of _____ (which he called the "war of nature") would make living things slowly _____, even though fi nally _____ wins. Th ose believing the Word of _____ rather than the words of Darwin have hope in Christ that _____ wins.

8. Relate each statement about God's world below to one of "4Cs" in God's Word:

   Creation   Corruption   Catastrophe   Christ

   _____ a. Flood conditions are ideal for forming fossils.
   _____ b. Many defects and diseases result from chance changes in heredity called mutations.
   _____ c. Adaptations are design features that suit each organism for its special role in the web of life.
   _____ d. Land animals saved on the Ark and the immune system healing deadly infections both illustrate God's deliverance from death and disaster.

Chapter 1

Gene Pools
and Variation within Kind

All the genes in an individual make up its genome; all the genes available for trade among members of a created kind make up its gene pool. Although any individual has no more than two ABO blood group alleles, for example, the human gene pool includes at least three alleles, L^A, L^B, and 1^O. "Non-tongue rollers" and "non-PTC tasters" possess only r and t genes respectively, but the human gene pool also includes R and T, along with melanin color alleles A, a, B, and b and many thousands of others. Think of the differences between the biblical twins Jacob and Esau: one was a "hairy man" who loved the outdoors, the other a "smooth man" who preferred to stay at home. Even the three basic singing ranges for men and women are influenced by one pair of genes in some combination, VV, Vv, and vv (e.g. tenor, baritone, bass in males).

What happens to the gene pool from one generation to the next? To find out, look again at the melanin skin color example, which started with two people, Adam and Eve, each with genes AaBb. Gene frequency is the percentage or fraction of a given allele among the total for a gene pool. So, the initial gene frequencies are 25 percent each for A, a, B, and b, since each is one-fourth (25 percent) of the skin color alleles in the first generation. Now look below at the Punnett square with 16 boxes that show the gene combinations in the second generation (in this case, the children of Adam and Eve). There was one melanin skin color in the first generation and five variations of melanin color in the second — yet the gene frequencies did not change at all! Count the A, a, B, and b genes in the Punnett square for the second generation and you'll find 16 each out of the 64 total — 16/64 = one-fourth = 25 percent! Lots and lots of individual variation but gene pool constancy: that's variation within created kind.

	AB	Ab	aB	ab
AB	AA BB	AA Bb	Aa BB	Aa Bb
Ab	AA Bb	AA bb	Aa Bb	Aa bb
aB	Aa BB	Aa Bb	aa BB	aa Bb
ab	Aa Bb	Aa bb	aa Bb	aa bb

Let's look at another example, the genes for tasting (T) and not tasting (t) the chemical PTC. Genetic studies have shown the gene frequency of the recessive t is 0.6 (60 percent) and of the dominant T is 0.4 (40 percent). What will the percentages be in the next generation? Will the frequency of the dominant gene increase? Population genetics treats one generation, or one gene pool, as the parents or ancestors of the next. Punnett squares can still be used, but the sex cell genes are written with their gene frequencies, and those numbers are multiplied together to show the percentage of the resulting gene pair in the next generation. Figure 2.1 shows a generation with T = 0.4 and t = 0.6 produces a generation that's 16 percent TT, 48 percent (24 percent + 24 percent) Tt, and 36 percent tt. What's the percentage of T in the next generation? The 16 percent TT individuals provide 16 percent T's, the 48 percent Tt provide 24 percent (1/2 of 48 percent) T, and the tt's provide no T's. So, the T total is 16 percent + 24 percent + 0 percent = 40 percent, or 0.4 — *exactly what it was in the first generation!* The frequency of the recessive t stays the same at 0.6, of course — 0.0 percent from the 16 percent TT, 0.24 from 48 percent Tt, and 0.36 from 36 percent tt = 0.0 + 0.24 + 0.36 = 0.6!

Note, by the way, there is no automatic tendency for dominant genes to replace recessive ones, or vice versa. *The gene percentages you have in one generation are the same as you wind up with in the next.*

Named after its discoverers, this tendency for genetic recombination to allow individual variation while keeping the group gene pool constant generation after generation is called the Hardy-Weinberg Law. It might also be called the Law of Conservation of Genetic Variability or genetic equilibrium. This fundamental law of population genetics is a superb illustration of "theme and variation," or variation in created kind. For evolutionists, who sometimes define *evolution as change in gene frequency,* this law of heredity is a stumbling block, a resistance to genetic change that might be called genetic inertia!

God, the Author of variety and the Creator of each kind, designed genetic recombination to both allow individual variation and keep the group constant.

Figure 2.1. Simple recombination keeps the gene pool constant from one generation to the next, although individuals vary -- variation within kind.

Human Gene Pool
Genes, and the fractions of each, that can be passed from one generation to the next

Unfortunately, however, we live in a fallen world, a creation corrupted by mankind and Darwin's "war of nature." There are factors in our world today that *do* affect genetic variability and group constancy.

Worst of all are mutations, random changes in genes that introduce new alleles into the gene pools of human beings and other created kinds. The created human gene pool, for example, included genes for adult hemoglobin (Hb^A) and for a fetal hemoglobin (Hb^F) designed to carry oxygen into the baby before birth. But "thanks" to mutation, the human gene pool now includes over 300 alleles for Hb^A, most associated with disease, and none as good at carrying oxygen in red blood cells as normal (created) adult hemoglobin. Many mutations knock out the normal function of a gene and so, at least in the double recessive form (e.g., aa), cause disease conditions related to loss of function, e.g., albinism, hemophilia ("bleeders disease"), PKU, etc. *Mutations do not help explain the origin of species,* but they do a great job of *explaining the origin of birth defects, disease, and disease organisms!*

Many of these mutations are held in check by the *struggle for survival* that also followed mankind's corruption of creation. As described by a creationist writing 24 years before Darwin, however, the *fittest* that survive are *not* some "new and improved species" but rather those *most like the original created kind and with the least number of defects and diseases!* On a more positive note, natural selection can help explain how and where

Parental Gene Pool
40% **T** (tasters); 60% *t* (non-tasters)
"Dads" **T*t*** x **T*t*** "Moms"
(.4)(.6) x (.4)(.6)

	T (.4)	t (.6)
T (.4)	TT .4 x .4 = .16	T t .4 x .6 = .24
***t* (.6)**	T t .4 x .6 = .24	t t .6 x .6 = .36

Children's Gene Pool

		T	t
.16 TT	....	.16	.00
.24 Tt	....	.12	.12
.24 Tt	....	.12	.12
.36 tt	....	.00	.36
H-W Law:		.40	.60

Simple recombination keeps gene frequencies the same "Conservation of Genetic variability" or "Genetic Equilibrium" varieties of a kind survive as they multiply into different environments. The fittest is often the hybrid with mixed (heterozygous) alleles (e.g., Aa), a phenomenon called hybrid vigor or *heterosis*. Only half the offspring of hybrids are also hybrid, so hybrid vigor may have been established by God as yet another means of maintaining genetic variability. Besides, as we saw with the high, medium, and low temperature-adapted flies, the offspring with alleles alike ("pure breeding" or *homozygous*, e.g., AA or aa) may also be fit to survive in slightly different environments.

Specialized, adapted subtypes of the "bear kind"

As described earlier, there does seem to be a tendency for generalized, adaptable *created kinds* to break up into specialized, adapted *sub-types* as they multiply and fill the earth (e.g., "bear kind" to black, brown, grizzly, and polar bears). When a large population breaks up into smaller ones, the small populations often include genes at frequencies different from those in the original population. Imagine a big bowl with equal numbers of all the M&M's® colors. Grab a handful and just by chance, you may have a higher percentage of reds and a lower percentage of blues than the percents present in the big bowl.

The tendency for chance to produce small populations with gene percents different from those in the original gene pool is called *genetic drift*. Just by chance (from the human point of view), some of the language groups moving away from the Tower of Babel carried genes for lots of melanin production (A and B) and dark skin tone while other groups took mostly genes for less melanin production (a and b) and light skin tone. Similarly, alleles for ABO blood groups are not distributed equally among all peoples, and differences can be used to trace migration patterns (migration, *not* evolution!). One advantage of genetic drift is making visible the invisible genetic variability God built into each created kind.

Genetic drift may or may not be accompanied by some form of reproductive isolation, the tendency of small groups to breed among themselves and not with other small groups or the larger original population.

Such reproductively isolated groups these days are often named as new species, but they are NOT new kinds. In fact, most such groups have far fewer alleles and less genetic variability than what was present in the original gene pool — a loss of information and variety that reduces the smaller group's ability to explore new environments or to meet changes in their existing environments. Genetic drift and reproductive isolation may produce groups called new "species," but the genetic loss and restriction are the exact opposite of evolutionary hopes and represents *only variation within created kinds*.

There is a tendency for genetic drift and reproductive isolation to produce specialized subtypes of created kinds properly called *subspecies*. Evolutionists like to call that process *speciation*, but if so, that means "speciation, yes; evolution, no."

The effects of genetic drift are well illustrated in the human population when a small group separates from the larger population and for whatever reason, marries only within the smaller group. We've already mentioned how one language group might end up with darker melanin skin tone, just by "chance" or genetic drift, than another language group. When their ancestors moved into different parts of Africa (only about 100 miles or 160 km apart), the Watusi "took with them" lots of alleles for tallness (e.g., C, D, E) and average nearly 7 feet (2.1 m) tall, while the Pygmies "took" alleles for shortness (e.g., c, d, e) and average under 5 feet (1.5 m).

People in China tend to be short with

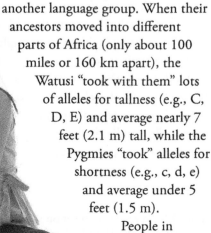

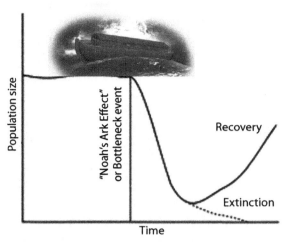

Figure 2.2. Example of the phenomenon known as the genetic bottleneck

San Luis Petos Kingsnake
(Central Mexico)

medium skin tone and straight black hair, while those in India vary considerably in height and melanin skin color and have hair from straight to curly. Why the difference? Geneticists call it the founder effect and trace it back to gene frequencies or percents that differed, just by "chance" or genetic drift, in the small groups that founded these two large populations. Some genetics books even refer to the founder effect as the "Adam and Eve Effect," differences among offspring that trace back to the traits in their first parents. Differences even developed among the tribes of Israel, so that, for example, one tribe could say "shibboleth" and another tribe only "sibboleth." In accord with the Hardy-Weinberg equilibrium, the new gene frequencies in a small founding population tend to be maintained among the descendants of those founders, as long as the group remains reproductively isolated.

Sometimes a major catastrophe reduces a large population to one or a few small ones, a phenomenon

called a genetic bottleneck or the "Noah's Ark Effect." Certainly Noah's Flood would have a dramatic impact on biological diversity, especially among land plants and animals and people. The visible expression of genetic variability in the pre-Flood world would have been reduced to that expressed by just eight people and one pair of each "unclean kind" and seven of the "clean kinds" of all living creatures. Still, those small groups could include as much genetic potential as God built into the first of each created kind, or even more, and it was God — who could see and choose the genes — who brought the animals to Noah. It's true, however, that the genetically distinctive sub-groups of each kind developing in new environments after the Flood would likely express traits visibly different from those expressed before the Flood. And any genetic disease or deficiencies (as well as any superlatives) in Noah's family would likely be found in higher percentages among post-Flood than pre-Flood peoples.

In our corrupted creation, genetic drift has the unfortunate effect of establishing certain disease conditions in isolated populations at much higher levels than those found in the larger population. One of the first 200 Germans who helped establish the Amish settlements in Pennsylvania (Strong Jacob Joder), for example, unknowingly carried a recessive gene for a blood disease. The gene was present at low levels (perhaps, e.g., 1 in 100,000) in the general German population, but it was established at 1 in 400 (200 settlers x two genes for each trait) in the founding Amish population. Other recessive disease conditions rare in the general human population but found in higher percentages in subpopulations include Tay-Sachs disease, traced back to a

Arizona Mountain Kingsnake

17

Jewish community in Czechoslovakia in 1925; porphyria among the Dutch in South Africa; and hemophilia in the royal families of Europe that is traceable back to a mutation in England's Queen Victoria.

Genetic drift causes plant and animal groups to break up into different sub-populations, too, as they multiply and fill the earth. Color markings on snakes and birds, for example, frequently differ between those living east or west, north or south, high altitude or low, wet or dry environments, etc. Leaf shape and bark texture on oaks in the Midwest can be quite different from that of oaks in California or South Florida. Percentages of antibiotic-resistant bacteria are all too often higher in hospitals than anywhere else. These differences, like the differences among sub-populations of human beings, do NOT require millions of years, but become apparent instead in just a few generations.

With so much genetic potential producing so much visible variability in so little time, are there any limits to biological change? Are scientists able to recognize boundaries between kinds and limits to variability, as creationists suggest? Or do scientists find evidence for limitless genetic expansion, the origin of all species from one, as evolutionists assert? Before we can know whether or not we've answered these questions, we have to come to some understanding of two important but controversial terms: species and kind.

Form your foundation.

Created kinds always the same, individuals always different: that's variation within kind. As people and other living things "multiply and fill the earth," the variability God built into the first of each kind comes to inspiring visible expression!

California oak leaves

White oak leaves

1. The "gene pool" is all the genes (and their allelic variations) that can be passed from one generation to the next. The number of alleles in one individual is usually (**less than/more than/the same as**) _____ than in the total population, somewhat like the cards in a deck include (**greater/lesser/the same**) _____ variation than the cards dealt to one person. When they are shuffled and dealt again, the cards individuals get are (**constantly changing/always the same**) _____, but the deck is (**constantly changing/always the same**) _____. Similarly, gene shuffling from one generation to the next (recombination) keeps the gene pool of each kind (**always constant/ever changing**) _____ while individuals in each new generation continually express (**the same old/ever new and unique**) _____ trait combinations, unfolding the creativity and diversity built in ahead of time by (**God/evolution**) _____.

2. The Punnett square on p. 9 shows a dramatic change from one skin color in Adam and Eve to every melanin color from very dark to very light in their children — but what change occurred in the gene pool? _____ Given the very first generation had genes AaBb, the fraction of A in their melanin color pool was (**0-none, ¼, ½, ¾, 1-all**) _____. Among the 16 boxes with 4 genes each (64 total) in the second generation, counting shows (how many?) _____ are A — and 16/64 reduces to (**1/8, 1/4, 1/2**) _____, which is (**dramatically different from/exactly the same as**) _____ the fraction of A in first generation. Group constancy plus individual variation — that's (**variation within/change between**) _____ kinds and illustrates (**creation/evolution**) _____. Creationists might call this Conservation of Genetic Variability genetic (**equilibrium/inertia**) _____, a positive term, while evolutionists see it as _____, or resistance to genetic change.

3. Below are non-evolutionary factors that can disrupt the gene pool constancy normally maintained by recombination and the Hardy-Weinberg Law. Match names and descriptions.

   genetic drift   **specialization**   **reproductive isolation**
   genetic bottleneck   **founder effect**   **mutations**

   _____ a. Only a few members of a species with a large gene pool survive a major disaster (e.g., animals aboard the Ark)

   _____ b. Several small groups separate from a large population, each with percentages of alleles different from those in the original gene pool (e.g., language groups moving away from the Tower of Babel).

   _____ c. Members of a kind separating into distinctive subtypes as they "multiply and fill" earth's environmental diversity (e.g., generalized bears leaving the Ark becoming black, brown, grizzly, and polar bears).

   _____ d. Barriers or preferences in the choice of a mate separate some parts of a gene pool from others (e.g., culture and language separate humans; size and temperament separate dogs).

   _____ e. Random changes in genes that often change normal genes into alleles producing defects or disease (e.g., sickle cell hemoglobin).

4. Breakup of the human gene pool at the Tower of Babel produced some groups with only AABB melanin control genes. Since they could only pass on A and B genes, their children were always (**very dark, dark, medium, light, very light**) _____. Children whose founders carried only aabb genes were always _____. Groups with AAbb founders always passed on A and b genes, so their children (like some Orientals, Polynesians, and Native Americans) are always _____. People migrating to India apparently took A, a, B, and b, so their children can be (**only medium/any shade of**) _____ melanin skin color.

5. "Hybrid vigor" means hybrids (e.g., Rr) are often hardiest. What fraction of off spring from a hybrid cross will also be hybrid? _____. If hybrids are "superior," can superior parents have only superior children? _____. Did Hitler know this? _____.

Chapter 2

Species, Kind, and the Mosaic Concept

Dogs have puppies, cats have kittens, cows have calves, and oak trees bear acorns. This phenomenon of plants and animals "multiplying after their kinds" is one of the most distinctive and best-known features of living systems. Genesis 1 explicitly states that God gave each of the kinds of life He created the ability to multiply after its kind, and this ability to interbreed is used today as the chief basis for defining species, the biological relative of the biblical term *kind*. Organisms are recognized as belonging to the same *species if they are members of a population that can freely interbreed in nature to produce fertile offspring.*

Problems in Defining Species and Kind

Although the definition of species as an interbreeding population seems to have the support of both Scripture and modern science, several problems arise in trying to apply this definition. First of all, this definition does not apply to life forms that reproduce only asexually. Certain amoebas, for example, only reproduce asexually, and so do some large organisms, such as banana plants and dandelions. It may be acknowledged that all amoebas and all banana trees descended from those forms of life originally created by God, but we recognize such asexually reproducing kinds today on the basis of their structural and genomic similarities, because we cannot do it on the basis of their interbreeding capabilities.

Normally, of course, species are identified on the basis of structural similarities anyway, but such data can occasionally conflict with information about breeding habits. For example, on the basis of striking differences in appearance and courtship rituals, we recognize several species of exotic tropical bowerbirds, such as the great bowerbird, the bird-of-paradise, and the cock-of-the rock (Figure 3.1). Given the chance, however, members of these different "*species*" can interbreed and produce fertile, hybrid offspring. In such a case, it may be that God created several different kinds of bowerbirds, but reproductive barriers have broken down to some extent in our fallen world. It is more likely, however, that the bowerbird *kind* is broader than *species*, including several varieties like the varieties among the dog, cat, and horse species/kinds.

Figure 3.1. Diverse bowerbirds: (A) bird-of-paradise; (B) cock-of-the-rock; (C) great bowerbird

Situations almost exactly opposite that illustrated by bowerbirds also occur. For example, something like 40 different "species" of fruit flies have been identified. Most of these look so much alike that only an expert would be able to tell them apart, yet minor differences in mating behavior prevent interbreeding among these obviously similar species, called *sibling species*. In this case, it might well be that God created only one species of fruit fly and that later developments such as mutations, chromosome fission and fusion, genetic drift, and reproductive isolation fragmented this original kind into non-interbreeding subgroups.

A situation somewhat between that illustrated by the bowerbirds and fruit flies is found among some frogs and many birds. The southern grass frog and the northern grass frog, for example, cannot interbreed, primarily because of differences in mating times. Both the northern and the southern frog, however, can interbreed with the frog variety in the Middle Atlantic states, and so indirectly these two "types" (kinds? species?) can still exchange genes.

At this point you may recognize the potential danger in equating the biblical term *kind* with the biological term *species*, if for no other reason than that the scientists have difficulties defining and identifying *species*. Indeed,

the term species has become severely abused, and is being applied arbitrarily and subjectively to an exploding number of ever more narrowly defined sub-groups, all too often for reasons that have to do more with personal whim or political preference than with scientific merit. *Putting biology and the Bible together may provide the basis for an objective definition of "kind," one that uses scientific tests, not subjective opinion, to assign organisms to their correct category (or "real species"?).*

Reproductive ability is the biblical basis for identifying created kinds, and scientists still want to apply that criterion to the definition of species. What about the multitude of problems described above for this simplistic approach? These problems may be solved or solvable with recent advances in *DNA technology* and our growing knowledge of how genes interact and are passed on in "sets" called *chromosomes*.

The simplest, most direct test of what belongs to which kind is carried out "jillions" of times by recognition proteins on the surfaces of egg and sperm cells. Jillions of egg, sperm, and other sexually uniting cells are released into the ocean at the same time, for example, but "multiplication after kind" is guaranteed because only those cells with complementary "docking proteins" will unite to produce the first cell of the next generation.

Modern advances in DNA technology allow DNA code sequencing to identify genes of the same kind and organisms of the same kind for both sexually and asexually reproducing forms. If the sequence is not available, similarity can be inferred by measuring the degree of pairing of single strands of DNA from the known gene with the complementary (base-paired) strand of the test gene, a "routine" experimental procedure called DNA hybridization.

Further scientific clues to the identities of the created kinds are provided by the way genes are usually linked together in long to very long

molecules of DNA-forming structures called chromosomes. The DNA in chromosomes of plants, animals, and people are bound up with proteins; the DNA in bacterial chromosomes form "naked" (protein-free) loops.

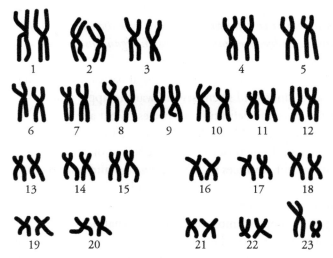

Figure 3.2. Chromosome set from a human male.

Figure 3.2 shows a specially prepared set of human chromosomes taken from a white blood cell. The blood donor was male, since the 23rd pair is the mismatched chromosome pair called "XY"; females have a matched "XX" 23rd pair of "sex chromosomes." Geneticists can diagnose certain conditions based on whether sections of chromosomes have been subtracted (*deletions*), added (*insertions*), or moved around (*translocations*), and on whether whole chromosomes have been added or subtracted from the set (*aneuploidy*) or multiple sets are present (*polyploidy*).

People with Down syndrome, for example, have "too much of a good thing," an extra copy of the 21st chromosome (trisomy 21), giving them 47 chromosomes total. Many cultivated crops have multiple sets of chromosomes — three, four, five, six, or seven in tri-, tetra-, penta-, hexa-, and heptaploid species like wheat!

There are 23 chromosomes in a human set or genome. Most human cells have two sets, or 46 chromosomes total, present as 23 pairs. Egg and sperm cells have only one set (the *monoploid* number, N = 23); when egg and sperm unite to start the life of a new human being, the "double set" (*diploid*, 2N = 46) number is restored. Egg and sperm in turn are formed by a special kind of cell division, *meiosis*, that separates chromosome pairs before later fertilization restores the double set in each generation.

The 23 chromosomes per genome in each human cell include about six feet (2m) of DNA. Much of that DNA

has regulatory, protective, and recognition functions, and functions yet to be discovered, but many long sections of this DNA serve as about *30,000* genes using GCAT bases as "letters" coding for protein production. That's enough information to fill 1,000 books of 500 pages each with small print! The small intestinal bacterium *E. coli* has over 5,000 genes in its naked loop of DNA. Viruses can have less than a dozen genes — but they have to "hijack" the genetic systems of more complex life forms in order to reproduce.

At one level, then, organisms of the *same kind* can be defined as organisms with *chromosomes of the same kind*. Each kind has a *characteristic number* of chromosomes in its set (*genome*), and *chromosomes of the same kind*, called homologous, can be identified by size, shape, and genetic content (and, as we'll see shortly, even breakage and reattachments changing chromosome size and number can be objectively identified).

Most importantly, in sexually reproducing organisms, the homologous chromosomes in diploid parents pair up gene-for-gene in the cell division process (*meiosis*) that halves the chromosome number before union of sex cells restores the diploid number.

Genes of the same kind can be defined chromosomally as segments of DNA that *occupy corresponding positions (loci; sing. locus) on homologous chromosomes.* Genes that pair up in meiotic cell division, therefore, can be identified as *genes of the same kind*. Genes of the same kind are also usually turned on and off by the same gene regulators. In these cases, it is not subjective human opinion that is telling us which genes are the same kind; it is objective, observable cellular processes.

Except for rare mistakes, genes produced by DNA *duplication* or base copying are genetically *identical*, but *homologous* chromosomes come from different parents and are only genetically *similar*. It is possible, for example, that each of the 30,000 coding gene sites (loci) in our first parents was occupied by four different alleles, two in Adam's homologous pair and two in Eve's. We've already looked at the stunning

variation within kind that results in human skin tone with far fewer alleles.

Mutations (random changes in the genetic code) do produce "new genes" not present at creation, but so-called new genes are still found at the same locus, still pair the same way in meiosis, and are still turned on and off by the same regulators. So they are really only *genes of the same kind* as the original, and represent only *variation within kind* (usually harmful variation in the case of mutations).

Notice the terms "new genes" and "different genes" can have two radically different meanings. As geneticists normally do, we have been calling genes of the same kind alleles. The genes for tongue rolling (R) and non-rolling (r) are *"different genes"* in one sense, but only variations of the *same kind* of gene — affecting the same trait, found in corresponding positions (loci) on homologous chromosomes, pairing up in meiosis, and turned on and off by the same regulators. They are NOT different genes in the sense that genes for tongue rolling and for making sickle-cell hemoglobin are! Similarly, the sickle-cell gene is a "new gene" in the sense that it was not present at creation, but it is only a new (and harmful!) *version of a pre-existing gene*, one that occupies the same chromosomal position, pairs the same way, and is turned on and off by the same regulators as the gene for making normal hemoglobin. In fact, the gene for sickle-cell hemoglobin differs in base sequence at only one position out of several hundred in the gene for making hemoglobin, again just *variation within kind* or *allelic variation*.

We need a new and different term to describe genes that are truly new and different — genes with information affecting a different category or trait — not just information on varieties of shirts, for example, but information on shoes (or motorcycles!). For genes that do NOT occupy the same locus on homologous chromosomes, that do NOT pair in meiosis, and that DO contain information on distinctive categories of traits, we will use the word *genon*. Genes for tongue rolling and non-rolling are different alleles, for example, but genes for tongue rolling and genes for making hemoglobin are different genons, with genes for normal and sickle-cell hemoglobin as alleles of the hemoglobin genon.

The human genome includes at least 30,000 different genons, each of which could have been created in four different allelic varieties. Genetic defects and diseases occurring since the corruption of creation have introduced *many new alleles but no new genons*.

All the genes in one generation available to be passed on to the next are called the gene pool. Members of the same kind *may also be defined* as organisms that share the same gene pool. The number of genes for different kinds of traits (genons) can be called *the depth of the gene pool*. Using earlier examples, we could say the human gene pool is 30,000 genons deep, the *E. coli* bacterial gene pool about 5,000, while the gene pool of a small virus may be only a dozen genons deep. The width of the gene pool refers to the amount of its "*horizontal*" allelic variation.

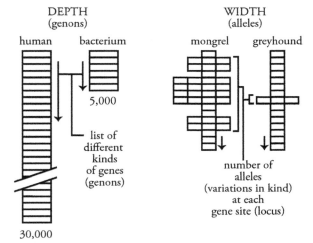

Figure 3.3. Gene pool concepts

Among dogs, for example, the width of a greyhound's gene pool is very narrow; crossing purebred greyhounds just gives you more greyhounds, all very similar in speed, color, intelligence, hair length, nose length, etc. Crossing two "mongrels," however, can give you big dogs and small dogs, dark and light and splotchy-colored dogs, dogs with long and short hair, yappy and quiet dogs, mean and affectionate dogs, and so on! Gene pools for greyhounds and mongrel dogs have the same depth (number of genons, and both are 100 percent dog), but the mongrel gene pool is much wider (has more allelic variation).

"Kind" is defined in terms of depth of the gene pool, the total number of different genons in a genome, and a list of the traits they influence. Variation within kind is defined in terms of the width of the gene pool, the number of alleles at each gene site (locus or genon).

It is becoming popular among creationists to use the term *baramin* for "created kind." Baramin (bah RAH min, or BARE ah min) is a combination of the Hebrew words for create (*bara*, pronounced bah RAH) and for kind (*min*). *Descendants of each of the created kinds belong to the same baramin.*

It is often obvious whether or not two organisms belong to the *same baramin*. A tawny cat and a black cat are certainly members of the same baramin or descendants from the same created kind; a cat and cardinal or red bird certainly belong to different baramins. But as living things multiply and fill the earth, they tend to break up into a *variety of sub-types*, and genetic tests may be required to assign an organism to its proper baramin.

Take the dozens of "sibling species" of fruit flies, for example. They all look alike, but they don't interbreed. In some cases, it is a mutation that affects the courtship ritual or mating dance. Fruit flies are very particular about those sorts of things, and only flies with compatible courtship rituals will mate. Such flies will *reproductively isolate* themselves from other members of their baramin, forming a sub-group that might be called a *fertilotype*.

Chromosomal changes are excellent for producing different *fertilotypes within a baramin*. The common "laboratory fruit fly" (*Drosophila melanogaster*, the "blackbellied fruit lover") has four pairs of chromosomes, three long chromosomes, and one very short. One "sibling species" has five chromosome pairs and another three. Organisms that have different chromosome numbers usually cannot mate and produce viable offspring, since chromosomes in their offspring cannot pair correctly during meiosis to form sex cells. Despite their present inabilities to interbreed, however, these various *fertilotypes* (or "sibling species") are easily seen to be members of the *same baramin*. Members of the different fertilotypes all have genetic instructions for the same kinds of traits. The depth of the gene pool, the list of genons in the genome, has not changed; each is a subset of the same gene pool.

Assignment of reproductively isolated fertilotypes to the same baramin can be done on the basis of genetic tests. The three chromosomes in one fly fertilotype result when the small fourth chromosome becomes attached to one of the larger chromosomes, as demonstrated by meiotic pairing, breeding results, patterns of chromosome

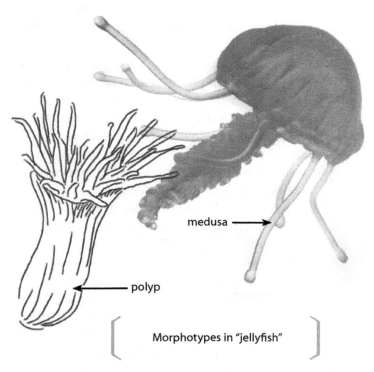

medusa

polyp

Morphotypes in "jellyfish"

bonding, etc. Similarly, fly fertilotypes with five chromosomes result when one of the large chromosomes breaks apart. Again, there is no change in genetic information, just the distribution of that information over five "pages" (chromosomes) instead of four.

It has been said that all the Hawaiian fruit flies ("drosophilids") were once part of a large, interbreeding population that has now broken up into perhaps 700 reproductively isolated subgroups. Although they are variants of the same baramin with the same gene pool depth, it's likely each fertilotype has a *narrower* gene pool width with *less* allelic variety than the original baramin — which means *less* ability to meet changes in their environment and less ability to explore new environments. On the positive side, however, the tendency for baramins to break up into fertilotypes does allow us to see more of God's creative potential (entelechy) expressed in unusual trait combinations that would be very rare in the large, more "average" population.

A cardinal and a cat belong to different baramins.

Remember the bowerbirds? These animals can all interbreed, but they exist in groups that are quite different in appearance from one another. Their interbreeding ability identifies them as members of the same baramin, but subgroups with distinctive appearances can be called *morphotypes*. Different sexes in a baramin often have different appearances (*sexual dimorphism*). Differences between males and females are obvious in human beings, of course; in those birds where only the males are brightly colored; and in the extreme case of a marine worm (*Bonellia*), the male lives "parasitically" in the reproductive tract of the female! Dramatic morphotypic variation is seen in plants and animals with "*alternation of generations.*" A fern, for example, can be either a sizable plant having fronds with many leaflets or a heart-shaped organism one-fourth inch (6mm) across, living in moist soil! These radically different plants have *the same genes*, but the small heart has only one chromosome set and produces egg and sperm cells while the big frond plant has two sets of *the same chromosomes* and produces spores by meiosis — an extreme, yet common, example of morphotypic *variation within kind!* Certain jellyfish also have alternating generations with quite different body forms (cylindrical "polyp" and umbrella-shaped "medusa").

Some baramins produce *ecotypes* whose appearance varies with environmental influences on the expression of their genetic potential. The Scottish red deer was on the verge of being classified as a species different from the red deer of the European mainland, for example, because it was consistently smaller with antlers very much smaller than the mainland form. But when Scottish red deer were taken to New Zealand and released, they grew to full size in that environment. A dwarf willow from the tundra will

A female marine flatworm

grow to much larger size if transplanted to a temperate climate. It's possible that some small plants today are ecotypes of plants that grew much larger under conditions in the pre-Flood world, and experiments with presumed pre-Flood conditions are being done. *Morphotypes do not change their appearance when transferred to a new environment, like ecotypes do.*

The familiar system of scientific naming was developed by a creationist, Carolus Linnaeus (or Karl von Linné). He developed the "two name

Scottish red deer

naming system" (*binomial nomenclature*). Each kind was given a broader name, the *genus* (plural, *genera*), followed by a more specific *species* name, e.g., *Homo sapiens* for human beings. The broader genus name is given first and capitalized, followed by the narrower species name in lower case, both in italics. Oaks, for example, belong to genus *Quercus*; the "more specific" red, white, and black oaks are *Quercus rubrum, Q. alba,* and *Q. niger*. Because of the extreme inconsistencies and arbitrary subjectivity involved in assigning species names today, a far greater degree of scientific objectivity might be obtained (and Linnaeus's original intentions fulfilled) by using the baramin/type as the two parts of a scientific name.

Our modern knowledge of genetics allows us to understand both the *dazzling diversity* and the *limits to variablilty* that God established in each of the created kinds or *baramins*. As living things multiplied and filled the earth, unfolding genetic potential (*entelechy*) diversified most *generalized, adaptable* baramins into a variety of more *specialized, adapted* subtypes: *fertilotypes* reproductively isolated by mutations or chromosomal changes; structurally distinct *morphotypes* separated by genetic drift or mating preference; and *ecotypes* reflecting environmental influence on genetic potential.

The Mosaic Concept of Kind

In the face of the difficulties cited above and the ambiguity of the scientific term species, how is the Christian to approach the scientifically important biblical term *kind*? Some Christians prefer to live with the difficulties cited, just as all scientists must, and are willing to equate kind with species, emphasizing that "multiplying after kinds" is the chief characteristic used in defining both terms. Although we can accept this as a legitimate view, we may also consider another view: the mosaic concept of kind.

"Mosaic" refers here to an artistic mosaic, such as a picture or mural formed of many little bits of colored stone. According to the mosaic concept of kind, God used several different genes or gene sets over and over again in different combinations and proportions to make a variety of life forms, somewhat like an artist might use several different kinds of colored stones over and over in different proportions and arrangements to make a variety of artistic designs. The different bits of stone in the artist's mosaic would correspond to the many different genes or gene sets in God's "mosaics," which are the various forms of living things.

According to this mosaic concept, God used a basic plan in making living creatures somewhat similar to the plan He used in making different non-living substances. All the countless chemical substances in the universe are made from different combinations and proportions of only about a hundred different elements, and each kind of chemical compound can be represented by a formula expressing the number, kind, and arrangement of elements within it. *Perhaps God used genes as "elements"* in making the various kinds of life, so that conceivably each different kind of life could be represented by a *"formula"* indicating the number, kind, and arrangement of different genes (genons) in its chromosomes. Such formulas would, of course, be much larger and much more complex than those for the most complicated chemical substances. Nevertheless, the mosaic concept does suggest that all the incredible variety and diversity of life forms we see about us may be constructed using only the information in a few thousand DNA segments turned on and off by cell

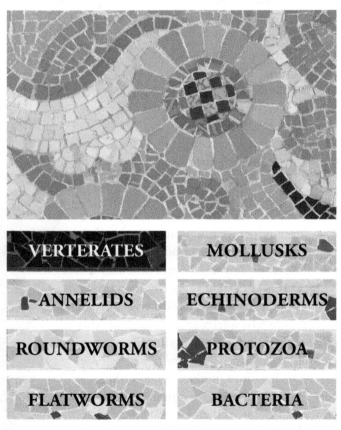

Figure 3.4. Hemoglobin is not distributed along branching lines of descent as postulated by evolution. It is distrbuted rather like a violet stone in an artist's mosaic, or like the element of molybdenum in a list of chemicals. The suggestion is that God used a relatively few genes and gene sets to make living things, somewhat like an artist forms different mosaics of only a few kinds of stones or a chemist many different compounds from just few elements. These genetic mosaic pieces are distributed according to their roles in God's total plan, not according to natural lines of descent in individual species.

regulators in relation to the development of a given trait, so that the regulators as well as the gene product and the function are necessary in defining the gene (or genon).

As an example of what might be considered a genetic "mosaic tile" or "element," consider the DNA segment or gene for making hemoglobin. Hemoglobin is the oxygen-carrying protein in the red blood cells of vertebrates, so the "formula" for vertebrates would include this gene. The hemoglobin gene, however, is also found in many segmented worms, some mollusks and echinoderms, a few insects, and some bacteria. The hemoglobin gene, then, might be compared to a violet-colored mosaic tile, a color that appears abundantly in only a few mosaics, but less obviously in many places. Or the hemoglobin gene might be compared to an element like molybdenum, again rare in general but found distinctively in one family of compounds (Figure 3.4).

Some genetic mosaic tiles or elements might be gene sets, groups of genes that must work together in producing some complex function. The sonar systems, or echolocation devices, of the bat, moth, and oil bird might be examples of such complex mosaic pieces. Echolocation requires the nervous and muscular connections to produce sounds, and the receptors and nervous apparatus to receive and interpret the reflected sound. Individual genes in such a set would be worthless, just as would isolated parts from a radio. Notice, too, that the sonar gene set occurs in widely different kinds of organisms (bat, moth, bird), but when it occurs, it occurs in a completely developed form. One problem, of course, is that a single mutation causing the loss of one protein or one gene in a gene set would

cause loss of the entire trait, so that the examination of the DNA itself, which is now possible, would be necessary for establishing the presence or absence of this gene set in an organism's original or created "formula."

As an example of a whole organism viewed in this mosaic perspective, consider the duckbilled platypus (Figure 3.5). The platypus has the genes and gene regulators for producing fur, a trait widely distributed among animals we call mammals. The platypus also, however, has the gene set required for producing a leathery-shelled egg, a gene set commonly present in reptiles but not in mammals. Like the mammals again, the platypus has a gene set for producing the complex chemical substance called milk, and it nourishes its young on this milk after they hatch from their eggs. The mouth structure, as the name implies, resembles the bill of a duck, yet it contains structures involved in detecting electrical impulses. The creature also has poisonous "fangs" like those we associate with snakes, but the "fangs" exist as spurs on the hind legs of the male. Certainly the combination of traits in the platypus is most unusual, and evolutionists are decidedly uncertain on how to interpret its relationship to other animals.

In this connection, notice that all the various traits and trait sets mentioned so far are fully developed in the platypus, and not in some state of change from some simpler structures or traits. Furthermore, none of the traits possessed by the platypus is unique in itself. Instead, the platypus is a *unique combination of non-unique traits.* In that sense, the platypus is like a mosaic, a unique arrangement of non-unique colored stones. Or it is like

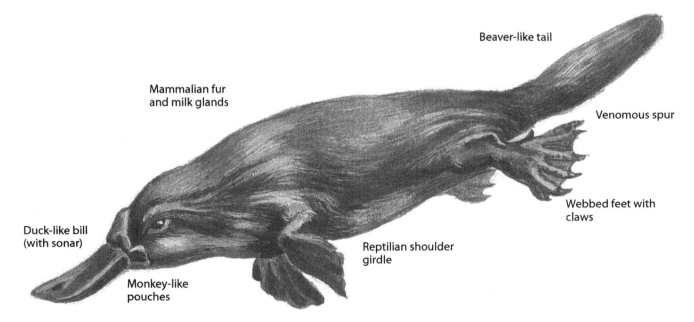

Figure 3.5. The platypus is a mosaic or mixture of several complete traits otherwise found scattered among quite different animals (reptiles, birds, and other mammals).

27

a chemical compound: the elements are not unique, but the number, kind, and arrangement of elements is, and that unique combination of non-unique elements is what makes that compound different from all others. It is perhaps in this way that we can look at the many different kinds of life as well: each unique, and yet each composed of a finite and potentially discoverable number of DNA elements.

If we speculate beyond the limits of our present knowledge, we can even dream of a biological system of classification that would be as well ordered and predictive as Mendeleev's periodic table of the chemical elements below. By someday identifying the genetic elements God used in the creation of the various kinds of life, we might also be able to identify and predict the existence of families of organisms somewhat like the chemist has been able to identify families of chemical compounds and to predict their characteristics. Advances in DNA analysis and computer technology may one day turn such a dream into a useful working concept.

At the present time, most scientists simply accept the term *species* as a rather arbitrary, subjective, ambiguous term. In practice, species names are simply the names agreed upon by conventions of biologists, and all scientists freely acknowledge the desirability of a more objective system. Perhaps a Christian working with the mosaic concept, or some other concept of created kind, will someday be able to propose such an objective concept of kind, both to the glory of God and to the service of the scientific community.

Form your foundation.

Each person and each created kind is a beautiful mosaic, a unique combination of non-unique traits that gives each person and each kind a special place in God's plan that no other can take.
God delights in diversity!

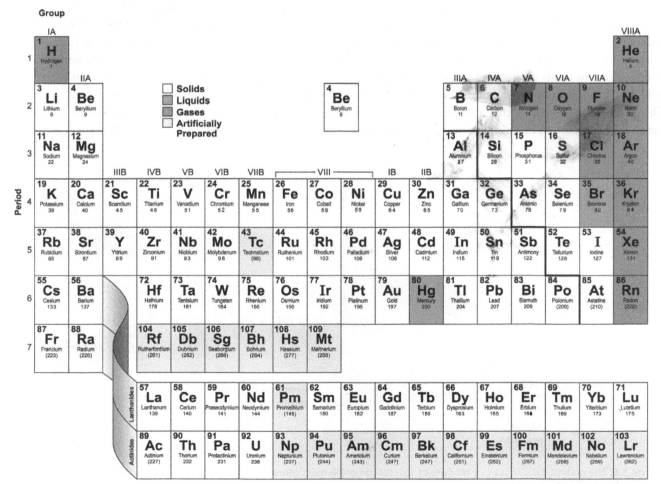

ʼBased upon ¹²C. () indicates the mass number of the most stable isotope.   For a description of the data, visit physics.nist.gov/data   NIST SP 966 (September 2002)

1. The basis for defining both species and kind is God's command that living things "_____."

2. Different kinds of genes (like those for hemoglobin vs. tasting) may be called (**genons/alleles**) _____. Genes of the same kind (like Hb^A vs. Hb^5 genes are _____, and they may be identified by such scientific tests as (a) chromosomal position, (b) meiotic pairing, (c) on-off regulators, (d) information content, (e) all of the above. _____ Organisms of the same kind can be objectively identified by all the following scientific tests except (choose one): (a) pairing of egg and sperm, (b) DNA hybridization, (c) matching chromosome sets; (d) pairing of homologous chromosomes; (e) genome studies; (f) branching lines of descent. _____

3. Created kinds may be called _____, a combination of the Hebrew words *bara* for _____ and *min* for _____.

4. This book uses the following terms for specialized subgroups formed as created kinds "multiplied and filled" the earth. Match them with examples below:

   fertilotype   morphotype   ecotype

   _____ a. Varieties that consistently look different but still interbreed
   _____ b. Differences in mating ritual or chromosomal rearrangements of the same genes (genons) prevent interbreeding
   _____ c. Can change appearance when moved to different environments
   _____ d. Look-alike species of fruit flies with different chromosome numbers
   _____ e. Effects on gene regulators make willow trees dwarfs in the Arctic
   _____ f. Black, brown, grizzly, polar, and panda bears

5. The scientific naming system used today was given to us by _____, a Christian creationist biologist. The two parts of a binomial scientific name are *genus* and *species*. (a) Which is more general (like a person's last name)?_____. (b) Which is more specific (like first names in the same family)?_____. (c) Which is written first in a scientific name? _____. (d) Which is capitalized (genus, species, neither, both)? _____. (e) Which may be abbreviated by its first letter and a period after its first use? _____. (f) Which is always underlined, italicized, or otherwise set off from surrounding print? _____. (g) Which may be abbreviated by its first letter and a period after its first use? _____. (h) What's the plural of genus? _____. (i) What's the singular of species? _____. (j) Correctly write the scientific name for mankind: _____ _____.

6. No single trait makes a person unique, i.e., different from all others (not hair, eye, or skin color; not height, weight, or nose length; etc.). Yet each person is a (**unique/non-unique**) _____ combination of traits that are separately _____, i.e., shared with others. Similarly, each created kind is a _____ combination of _____ traits shared with other kinds, somewhat like each molecule is a _____ combination (CO_2, CH_4, NH_3) of _____ atoms (C, O, H, N). Similarly, bits of (**unique/non-unique**) _____ colored stones may be artistically arranged to form a _____ mosaic artwork — and each created kind may be a unique _____ of non-unique genetic elements put together by God.

7. The platypus has several major non-unique traits, some shared with other mammals, reptiles, or birds. To decide whether the platypus is a created mosaic or evolutionary link, a scientist could consider whether the non-unique traits are complete and complex (creation) or incomplete and gradational (evolution):
   _____ a. Is the platypus hair 100% hair (creation), or partly mammalian hair and reptilian scale (evolution)?
   _____ b. Is the milk 100% milk (creation), or a combination of features of milk and sweat (evolution)?
   _____ c. Is the egg 100% egg (creation), or does it show evidence of forming an attachment to its mother (evolution)?

Chapter 3

"Change through Time" vs. Darwinian Change

It's obvious from the foregoing discussion of "Genes and Genesis" that the creation model includes many types of "change through time" — lots and lots of change, some of it happening quite rapidly!

In their *second greatest propaganda ploy*, evolutionists tried to convince the world that creationists believe in "fixity of species." Taken to the extreme, that was supposed to mean belief that God created each species looking exactly as it does today and living in exactly the environment where it lives today — a notion totally false. It's doubtful that any Christian ever believed a view like that, and such a concept of fixity is totally anti-biblical. It would deny the variability that God built into each kind so that they could multiply and fill the earth with diversity and individuality (entelechy). It would deny the major changes that occurred when mankind corrupted God's creation; e.g., plants producing thorns, and animal predators beginning to kill and eat other animals. It would deny the re-diversification into radically changed environments among the animals that got off the ark. Finally, it would deny the fantastic re-creation that occurs when Christ returns, and once again *"the wolf shall dwell with the lamb, and the leopard shall lie down with the kid. . . . they shall not hurt nor destroy in all my holy mountain; for the earth shall be filled with the knowledge of Jehovah, as the waters cover the sea"* (Isa. 11:6–9; ASV). Wow, do creationists believe in "change through time" — more change than evolutionists dare dream, and faster, too!

Perhaps the evolutionist's most successful propaganda ploy has been to define *evolution* as *"change through time,"* and then to *equate "change" with "evolution."* People may sometimes try to get you to accept evolution by saying, "You believe in change, don't you?" You might like to say, as you jingle some coins, "Of course I believe in change; I've got some in my pocket." They will say, "I don't mean that kind of change." But that's the point. NOT every kind of change is evolution. People growing old and feeble, a young child growing up, road kill decomposing, leaves turning color in autumn, a storm devastating a reef, weeds taking over an unmowed

God built a variability into each kind so they could multiply and fill the earth.

yard — all of these are change through time, yet NONE of them is evolution! So what kind of change is evolution anyway?

Most people associate "evolution" with the belief that over millions of years natural processes (*time, chance, struggle,* and *death*) have changed some single-celled organisms through stages into fish, then apes, and now mankind and all the other life forms on earth. Such a grand sequence of generally progressive change would involve, of course, a tremendous and continuous increase in genetic information. Not only do we have *more genes* than bacteria, for example, but we also have *different kinds of genes* — genes for features and functions bacteria don't even have. This kind of change, adding new genes (genons) for new features and functions so that one initial life form gradually filled the earth with more and more complex and varied life forms, is properly called MACROevolution!

Macro means "big," and the changes pictured in macroevolution certainly are big: non-life to life, one-celled life to multicellular, asexual reproduction to sexual, invertebrates to vertebrates, apes to man. But evolution

has a *radically different meaning* when it's coupled with the prefix "micro" as MICROevolution. Macroevolution is about "molecules to man," as the subtitle of an old government biology textbook put it, or "fish to philosopher" (another book title), or at least reptile to bird. But microevolution is only about big dogs vs. little dogs, race horses vs. work horses, pink flowers vs. white flowers.

Macroevolution	adding genes that never existed before
Microevolution	shuffling existing genes and their alleles into various combinations

So-called *microevolution* actually involves no processes or results different from those already described by creationists for producing *variation within the created kinds.* So, *unless otherwise stated, we will use the term* evolution *to mean macroevolution,* since that's the point of difference between creation and evolution models.

For the far, FAR lesser amounts of variability on which both sides agree, creationists prefer the term *variation within kind* (or entelechy), while evolutionists prefer the term *microevolution.* Creationists want to emphasize, of course, both scientific and scriptural limits to diversity; evolutionists want to suggest that (*contrary* to the evidence we'll discuss later) little changes (microevolution) plus LOTS of time add up to big changes (macroevolution).

Creationists and evolutionists agree on the kinds of changes we see being produced in the present by

Changes through time

Which of these "changes through time" are examples of evolution?

  a. growth of child into adult
  b. old man losing ability to walk
  c. road kill decomposing
  d. weeds growing in abandoned yard
  e. none of the changes above

31

such processes as genetic recombination, mutation, genetic drift, Darwinian struggle, speciation, etc. But they strongly disagree on how much change those same processes could produce even over vast amounts of time.

The potential connection between observed variation within kind and *hypothetical* macroevolution from one kind to others is called extrapolation, following a trend to its logical conclusion. Scientists extrapolate from population records, for example, to predict changes in the world population. If world population growth continued at the rate observed in the 1960s, statisticians said, then the world population by AD 2000 would be over six billion. Similarly, if variation continued over very long periods of time, evolutionists say, the same process that changes moths from mostly light to mostly dark forms will gradually change fish to philosophers or molecules to man.

Now there's nothing wrong with extrapolation in principle. But there are things to watch for in practice. For example, simple extrapolation would suggest a population of a "zillion" by AD 3000. But, of course, there will come a point when the earth is simply not big enough to support any more people. In other words, there are *limits*, or *boundary conditions*, to logical extrapolation. Runners have broken the four-minute mile, but the limit for human runners will be reached before anyone breaks the one-minute mile (60 miles/hr or 96 km/hr)!

Professional evolutionists are aware of the problem. In their classic textbook, *Evolution*, the late Theodosius Dobzhansky and three other famous evolutionists distinguish between SUB*speciation* and TRANS*speciation*. "Sub" is essentially variation within species, and "trans" is change from one species to another. The authors state their belief that one can "extrapolate" from variation *within* species to evolution *between* species. But they also admit that some of their fellow evolutionists believe that such extrapolation goes beyond all logical limits, like running a one-minute mile.

What does the evidence suggest? Can evolution from "molecules to man" be extrapolated from selection among dark and light moths? Or are there boundary conditions and logical limits to the amount of change that time, chance, struggle, and death (Darwin's "war of nature") can produce? *Which side of the debate currently enjoys the best scientific support?* Have creationists been able to identify the scientific processes and factors that limit *variation to within kind?* Or have evolutionists found the scientific processes that would produce limitless *genetic expansion* from simple beginnings?

Charles Darwin

We've looked at genetic variability in creationist perspective. Let's look now at what evolutionists have to say.

Darwinian Change

Both genes and Genesis allow for fantastic variability within the created kinds. But evolutionists wanted more. From ancient times, evolutionists had dreamed of finding some natural process that would change one or a few simple life forms into many complex and varied ones — all without any outside "help" or "interference" from some "creator." They wanted change between kinds, not just variation within kind. In 1859, long before scientists discovered the laws of heredity or deciphered DNA's genetic code, evolutionists believed they had found such a process in the book by Charles Darwin, *On the Origin of Species by Means of Natural Selection, or the Preservation of Favoured Races in the Struggle for Life* (usually shortened to *Origin of Species*).

Natural selection. As described by the evolutionist debater in Volume 1 (*Building Blocks in Science*), natural selection is a fact. It's based on two obvious observations leading to one logical conclusion: (1) there is an incredible amount of heritable variation among the members of a species; (2) there is a constant *struggle* for *survival*, which only a few of each species survive; (3) those varieties that do survive may be called the *fittest*, so there will be a *survival of the fittest*. Darwin, himself a pigeon breeder, was well aware of all the specialized varieties of dogs, cats, horses, pigeons, etc., produced by the artificial selection of plant and animal breeders, so he called his three-part process natural selection, i.e., selection by nature, without help from man or God, as a consequence of (1) variety + (2) struggle = (3) survival of the fittest.

Since the 1950s, the classic example used in almost all biology textbooks to illustrate natural selection involves the peppered moth, *Biston betularia*. Peppered moths came in several varieties, from light forms "peppered" with black flecks to the solidly dark-colored forms (Figure 4.1). These moths are common in the forests of the British Isles, and collectors have long kept records of the moths. Over a hundred years ago, most of the moths collected around London were of the light-colored variety. In those days, most of the trees were covered with a light gray lichen growth, on which the light-colored moths were well camouflaged from predatory birds. By contrast, the dark-colored form was fairly obvious and presumably much more noticeable to predators. At that time only about two moths in a hundred were dark colored.

Then pollution changed the environmental situation. Pollutants killed the lichens on the trees, causing the natural dark color of the trees to show through. In this new situation, the dark-colored moths seemed to be better camouflaged and consequently, more "fit to survive." Over a period of a hundred years, the population shifted from 98 percent light to 98 percent dark. Light forms still predominate in the unpolluted forests of Scotland, and now that pollution controls are in effect in the London area, the light forms, as expected, are again becoming predominant there, too.

Recently the peppered moth story has come under considerable fire. The classic pictures contrasting light- and dark-colored forms on tree trunks were made of dead moths glued to the tree trunks. The moths seem to rest instead high in the branches where both dark and light backgrounds exist, and the moths have a complex instinct for searching out a background matching their color, a phenomenon called *habitat choice*. Besides, rather than staying in polluted forests to be eaten, many migrated to other areas. Furthermore, moth color is polygenic, grading through several shades from very light to very dark, like human skin color does. In fact, the moth's coloring agent, like ours, is melanin, and the increase in dark forms in polluted areas is often called industrial melanization. Despite all these difficulties with the story, we'll continue to use the classic story of the peppered moth to illustrate natural selection.

It's becoming increasingly common, however, for evolutionists to illustrate natural selection with increasing numbers of resistant forms; e.g., increasing *antibiotic resistance* among bacteria, *herbicide resistance* among plants, and *pesticide resistance* among insects. Populations of bacteria, plants, and insects usually include a variety of forms, grading from those very sensitive to various poisons used against them to those that are very resistant. Widespread use of antibiotics, herbicides, and pesticides kills off sensitive forms, leaving the more resistant forms for survival in greater numbers (and that has very important consequences for health, agriculture, and even, some say, human survival). Evolutionist call the greater survival of resistant forms in a toxic environment "natural selection."

Figure 4.1. The famous peppered moth, *Biston betularia*, in its darkest form (middle) and its lightest form (bottom)

The peppered moth and antibiotic resistance do illustrate Darwin's "war of nature," but that should also make one ask this question:

Question	What is so significant about a theory that explains, in rather obvious fashion, why preexisting camouflaged and resistant varieties survive to produce more offspring?

The answer to this pointed question is probably found in both the philosophic mood of the times, since Darwin's theory had far more philosophic impact than scientific, and also in the low degree of development in some of the life sciences. Had the sciences of genetics and ecology been developed in Darwin's time, natural selection would probably have rated a section or chapter along with other technically important concepts, such as the Hardy-Weinberg Law. That is, Darwin's theory would have been considered a valuable piece of scientific work, but never a revolutionary concept of philosophic importance.

In the roughly 150 years since Darwin's concept of natural selection became popular, scientists have

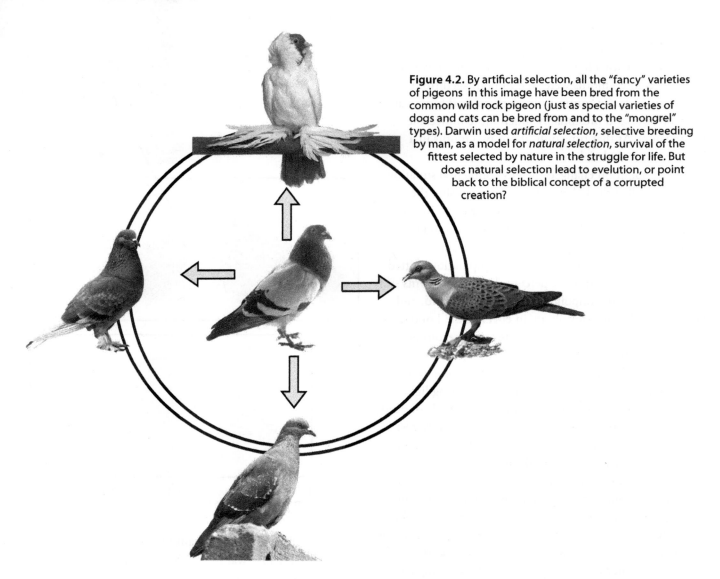

Figure 4.2. By artificial selection, all the "fancy" varieties of pigeons in this image have been bred from the common wild rock pigeon (just as special varieties of dogs and cats can be bred from and to the "mongrel" types). Darwin used *artificial selection*, selective breeding by man, as a model for *natural selection*, survival of the fittest selected by nature in the struggle for life. But does natural selection lead to evelution, or point back to the biblical concept of a corrupted creation?

discovered a long list of factors, both logical and scientific, that set definite *limits to the kind and amount of change natural selection can produce — no matter what the time involved.* You could calculate how long it would take you, pedaling a bicycle at 10 mph (16 kph), to reach the moon, but such a calculation would ignore serious limits to getting to the moon on a bicycle — even if you had zillions of years to do it!

Following are some of the limits that prevent extrapolation from natural selection to evolution — limits causing a growing number of scientists to say, "Natural selection, yes; evolution, no."

Form your foundation.

His followers agree that what Darwin called "the war of nature, famine, and death" would make things better, leading to "the production of higher animals" (evolution). Science and logic tell us Darwin's "war of nature" makes things worse, and Scripture tells us struggle and death began only after man's sin corrupted God's perfect creation.

1. Suppose someone challenges you this way: "You've got to believe in evolution. Evolution is just 'change through time.' You believe in change, don't you?" Respond by "giving a reason for the hope that is in you" (1 Peter 3:15), using evidence and logic.

   _____

   _____

   _____

   _____

2. Explain what Darwin's followers mean by MICRO- vs. MACROevolution, and give at least a hypothetical example of each. What would a creationist say about these two terms?

   _____

   _____

   _____

   _____

3. Explain why no Christian familiar with the 4 Cs of biblical history would ever have accepted "fixity of species." Why do many evolutionists say that's what Christians believe?

   _____

   _____

   _____

   _____

4. Suppose Darwin was right about the "war of nature" (time, chance, struggle, and death, or TCSD), and suppose Darwin's followers are right that (1) variety + (2) struggle = (3) survival of the fittest. Does that mean they are right about evolution? Use the famous peppered moth example to help you explain why or why not.

   _____

   _____

   _____

   _____

5. What does "molecules to man" evolution need that neither microevolution nor natural selection provide?

   _____

   _____

   _____

   _____

6. Why did Darwin call his view "natural selection"? Why do Darwin's followers prefer this term to "war of nature"?

   _____

   _____

   _____

   _____

Chapter 4

Natural Selection, Yes; Evolution, No

Logical Limits to Natural Selection

What does "fittest" mean? The definition of "fittest" guarantees that *natural selection must be accepted as a fact*. Most people assume that "fitness" refers to features of structure, function, or behavior that suit an organism for a particular role in its environment. *It doesn't*. Fitness is defined by scientists solely in relation to relative reproductive success. *Members of a population that leave the most offspring to the next generation are fittest by definition.*

You may have thought the dark-colored peppered moth was fittest to survive in a polluted forest because it was most camouflaged. But what if the extra melanin production interfered with, say, sex hormone production and made the dark-colored moths sterile? Obviously, the superior camouflage would *not* make such a moth fittest to survive! Evolutionists think the camouflage helped, of course, but the dark moths were really determined to be "fittest to survive" because a greater percentage of their offspring survived in polluted forests than the percentage for any other color form.

So the only way to determine fitness is to make notes on organisms in the first generation, wait for the *struggle for survival* to take place, then see which organisms actually left the most offspring to the next generation. To see how scientists calculate fitness, let's work through Figure 5.1 (following page), a simple example involving one pair of alleles, A and a, which produce three varieties of organisms: AA, Aa, and aa (which could be, for example, tall-medium-short, red-pink-white, fast-moderate-slow, etc.).

We'll start the first generation (G_1) with 40 AA, 40 Aa, and 20 aa individuals. The second generation (G_2) coming through the struggle for survival includes 20 AA, 60 Aa, and 20 aa. It's already obvious that organisms in the genotype Aa were fittest, winning the struggle for survival, since they're the only group that increased in numbers. The numerical fitness of each group can be easily calculated. First, divide the number in the second generation in each category by the number in the first (G_2/G_1); that gives $^{20}/_{40} = 0.5$ for AA; $^{60}/_{40} = 1.50$ for Aa; and $^{20}/_{20} = 1.00$ for aa.

Note the highest G_2/G_1 ratio is the 1.50 for the Aa fittest, or winners, in this example. Calculate the

CALCULATION OF FITNESS, OR NET RELATIVE REPRODUCTIVE EFFICIENCY											
	A. Static Population				B. Increasing Population				C. Decreasing Population		
Trait categories	AA	Aa	aa	Total	AA	Aa	aa	Total	AA	Aa	aa	Total
First generation, G_1	50	30	20	100	50	30	20	100	50	30	20	100
Second Generation, G_2	20	60	20	*100*	40	120	40	*200*	10	30	10	*50*
G_2 / G_1 ratio	20/50	60/30	20/20		40/50	120/30	40/20		10/50	30/30	10/20	
"Numerical fitness," NF	0.4	2.0	1.0		0.8	4.0	2.0		0.2	1.0	0.5	
H, highest ratio, (survival winner)		*2.0*				*4.0*				*1.0*		
NF ÷ H	0.4/2	2/2	1/2		0.8/4	4/4	2/4		0.2/1	1/1	0.5/1	
"Standardized fitness"	0.2	1.0	0.5		0.2	1.0	0.5		0.2	1.0	0.5	
Fittest		**1.0**				**1.0**				**1.0**		

Figure 5.1. The calculations above compare the fitness of three variations of a trait (AA, Aa, aa, which could represent, for example, "large-medium-small" or "red-pink-white," etc.). Dividing numbers in the second generation by the first (G_2/G_1) gives the "numerical fitness," which is standardized by dividing each by the highest ratio (H). Based on counts of survivors (and not on any particular adaptation, such as intelligence, speed, or camouflage), standardized fitness values range from 0 (no survivors) to 1.0 (top survivor). Note that Aa is the top survivor above (fitness = 1.0) whether the population of its species is static (A), increasing (B), or decreasing (C). In case C, Aa is the "high scorer" on a "losing team," *winning the natural selection battle* **within** its species, but possibly becoming extinct as its species is *losing the ecological war* with others.

standardized fitness value by dividing each "survival ratio" (G_2/G_1) by the highest (H). This last step always gives the winner a fitness value of 1.00 (H/H) and ranks other groups from 0 (a loser with no survivors) to some fraction of 1.00. The AA fitness here is $^{0.50}/_{1.50}$ or 0.33, meaning the AA's survived about "one-third as well" as the fittest Aa's. The aa's did better at $^{1.00}/_{1.50}$ = 0.67, surviving about "two/thirds as well" as the fittest.

Several profound and often misunderstood consequences follow from the simple calculation of fitness:

(1)   *Survival of the survivors.* The definition of fitness is grounded ultimately in reproductive success, so it is sometimes called differential reproduction or net relative reproductive efficiency. In far less pompous-sounding phrases, what that boils down to is survival of the survivors. *Now you can see why natural selection, or survival of the fittest, is a fact.* How is it determined which organisms will be "naturally selected" as fittest? Wait for the struggle for survival to play out from one generation to the next, then count who survived in greatest numbers! An organism may be ugly, slow, or stupid, but if its offspring survive in greatest numbers, it's the fittest!

Notice that natural selection is NOT some awesomely powerful scientific theory that enables scientists to predict future changes in population. *"Natural selection" is really just a high-sounding, misinforming term* applied to the observation that some organisms in a varied population survive in greater numbers than others do: *survival of the survivors.* After scientists observe which organisms are "fittest" (i.e., survived in greatest relative numbers), then they can begin to *speculate on why.* Was it camouflage, speed, intelligence, fecundity (having lots of offspring easily), disease resistance, some combination, or none of these, or just "blind luck"? Ecclesiastes 9:11 says, "The race is not to the swift, nor the battle to the strong [in our fallen world] . . . but time and chance happeneth to them all" (ASV).

Natural selection is a fact because it's a tautology or truism, a form of circular reasoning. *It is argued that the fittest are those that survive in greatest relative numbers, and those that survive in greatest relative numbers are defined as the fittest.* That's definitely true, but it may be trivial. It's really an observation, not a profound theory, and *begs the question of what makes some organisms fitter than others.*

The story is told of a student walking to school who saw in the grass a mouse that remained absolutely motionless as a hawk soared overhead. When she asked her teacher why, the teacher explained that mice that ran were seen and killed by the hawk, so natural selection produced those that remained motionless. The next day, the student saw a mouse running to its burrow as a hawk soared overhead. Her teacher explained how mice that remained motionless were easy targets for the sharp-eyed hawk that killed and ate them, so natural selection favored survival of the mice that ran. The "nice" thing about "survival of the survivors" is that it can explain anything: why mice run or stay put, why some species (e.g., horseshoe crabs) never changed in "600 million years" while others changed rapidly and quickly (e.g., an insect eater thought to have evolved into horses, whales, and bats in less than "5 million years"). The so-called proof that natural selection produces evolution is merely the circular argument that survivors survived!

(2) *Fitness vs. adaptation.* Adaptations are *features and functions that suit an organism for its role in its environment.* Fitness is determined by counting survivors in Darwin's "war of nature." Adaptation is determined by engineering or design analysis. A woodpecker is admirably designed for drilling holes in wood regardless of how well it is surviving. Professional evolutionists freely admit that *fitness and adaptation are quite different concepts determined in quite*

different ways, but that major difference is almost always overlooked in popular nature programs and children's literature, and it's often ignored in introductory college biology textbooks. Professional evolutionists do go on to say that at least some of the time well-adapted organisms should show greater fitness (i.e., leave more offspring to the next generation than their competitors). Creationists already believe, of course, that organisms God created with adaptations were designed with survival value so they could multiply and fill the earth.

There is no convincing evidence or argument that fitness or natural selection leads to adaptation, but there is ample evidence and logic for the *reverse: adaptation can lead to natural selection!* If organisms already have certain adapted or adaptable traits, then, as they multiply over the earth, they will more likely survive and be "fittest" or "naturally selected" in some environments rather than others. In his article entitled "Adaptation" in the *Scientific American* book *Evolution,* Richard Lewontin emphasizes this point over and over again:

> Evolution cannot be described as a process of adaptation because all organisms are already adapted. . . . Adaptation leads to natural selection, natural selection does not necessarily lead to greater adaptation.[1]

That is, adaptation has to come *first, before* natural selection can act. Natural selection obviously cannot explain the *origin* of traits or adaptations if the traits have to be there first.

Lewontin recognizes that this simple (but crucial) point is often overlooked, so he gives an example. As a region becomes drier, he says, plants can respond by developing a deeper root system or a thicker cuticle (waxy coating) on the leaves, but "*only if* their gene pool contains genetic variation for root length or cuticle thickness"

1. Richard L. Lewontin, "Adaptation," *Scientific American,* Sept. 1978.

(emphasis added). Here again, the adaptation for deep roots and thick, waxy coats must be present among the genes of a kind *before* natural selection can select them. And if the genes are already there, we are talking only about variation within kind, i.e., creation, not evolution. As creationists were saying *even before* Darwin's time, natural selection does *not* explain the *origin of* species or traits, but only how and where certain varieties survive as they multiply and fill the earth.

Lewontin is an evolutionist and outspoken anti-creationist, but he honestly recognizes the same limitations of natural selection that creation scientists do:

> Natural selection operates essentially to enable the organisms to *maintain* their state of adaptation rather than to improve it [emphasis added].[2]

Natural selection does not lead to continual improvement (evolution); it only helps to maintain features that organisms already have (creation). Lewontin also notes that extinct species seem to have been just as fit to survive as modern ones, so he adds:

> Natural selection over the long run does *not* seem to improve a species' chances of survival, but simply enables it to "track," or *keep up with*, the constantly changing environment [emphasis added].[3]

Adaptation leads to natural selection because kinds were created with design features and sufficient variety to multiply and fill the earth in all its ecologic and geographic variety. Without realizing it at the time, Darwin actually discovered important evidence pointing to both God's *creation* (adaption and variation) and the *corruption* of creation (struggle and death).

(3)　*Natural selection vs. ecological competition.* Most people just assume "natural selection" for the "fittest" means the selected population must be increasing. Actually, natural selection has nothing

to do with whether a species as a whole is increasing or decreasing in numbers or staying the same (static or stable). Look back at the calculation of fitness in Figure 5.1. In Case A, the population was static or stable; the second generation (G_2) had 100 individuals like the first one did (G_1). Now imagine the population doubled to 200 (Case B), and G_2 consisted of 40 AA, 120 Aa, and 40 AA. Let's start, as before, with a G_1 of 40 AA, 40Aa, and 20 aa. What would the new fitness values be? The winner ("fittest") being "naturally selected" is still Aa, and its G_2/G_1 ratio is $120/40 = 3.0$, which is the highest value (H). That means the fitness of Aa, $3.0/H$, is 3.0/3.0 or 1.00, the maximum value, just as it was in the static population. The fitness values for the AA and aa groups are also exactly the same in the expanding population (Case B) as they were for the static Case A. For AA, $G_2/G_1 = 40/40 = 1.0$, and $1.0/H = 1.0/3.0 = 0.33$, "one third" the maximum fitness as before. For aa, $G_2/G_1 = 40/20 = 2.0$, and $2.0/H = 2.0/3.0 = 0.67$, the same "two-thirds" maximum as in the static population.

What if the species population is decreasing? Who's the fittest then? Imagine the population declined by half (Case C), and the second generation was 10 AA, 30 Aa, 10 aa (50 total) with G_1 again 40AA, 40Aa, and 20 aa. Still, Aa is the best survivor or fittest, this time because it declined the least in population. The best G_2/G_1, or H, is $30/40 = 0.75$ for Aa. The AA's again did only one-third as

2. Richard L. Lewontin, "Adaptation," *Scientific American*, Sept. 1978.
3. Ibid.

well: $^{10}/_{40} = 0.25$ and $^{0.25}/H = ^{0.25}\%_{.75} = 0.33$. The aa's again did two-thirds as well: $^{10}/_{20} = 0.50$, and $^{0.50}/H = ^{0.50}\%_{.75} = 0.67$. Notice, however, the species population is decreasing dramatically. In Case C, being the fittest only means being the high scorer on the losing team!

Being the fittest, then, is no guarantee of survival at all. *It may only mean you are likely to be the last of your kind to die out!* Fitness has to do with competition *within a group*; survival of the group often depends on competition *between different groups*, often related to changing environmental factors — loss of habitat, increase or decrease in temperature or moisture levels, changes in the saltiness of aquatic and soil environments, catastrophes like fires, floods, earthquakes, underwater landslides, etc. So, for example, it's NOT natural selection that determines whether the dull and sluggish opossum or the sleek and daring cheetah survives; it's ecology, interaction among different groups and the environment (and at present the opossum is out-surviving the cheetah — putting "ugly, slow, and stupid" in the lead!).

(4)   *Intra- vs. interspecific competition.* Many people have the mistaken notion that natural selection involves, for example, competition between lions and zebras. Not at all. Natural selection is NOT lion vs. zebra; it's *lion vs. lion* (who can catch a zebra) and *zebra vs. zebra* (who can escape the lion). In other words, natural selection is NOT INTER*specific* competition (between species); it's INTRA*specific* competition (within species). By analogy to human kind, natural selection is competition among classmates and friends for dates on a Saturday night and jobs at McDonald's, or competition among brothers and sisters for family favors. Natural selection is the ultimate sibling rivalry, a struggle to the death among members of the same species.

Even members of a plant species compete with one another (not consciously, of course) for water and minerals from the soil and a place in the sun. Some variants of a species are more likely to leave more offspring to the next generation than others, but at most the intraspecific competion of natural selection

produces variation within kind, NOT change from one kind to another. *Natural selection, yes; evolution, no.*

A classic lab kit sold to demonstrate natural selection does nothing of the sort. The kit includes *two different species* of flour beetle, *Tribolium confusum* and *T. castaneum*. By changing temperature and moisture conditions and adding predators and different hiding places, students can see one beetle survives under this condition, the other beetle species under another. Competition between different species as conditions change is ecological competition, not at all natural selection among members of the same group.

Evolutionists, however, did report an example of natural selection that once occurred in a flour beetle experiment. A mutant beetle occurred in one species, and offspring of that beetle eventually wiped out other members of that species — natural selection in action. But the "new and improved" beetle species then lost the ecological competition with the other beetle species under conditions that the pre-mutant beetle species *formerly won*. As evolutionists recognize, winning the natural selection battle can lead to losing the ecological war — *"mischievous results"* of natural selection one evolutionist called it.

(5)   *Succession vs. evolution.* Evolution is a hypothetical process that is supposed to change a few simple forms over time into many complex and varied forms. There is a real process of change through time in which a few life forms are followed by a series of more and more complex and varied forms, but the real process is ecological succession, NOT evolution. If you watched a certain area of bare rock over time, as scientists have, you could observe a series of changes from lichens to moss, ferns, shrubs, and trees. But the lichens didn't evolve into the moss, nor the moss into the ferns, etc. Rather, each living community changed the environment in ways that paved the way for the next community to move

in. (Plants "move" by scattering spores and seeds that sprout when conditions are right.) Lichens can break down rock, producing enough soil for mosses. Mosses build more soil, and hold moisture, paving the way for ferns and shrubs. These break up the rock further, anchor the soil, and provide shade to decrease moisture loss, paving the way (in the proper climate) for trees.

It is environmental change, NOT *natural selection* or *evolution*, that produces the progressive changes in ecological succession. It is migration of different kinds, NOT *mutation* of one kind into others, that produced the sequence. And succession involves only *tens* or *hundreds of years*, NOT millions.

As the plant communities change, so do the animals. Protozoans are followed successively by worms, insects, birds, and mammals. *Existing species* from another area move in as conditions become favorable — ecology, not evolution.

Ecological succession on a global scale would have followed both creation (multiply and fill) and the Flood (migration from Ararat). As discussed later, dramatic environmental changes caused by the Flood would favor both (a) selection for different adaptations among pre- and post-Flood members of the same kind, and also (b) survival of different kinds in different proportions in the pre- and post-Flood ecologies.

Natural selection and ecological competition may not help explain evolutionary changes, but they do help explain changes important in the creation model.

(6) *Long-term vs. short-term advantage.* Richard Dawkins, Great Britain's leading spokesman for evolution, refers to evolution by natural selection as the "blind watchmaker." In contrast to creation by plan and purpose looking toward a goal, natural selection, Dawkins asserts, is a "blind" process that does not plan, has no purpose, and can't look ahead toward goals. Natural selection is merely opportunistic, rewarding chance combinations of traits with a slight advantage in Darwin's ceaseless "war of nature."

Dawkins is right about selection but wrong about the nature of the living world. *Natural selection cannot plan ahead*; selection is only the observation that certain trait combinations will win the immediate struggle for survival, becoming, by definition, the fittest — *no matter*

what that does to the future of the species. That can have a devastating impact on living things, the exact opposite of the evolutionist's hopes and dreams.

Consider territorial population control. Many birds and mammals regulate their populations through a series of complex instincts and "ritualistic combat" in which no death occurs and no predators are necessary. Sea lions, for example, limit their population by "allowing" breeding only on certain restricted territories on small beaches. Males who fail to stake out a territory one year must wait until later years to breed. That guarantees plenty of food for the species as it cruises the Pacific. But suppose a chance mutation knocked out the instinct for territorial recognition. Such a mutant male might establish a new breeding colony on another island and pass on his unrestricted urge to breed. Descendants of such a male would automatically win the struggle for survival in the short term, but the long term effects might include over-hunting their range and even bring the species to extinction — or at least replace gentle territorial control with harsher predatory control.

In a given environment, specialists are usually more efficient at exploiting food sources than generalists, and evolutionists recognize the tendency for natural selection to convert generalized ancestral populations into ever more specialized descendants. But when the environment changes, highly adapted, specialized varieties tend to lose out to the adaptable, generalized forms — if there are any left. Again, *natural selection seems to promote short-term survival at the expense of long-term extinction.* As we shall see in the unit on fossils, the long-term survivors over and over again are the generalized, adaptable forms like those God created to multiply and fill the earth, NOT the specialized forms natural selection generated to exploit short-term advantage. Once again, it's "(sub) speciation, yes; evolution, no."

Dawkins is right about the blindness and failure to plan by natural selection, but that makes him wrong about evolution and life.

Eliminating the defects of an old car will never turn it into a race car.

(7) *Brake or accelerator?* Remember, evolution may not be true, but natural selection is. *Natural selection is a process at work in our fallen world; it is a description of what happens when different varieties of the same gene-trading species compete for limited resources.* But as we have seen, the results of natural selection in action are often the opposite of what evolutionists expected, and the exact opposite of what the public is told.

Calling natural selection "survival of the fittest" conjures up an image of a positive, progressive process. But natural selection really operates as the "great eliminator" or "terminator," and might be better called "unsurvival of the unfittest." Think back on the famous peppered moth case. Natural selection did NOT produce a "new and improved moth"; the dark moth was already present. Pollution made the light form less camouflaged, and so (presumably) natural selection eliminated more light than dark moths. Had natural selection "gone to completion" and totally eliminated the light moth, the species might now be well on the road to extinction, since reduction in pollution has now made the dark moth less camouflaged. Were there no death at all, the genes for dark and light colors would continue at the same percentages "forever" (the Hardy-Weinberg Law). By eliminating or reducing some genes, natural selection can reduce genetic variability and thus reduce long-term survival, but it did nothing to produce the dark-colored moth that already existed.

Mutations are supposed to produce new traits for selection to select, but known mutations are either neutral (having no effect) or harmful, producing defects, disease, and disease organisms. Perhaps the most important role of natural

selection in a fallen world (corrupted creation) is acting as a brake, slowing down the accumulation of harmful mutations, eliminating or reducing genetic decay by producing "unsurvival of the unfittest."

All scientists agree that *elimination of the unfit* is a major consequence of natural selection in our present world, but a process that works at best to make tomorrow no worse than today is no process for producing the evolutionist's dream of upward, onward progress. Eliminating defects to repair an old car and keep it running is good, but it will never turn a minivan into a Formula 1 race car!

The seven points above are all logical limits to *extrapolating* the hypothetical process of evolution (macroevolution) from the observable process of natural selection. It really looks like using natural selection to "reach" evolution is like using a bicycle to reach the moon; the barriers are insurmountable, *no matter how much time you take.* But evolutionists face two even more serious difficulties in trying to explain evolution as a result of natural selection: "compound traits" and "origin" of new traits.

Form your foundation.

Don't be fooled by evolution's "word games." "Survival of the fittest" does NOT explain change from one kind to another, but only helps explain how and where varieties thrive as descendants of each created kind "multiplied and filled the earth" after sin.

1. Describe how "**fitness**" is determined so that "**survival of the fittest**" is a fact. Then explain why fitness may be a "frivolous fact," or circular argument, that "sounds scientific" but explains nothing.

   _____
   _____
   _____

2. What's the difference between **fitness** and **adaptation**? Give (or make up) an example of a well-adapted plant or animal with low fitness, then one with high fitness that's poorly adapted.

   _____
   _____
   _____

3. According to famous evolutionist Lewontin, does natural selection lead to adaptation, or adaptation to natural selection? What would a creationist say?

   _____
   _____

4. Can an organism win the "struggle for survival" with natural selection's highest fitness—and then go extinct? Explain. (Think high scorer, losing team.)

   _____
   _____
   _____

5. Use lions chasing zebras to explain the difference between natural selection and ecological competition.

   _____
   _____

6. Use mosses, ferns, and shrubs to explain the differences between real simple-to-complex change, ecological succession, and imaginary evolutionary change by natural selection.

   _____
   _____

7. Explain how a mutant sea lion "ignoring" territorial population limits would be "rewarded" by natural selection — but then bring its species to extinction.

   _____
   _____
   _____

8. Explain why creationists think that "natural selection" works best as "unsurvival of the unfittest."

   _____
   _____

9. Darwinian competition may help change a generalized, adaptable population into several specialized, adapted subpopulations. How is this useful to creationists?

   _____
   _____
   _____

Chapter 5

Design vs Darwin
Compound Traits or "Irreducible Complexity"

Many believe any genius Darwin had is found in explaining how all the complex and varied structures and functions of living things could be produced *one step at a time* by the process of natural selection. Imagine you are standing at the bottom of the Empire State Building. Getting to the top looks impossible, especially if you have to do it in one huge jump. But then someone shows you the stairway. What looked like an impossibility now seems like a certainty. The climb may be long and hard, but you could make it from the bottom to the top if you took one step at a time. That's the way most people now look at the world of living things. Producing life without the outside help of a Creator once seemed *impossible*. But now, say the evolutionists, the production of all life forms from simple beginnings is a virtual *certainty — IF each feature is produced slowly and gradually, one step at a time.*

Perhaps Darwin's real genius was recognizing that adaptations in living systems often depend on many parts working together simultaneously. Darwin called such features *"difficulties with the theory."* Such compound traits, or systems of irreducible complexity, are considered the most powerful argument against Darwinism and have fostered the burgeoning growth of the "Intelligent Design" (ID) movement among secular scientists today.

	Natural selection can be used to turn the impossible into the highly probable IF AND ONLY IF each step in the development of an adaptation has survival value, allowing it to increase in numbers relative to its competitors.
Remember	

In the *Scientific American* book *Evolution*, Harvard evolutionist Richard Lewontin says, "The marvelous fit of organisms to their environment . . . was [and I say is] the chief evidence of a supreme Designer." In fact, Lewontin says that organisms "appear to have been carefully and artfully designed."[1] Lewontin himself sees it only as a tough case to be solved by evolutionary theory, but other scientists might logically infer from their observations that living things were "carefully and artfully designed."

---

1. Richard L. Lewontin, "Adaptation," *Scientific American*, Sept., 1978.

Chapter 6

Take the woodpecker, for instance. Here's a bird that makes its living banging its head into trees. Whatever gave it the idea to do that in the first place? Was it frustration over losing the worm to the early bird? How did banging its head into trees increase its likelihood for survival — until *after* it had accumulated (by chance?) a thick skull with shock-absorbing tissues, muscles, etc.? And what would be the survival value of all these features (and how could they build up in the population) until *after* the bird started banging its head into trees?

The woodpecker is a marvel of interdependent parts, "irreducible complexity," or "compound traits" — traits that depend on one another for *any* to have functional value. When a woodpecker slams its head into a tree, the deceleration experienced is many times that of gravity. The nerve and muscle coordination must produce a dead-on hit; a slip to one side or the other could virtually wrench the cover off the brain! The eyelids snap shut when the beak strikes its target. Some scientists say that's to keep wood chips out of the eyes; others say it's to keep the eyeballs from popping out of their sockets! Both may be right!

For such drilling, a woodpecker obviously needs a tough bill, heavy-duty skull, and shock-absorbing tissue between the two. But if the woodpecker were put together by time and chance, without any planning ahead, which part came first? Suppose, just by chance, a baby bird is born with a tough bill. It decides to try it out. WHACK! It throws its head into a tree. The bill is just fine, but it squishes in the front of its face. One dead bird; end of evolutionary story!

Perhaps we should start with a different feature. Maybe, just by chance, a baby bird was born with a heavy-duty skull. WHACK! It throws its head into a tree. This time its skull is okay, but its bill folds up like an accordion. There's no evolutionary future in that either!

In fact, neither the tough bill nor the heavy-duty skull would have any functional survival value until both occurred together — along with the shock-absorbing tissue, nerve and muscle coordination, etc.! That's no problem if the woodpecker were put together by plan, purpose, and a special act of creation. We expect drilling tools created by people to have interdependent parts that must all be completely assembled before the machine works. That's just good sense and good science. We would surely expect no less from the perfect devices created by

God! But, as Dawkins insists, natural selection is a "blind watchmaker" that cannot plan ahead or put parts together on purpose.

And there's more. Since death entered the world, some woodpeckers are doing more than just drilling holes to store acorns. They're looking for bark beetles. The beetles hear all this pounding, of course, so they just crawl farther down their tunnels. To reach the beetles, the woodpecker needs more than just drilling tools; it needs a long, sticky tongue.

But if a bird gets a long, sticky tongue just by chance, what's it going to do with it? Dangling out of the bill, the tongue gets bitten or even stepped on. As the bird is flying over a twig, the tongue could wrap around the twig and hang the hapless "pre-woodpecker." The answer for the woodpecker is to slip its tongue into a muscular sheath that wraps around the skull under the scalp and inserts into a nostril! That makes good sense (and good science) if you're planning ahead, but poses real problems if your faith is in time and chance, trial and error. (You don't get

The intricately designed woodpecker

Albert Szent-Gyorgyi

another trial if the error is fatal!) Nobel prize winner Albert Szent-Gyorgyi writes the following about a system much simpler than the "drilling tools" and sticky tongue of the woodpecker. He is talking only about how a young herring gull pecks at a red spot on the beak to get the adult to spit up some food (if you'll pardon the example). He says, "All this may sound very simple, but it involves a whole series of most complicated chain reactions with a horribly complex underlying nervous mechanism. . . . All this had to be developed simultaneously."[2] It's the same thing for the woodpecker. So what are the odds of getting all the chance events required for an advantageous behavioral response at the same time? Szent-Gyorgyi says that the probability is. . . .

What will he say here? That probability is one, that is, a certainty, given natural processes like selection and vast amounts of time? Some low figure like $10^{-3,000,000}$ (odds Huxley gave against the evolution of the horse)? Szent-Gyorgyi says that a coordinated behavioral adaptation such as the woodpecker's drilling and probing, as "random mutation, has the probability of zero."[3] Just zero. Nothing. Its survival value, he says, just cannot come about by time, chance, struggle, and death. Then Szent-Gyorgyi goes on to say, "I am unable to approach this problem [compound traits] without supposing an innate 'drive' in living matter to perfect itself."[4] That innate drive he calls "syntropy," the opposite of "entropy" (the universal law

of disorder). In other words, here's a brilliant scientist, sympathetic to evolution, whose observations of the living world force him to postulate at least an *impersonal creative force*. Here's a scientist who recognizes that creation can be logically inferred from observations of certain kinds of order, even if he didn't know who or what the creative agent is.

Garrett Hardin, a noted biologist and textbook author, seems to go even further than this in an old but timeless Scientific American book on adaptations and ecology, *39 Steps to Biology*[5]. The first section, titled "Fearfully and Wonderfully Made" (a phrase from Psalm 139), describes several marvels of adaptation often used as evidence of creation. In the second section, "Nature's Challenges to Evolutionary Theory," Hardin discusses other remarkable relationships that, he says, "are only a few of the unsolved puzzles facing biologists who are committed to the Darwinian [evolutionary] theory." Then he openly wonders, "Is the [evolutionary] framework wrong?" That is, do our observations of the living world force us, at least for the present, to rule out evolution as an explanation for origins?

But Hardin doesn't stop there. He goes on to ask, "Was Paley right?" You have probably never heard of William Paley. But Hardin explains. Paley was a thinker in the 18th century who argued that the kind of design we see in the living world points clearly to a Designer. Then the evolutionists came along in the 19th century and argued that they could explain design on the basis of time, chance, and properties of matter that did *not* require a Designer. Now, Hardin said in the 20th century, "Was Paley right" after all? Do the kinds of design features we see in the living things point clearly to a Designer? And Paley was not thinking of an "impersonal creative force" like Szent-Gyorgyi; he was thinking, instead, of a personal Creator God.

Hardin's conclusion? *"Think about it!"* (emphasis added).

2. Albert Szent-Gyorgyi, "Drive in Living Matter to Perfect Itself," *Synthesis 1* (1), 1977.
3. Ibid.
4. Ibid.

5. Garrett Hardin, *39 Steps to Biology* (San Francisco, CA: W.H. Freeman, 1968).

In the 21st century, scientists willing to think about design versus evolution have focused their study of compound traits on stunning examples of *irreducible complexity* found in the "molecular machinery" of living cells: the astonishing rotary motor of the bacterial flagellum, the ribosome that "reads" genetic messages (see chapters 17 and 18), photoreceptor/ effector systems ("eyes"), complex stimulation/ inhibition interactions in blood clotting and the immune system, etc.!

Throwing dynamite into the fire started by Michael Denton (*Evolution: A Theory in Crisis*,[6] 1986) and Phillip Johnson (*Darwin on Trial*,[7] 1993), biochemist Michael Behe brought popularity to the "Intelligent Design" (ID) movement among secular scientists with the publication of his book, *Darwin's Black Box*,[8] (1996), describing myriad examples of irreducible complexity at the biomolecular level. (Check out Behe's 2007 book *The Edge of Evolution*[9] too.) Christian creationist scientists, whose publications of such concepts years ago were largely ignored, are thrilled to see discussion of such topics finally reaching a broader academic community. We'll examine examples of molecular evidence of design in the unit on life's origin, where the molecular stage is set. Right now, let's look at other examples of compound traits on a larger scale.

Since death entered the world, there are many large, predatory fish that roam the oceans. But as they feed on smaller fish and shrimp, their mouths begin to accumulate food debris and parasites. Lacking recourse to a toothbrush, how is such a fish going to clean its teeth?

For several kinds of fish, the answer is a visit to the local cleaning station. These are special areas usually marked by the presence of certain shrimp and small, brightly colored fish, such as wrasses and gobis. Often fresh from chasing and eating other small fish and shrimp, a predatory fish may swim over to take its place in line (literally!) at the nearest cleaning station. When its turn comes, it opens its mouth wide, baring the vicious-looking teeth.

You might suspect, of course, that such a sight would frighten off the little cleaner fish and shrimp. But no, into the jaws of death swim the little cleaners. Now even a friendly dog will sometimes snap at you if you try to pick off a tick, and it probably irritates the big fish to have a shrimp crawling around on its tongue and little fish picking parasites off the soft tissues of the mouth. (Try to imagine shrimp crawling around on your tongue!) But the big fish just hovers there, allowing the cleaners to do their work. It even holds its gill chambers open so that the shrimp can crawl around on the gill filaments picking off parasites!

At the end of all this cleaning, the second "miracle" occurs. You might think the big fish would respond, "Ah, clean teeth; SNAP, free meal!" But, no. When the cleaning is done, the big fish lets the little cleaner fish and shrimp back out. Then the big fish swims off — and begins hunting again for little fish and shrimp to eat!

The fantastic relationship just described is called cleaning symbiosis. Perhaps you have seen cleaner fish in a major public aquarium, or seen pictures of their behavior in television footage or nature magazines. Cleaning symbiosis is a well-known example of mutualism an intimate relationship of benefit to both types of species involved, in this case, the "cleaner and the cleanee."

Obviously, cleaning symbiosis has survival value for both types of species involved. But does survival value explain the *origin* of this special relationship? Of course not. It makes sense to talk about survival value only after a trait or relationship is already in existence.

> **Question**
>
> Did the survival value of this cleaning relationship result from time, chance, struggle, and death or from plan, purpose, and special acts of creation?

The major problem with using Darwinian fitness to explain traits with many interdependent parts is that none of the separate parts have *any* survival value. There's certainly no survival value in a small fish swimming into a large fish's mouth on the hope that the big fish has

6. Michael Denton, *Evolution: A Theory in Crisis* (Bethesda, MD: Adler & Adler, 1986).
7. Phillip E. Johnson, *Darwin on Trial* (Downers Grove, IL: Inter Varsity Press, 1993).
8. Michael Behe, *Darwin's Black Box* (New York, Free Press, 1996).
9. Michael Behe, *The Edge of Evolution* (New York: Free Press, 2007).

somehow evolved the desire to let it back out! Sea creatures don't provide the only examples of cleaning symbiosis, either. A bird, the Egyptian plover, can walk right into the open mouth of a Nile crocodile — and walk back out again after cleaning the croc's mouth! On an evolutionary basis, each cleaning relationship would have to be explained separately on the basis of time, chance, struggle, and death operating on variants of each species involved.

> **Remember**
> Natural selection can help explain the origin of compound traits one step at a time IF AND ONLY IF each separate step has survival value on its own.

The situation is even more dangerous for the famous "bombardier beetle." The bombardier is an ordinary-looking beetle, but it has an ingenious chemical mechanism. Imagine: Here comes a mean ol' beetle-eater, a toad, creeping up behind the seemingly unsuspecting beetle. Just as he gets ready to flash out that long, sticky tongue, the beetle swings its cannon around, and *boom*! It blasts the toad in the face with hot noxious gases at the

boiling point of water, and coats the toad's tongue with a foul-tasting residue. Now that doesn't actually kill the toad, but it surely kills its taste for beetles! Pictures show the toad dragging its tongue across the sand trying to get rid of the foul taste.

Successful firing of the bombardier beetle's cannon requires two chemicals (hydrogen peroxide and hydroquinones), enzymes, pressure tanks, and a whole series of nerve and muscle attachments for aim and control. Try to imagine all those parts accumulating by time, chance, and natural selection. One crucial mistake,

of course, and *boom*! The would-be bombardier beetle blows *itself* up, and there's surely no evolutionary future in that! Trial and error can lead to improvement only if you survive the error!

Creationists and evolutionists agree that adaptations such as the woodpecker's skull, cleaning symbiosis, and the bombardier beetle's cannon all have survival value. The question is, how did they get that way: by time, chance, and the struggle for survival, or by plan, purpose, and special acts of creation? When it comes to adaptations that require several traits all depending on one another, the more logical inference from the evidence seems to be creation.

Darwin himself was acutely aware of this evidence of creation and the problem it posed for his theory. His chapter in *Origin of Species* on adaptations was NOT titled "Evidence for the Theory" but "Difficulties with the Theory." In it, he discussed traits that depend on separately meaningless parts. Consider the human eye with the different features required to focus at different distances, to accommodate different amounts of light, and to correct for the "rainbow effect." Regarding the origin of the eye, Darwin wrote these words:

> To suppose that the eye [with so many parts all working together] . . . could have been formed by natural selection, seems, I freely confess, absurd in the highest degree.[10]

"Absurd in the highest degree." That's Darwin's own opinion of using natural selection to explain the origin

10.Charles Darwin, *The Origin of Species*, Washington Square Press, Inc., New York, 1963 (original edition 1859), pp. 154–155.

of traits that depend on many parts working together. Nevertheless, Darwin thought such difficulties could be overcome. It was even more absurd, in Darwin's mind, to believe a Creator put the eye together on purpose.

Modern evolutionists continue to recognize these "difficulties with the theory" of evolution. Harvard's Stephen Gould wrote, for example, "What good is half a jaw or half a wing?"[11] Gould also recognized that many people (especially artists employed by museums and textbook publishers) have tried to present a hypothetical series of gradual changes from one kind to others. So he adds, "These tales, in the 'Just-So Stories' tradition of evolutionary natural history, do not prove anything. . . . Concepts salvaged only by facile speculation do not appeal much to me." Even though Gould was an ardent evolutionist, he recognized that the classic textbook concept of gradual evolution rests on made-up stories and "facile speculation," and not on facts.

In another article, Gould pointed out that the perfection of complex structures has always been one of the strongest evidences of creation. After all, he said, "Perfection need not have a history."[12] No trial-and-error development over time from chance trait combinations and selection. So, Gould continued, evidence for evolution must be sought in "oddities and imperfections" that clearly show the effects of time and chance.

But creationists recognize imperfection, too. The Bible clearly indicates that "time and chance and struggle"

have indeed corrupted what God originally had created in perfection. Imperfection, then, is not the issue; perfection is. And evolutionists from Darwin to Lewontin and Gould admit that "perfection of structure" has always been "the chief evidence of a Supreme Designer." Much more evidence is provided by Jobe Martin in a fabulous series of videos, "Incredible Creatures that Defy Evolution."

Darwin said that his theory would be disproven by the existence of even one biological feature that could not be explained by the slow, steady accumulation of small changes. The plethora of compound traits, then, disproves Darwin's theory thousands of times over. Natural selection, yes; evolution, no.

In addition to the limitations on natural selection provided by logic and compound traits, there is yet a third kind of limit, which may seem surprising in light of the shortened title of Darwin's book.

Selection vs. the Origin of Traits

Take the famous example of "Darwin's finches." On the Galapagos Islands about 600 miles (nearly 1,000 km) west of Ecuador, Darwin observed a variety of finches, some with small beaks for catching

11. Stephen Jay Gould, "The Return of Hopeful Monsters," *Natural History*, June–July, 1977.
12. Stephen Jay Gould, *The Panda's Thumb*, W. W. Norton and Co., Inc., New York, 1980.

"Darwin's Finches" on the Galapagos Islands

insects, others with large beaks for crushing seeds, and one with the ability to use spines to pry insects from their tunnels. How did Darwin explain the "origin" of these various finches? Exactly the same way a creationist would. He saw finches with variation in beak type on the South American mainland and presumed these finches might have reached the islands on a vegetation mat or something similar. The ones with seed-crushing beaks survived where seeds were the major food sources, and those with insect-catching beaks out-reproduced others where insects were the major source of food. Given finches with a variety of beak types, then, natural selection helps us to explain *how* and *where* the different varieties *survived* as they multiplied and filled the earth. That, of course, is just what a creationist would say — except that a biblical creationist would add that the "struggle and death" part of migration did not begin until man's rebellion ruined the world God had created without death.

The full title of Darwin's book was *On the Origin of Species by Means of Natural Selection, or the Preservation of Favoured Races in the Struggle for Life*. Darwin's finches, like all the other examples of natural selection, fall under only the second half of the title, "*. . . the Preservation of Favoured Races* [varieties] *in the Struggle for Life.*" Left unanswered are the questions of origin.

Question	Where did the finches get their different beak sizes or the peppered moths their different colors, etc.?

Pangenesis: Use and Disuse — When it came to the actual origin of new traits, Darwin wrote that it was "from use and disuse, from the direct and indirect actions of the environment"[13] that new traits arose. About 40 years before Darwin, a famous French evolutionist, Jean Lamarck, argued for this kind of evolution based on the *inheritance of traits acquired by use and disuse*. Most books on the subject hint that we should laugh at Lamarck — but Darwin believed exactly the same thing.

Consider the supposed origin of the giraffe. According to both Darwin and Lamarck, the story begins back on the African prairies a long time ago. Because of prolonged drought, the prairie dried up. But there were green leaves up in the trees, and some of the animals started stretching their necks to reach them. As a result, their necks got a

13.Charles Darwin, *The Origin of Species*, Washington Square Press, Inc., New York, 1963 (original edition 1859), p 470.

Jean Lamarck

little longer (Figure 6.1). Now that could be partly true. If you really work at it hard enough and long enough, you could add a little bit to your height. People used to do that to get into the army or some special service where you have to be a certain height. The problem, however, is that the offspring of "stretched" parents start off just as small as all the others. The long neck could not be passed on to the next generation.

Like others of his time, Darwin didn't know about the mechanism of heredity. He thought that at reproduction each organ produced "*pangenes*" that would collect in

Figure 6.1. For the *origin* of new traits, Darwin (like Lamarck) resorted to "use and disuse" and the inheritance of acquired characteristics. Giraffes got longer necks, for example, because their ancestors stretched for leaves in trees, then passed on more neck "pangenes" to their offspring. This idea of "progress through effort" contributed to the early popularity of evolution, but has since been disproved.

the blood and flow to the reproductive organs. So a bigger neck made more neck pangenes. Some people still believe this sort of concept. You've probably run into people who say, for instance, that people will eventually have bigger heads because we think a lot, and no toes because we wear shoes all the time. Darwin even used pangenes to "explain" why (in his opinion) wives grew to resemble their husbands as both got older.

It seems Darwin knew as little about giraffes as he did about heredity. Because their neck is so long, there's a huge distance between a giraffe's heart and its brain. It needs auxiliary pumps to get blood to the brain so it won't faint when it raises its head up — and it needs pressure reducers so that when it bends its head down to take a drink, it won't blow its brains out!

Science has since disproved these early evolutionary thoughts, but back in Darwin's time, pangenes captured people's imaginations probably even more than natural selection did. To some, Darwin's original theory of evolution suggested continual progress. How do you make something happen? By use and disuse. If you want to get smarter, use your brain, and both you and your children will be smarter. If you want to be strong, use your muscles, and not only will you get stronger, but so will your children.

Well, almost unfortunately, that's not the modern theory of evolution. The use-disuse theory didn't work and had to be discarded. A man named Weismann, for example, cut off the tails of mice for 20-some generations, only to find that baby mice were still born with tails. Traits acquired by use and disuse just don't affect heredity. (By the way, if God took one of Adam's ribs to form Eve, would we expect men today to have one less rib than women? Of course not.)

Mutations — The modern evolutionist is called a *neo*-Darwinian. He still accepts Darwin's ideas about natural selection, but something new (neo-) has been added. The modern evolutionist believes that new traits come about by chance, by random changes in genes called "mutations," and *not* by use and disuse.

Almost everyone has heard about mutations — from Saturday morning cartoons or horror movies, if nowhere else. In those flicks, some atomic disaster produces people with gnarled skin, one big bulging eye, and other "new traits." In the real world, mutations are responsible for a number of genetic defects, including hemophilia (bleeders'

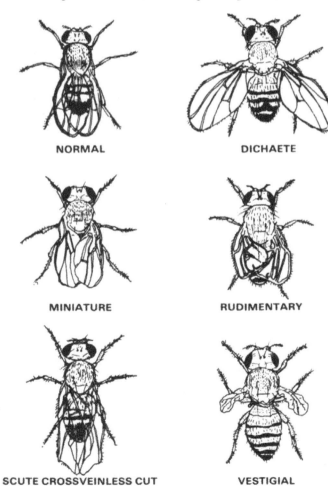

NORMAL   DICHAETE

MINIATURE   RUDIMENTARY

SCUTE CROSSVEINLESS CUT   VESTIGIAL

Figure 6.2. Mutations are random changes in genes (DNA), often caused by radiation. The mutations in the wings to the right were produced by x-raying fruit flies. According to the modern, neo-Darwinian view, mutations are the source of new traits for evolution, and selection culls out the fittest combinations (or eliminates the "unfittest") that are first produced just by chance. Mutations certainly occur, but are there limits to extrapolating from mutational changes to evolutionary changes (e.g., "fish to philosopher")?

disease), loss of protective color in the skin and eyes (albinism), and certain kinds of cancer and brain malfunction.

We have abundant evidence that various kinds of radiations, errors in DNA replication, and certain chemicals can indeed produce mutations, and mutations in reproductive cells can be passed on to future generations. Figure 6.2 shows some of the changes that have been deliberately brought about in the fruit fly wings: curled wings, spread-apart wings, miniature wings, wings without cross veins. Students in genetics classes work with these fruit flies, crossing different ones and working out inheritance patterns.

Consider the flu virus. Why haven't we yet been able to solve the flu problem? Part of the problem is that this year's vaccine and your own antibodies are only good against last year's flu. (They don't usually tell you that when you get the shot, but it's already out of date.) The smallpox virus has the common decency to stay the same year in and year out, so once you're vaccinated or build up an immunity, that's it. But the flu virus mutates quite easily, so each year its proteins are slightly different from last year's. They are still flu viruses, but they don't quite fit our antibodies, so we have to build up our immunity all over again. When it recombines with animal viruses (on the average of once every ten years), the problem is even worse, as in the cases of so-called bird flu and swine flu (H1N1).

Mutations are certainly real. They have profound effects on our lives. And, according to the neo-Darwinian evolutionists, *mutations are the raw material for evolution*. But is that evolutionary belief (and textbook assertion) really true? Is there any scientific evidence to support it? Is there scientific evidence to refute it? (On a more personal and constitutional note for American students: are you allowed — even encouraged — to discuss the scientific evidence pros and cons in your science classroom?)

The scientific evidence presented in the next chapter suggests *mutations, yes; evolution, no*. Read it, and then explain to yourself and others why you agree or disagree. Think also: if mutations are real but don't support evolution, what do they mean?

Form your foundation.

It's no wonder Darwin called adaptations "difficulties with the theory" that traits evolve one small step at a time. From the woodpecker's drill to a beetle's cannon and cleaning symbiosis, "compound traits of irreducible complexity" require multiple parts to produce one function, providing evidence of plan, purpose, and special acts of creation.

Building Inspection

1. T or F: Darwin's belief that big evolutionary changes (e.g., "amoeba to man") could result from selection for a great many small changes requires each small step to have its own survival value. _____

2. "Compound traits" of "irreducible complexity": Use the woodpecker, bombardier beetle, or cleaning symbiosis to explain why Darwin called features with many interdependent parts "difficulties" with his evolutionary belief, then tell why many scientists call such features evidence for creation or "intelligent design" (ID).

_____

_____

_____

_____

_____

_____

_____

_____

_____

_____

_____

3. The "late, great" evolutionist S. J. Gould called imperfections in living things evidence of _____; creationists call them evidence of _____.

4. Compare creationist and evolutionist explanations for variation in beaks among Galapagos ("Darwin's") finches.

_____

_____

_____

_____

_____

_____

_____

_____

_____

_____

5. Tell how Darwin used "pangenes" or "use and disuse" to explain the origin of the giraffe's long neck — then cite several scientific blunders in Darwin's explanation.

_____

_____

_____

_____

_____

_____

_____

6. Darwinists in the 1800s based their belief in evolution on pangenesis (use and disuse) + "selection"; evolutionists in the 20th and 21st centuries put their faith in neo-Darwinism, i.e. _____ + "selection."

Chapter 6

53

Mutations: Yes;
Evolution: No

Can mutations produce real evolutionary changes? Don't make any mistakes here. Mutations are real; they're something we observe; they do make changes in traits. But the question remains: do they produce *evolutionary* changes? Do they produce really new traits? Do they produce new genons, not just new alleles? Do they really help to explain that postulated change from molecules to man, or fish to philosopher?

The answer seems to be: "*Mutations*, yes; *evolution*, no." In the last analysis, mutations really don't help evolutionary theory at all. There are three major problems or limits (and many minor ones) that prevent scientific extrapolation from mutational change to evolutionary change.

Mathematical Challenges

One problem is mathematical. I won't dwell on this one, because it's written up in many books and widely acknowledged by evolutionists themselves as a serious problem for their theory.

Fortunately, mutations are very rare. They occur on an average of perhaps once in every ten million duplications of a DNA molecule (10^7, a one followed by seven zeroes). That's fairly rare. On the other hand, it's not that rare. Our bodies contain nearly 100 trillion cells (10^{14}). So the odds are quite good that we have a couple of cells with a mutated form of almost any gene. A fertilized human egg cell probably contains one or two genes different by mutation from any gene in either

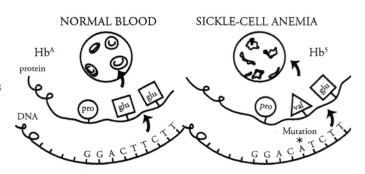

Figure 7.1. Radiation and chemical accidents can cause "typographic errors," called mutations, in the genetic code. A change of one letter among a thousand in DNA, for example, can change one amino acid among hundreds in hemoglobin, the protein that carries O_2 in red blood cells, and a serious blood disease results from that mutation.

parent — and new research suggests the number may be much larger (Sanford, 2005). A test tube can hold billions of bacteria, so again, the odds are quite good that there will be mutant forms among them.

The mathematical problem for evolution comes when you want a *series* of *related* mutations. The odds of getting two mutations that are related to one another is the product of their separate probabilities: one in 10^7 x one in 10^7 equals one in 10^{14} (which may be written more directly as 10^{-7} x 10^{-7} = 10^{-14}) — 10^{14} is a one followed by 14 zeroes, a hundred trillion! And any two mutations might produce no more than a fly with a wavy edge on a bent wing. That's a long way from producing a truly new structure, and certainly a long way from changing a fly into some new kind of organism. You need more mutations for that. So what are the odds of getting *three* mutations in a row? That's one in a billion trillion (10^{21}). Suddenly the ocean isn't big enough to hold enough bacteria to make it likely for you to find a bacterium with three simultaneous or sequential related mutations.

What about trying for *four* related mutations? One in 10^{28}. Suddenly the earth isn't big enough to hold enough organisms to make that very likely. And we're talking about only four mutations. It would take many more than that to change a fish into a philosopher, or even a fish into a frog. Four mutations don't even make a start toward any real evolution. But already at this point some evolutionists have given up the classic idea of evolution, because it just plainly doesn't work. Michael Behe's 2007 book, *The Edge of Evolution*[1], provides details.

Probability of a series of related mutations	
2 — one in a hundred trillion	10^{-14}
3 — one in a billion trillion	10^{-21}
4 — one in ten million billion trillion	10^{-28}

It was at this level (just four related mutations) that microbiologists gave up on the idea that mutations could explain why some bacteria, once presumed to reproduce only asexually, are resistant to four different antibiotics at the same time. The odds against the mutation explanation were simply too great, so they began to look for another mechanism — and they found it.

First of all, using cultures that are routinely kept for long periods of time, they found out that bacteria were resistant to antibiotics, even before commercial antibiotics were "invented." When the remains of Arctic explorers

1. Michael Behe, *The Edge of Evolution* (New York: Free Press, 2007).

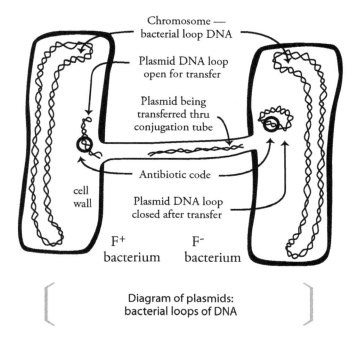

Chromosome —
bacterial loop DNA

Plasmid DNA loop
open for transfer

Plasmid being
transferred thru
conjugation tube

Antibiotic code

cell
wall

Plasmid DNA loop
closed after transfer

F+
bacterium

F-
bacterium

Diagram of plasmids:
bacterial loops of DNA

in the Franklin party were found 150 years after they froze to death, bacteria resistant to modern, commercially produced antibiotics were found in their bodies. Genetic variability was "built right into" the bacteria.

Did the nonresistant varieties get resistant by mutation? No. Resistant forms were already present. Furthermore, certain bacteria have little loops of DNA, called *plasmids*, which they trade around among themselves, and they passed on their resistance to antibiotics in that way (see diagram above). It wasn't mutation and asexual reproduction at all, just ordinary recombination and variation within kind.

Bacteria *can* be made antibiotic-resistant by mutation, but biologist Novick calls such forms "evolutionary cripples." The mutation typically damages a growth factor, so that the mutationally crippled bacteria can scarcely survive outside the lab. The antibiotic resistance carried by plasmids results from enzymes produced to break down the antibiotic. Such bacteria do not have their growth crippled by mutation. Their resistance is by design.

But, why, you might well ask, would God create antibiotic resistance? It's possible God designed antibiotic resistance in bacteria, and antibiotic production in fungi, to balance the growth of these prolific organisms in the soil. Only after the corruption of creation did some bacteria become disease causers, making antibiotic resistance "inadvertently" a medical problem.

Contrary to popular opinion, drug resistance in bacteria does *not* demonstrate evolution. It doesn't even demonstrate the production of favorable mutations. Mutational resistance is only "favorable" in an artificial environment, like a hospital, where the weakened yet resistant bacteria are protected by hospital procedures from competition with sensitive forms that survive better in the "outside world" because their growth systems have not been damaged.

Drug resistance *does* demonstrate natural selection (or a sort of artificial selection, in this case), but only selection among already existing variations within a kind. It also demonstrates that when the odds that a particular process will produce a given effect get too low, good scientists normally look for a better explanation, such as the plasmid explanation for resistance to multiple antibiotics.

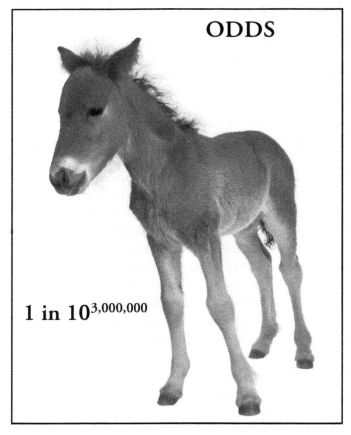

ODDS

$1 \text{ in } 10^{3,000,000}$

At this point, evolutionists often say, "Time is the hero of the plot. Sure, the odds are low, but there's all that time, nearly five billion years!" But five billion years is only about 10^{17} seconds, and the whole universe contains fewer than 10^{80} atoms. So even by the wildest "guesstimates," the universe isn't old enough or big enough to reach odds like the 1 in $10^{3,000,000}$ that Huxley, an evolutionist, estimated as the odds against the evolution of the horse. The odds against forming just one average, functional protein by chance are about one in 10^{100}.

Statisticians have estimated that, even if our huge universe were as old as evolutionists say, anything with odds lower than one in 10^{50} (10^{-50}) can be classified as "impossible." Yet Darwin's followers would rather believe the impossible than consider the possibility of God. Such *evolutionists believe in miracles; they just don't believe in the Miracle Worker.*

In his chapter "Beyond the Reach of Chance," Michael Denton[2] discusses attempts to simulate evolutionary processes on computers. He concludes with these strong words:

> If complex computer programs cannot be changed by random mechanisms, then surely the same must apply to the genetic programs of living organisms. *The fact that systems in every way analogous to living organisms cannot undergo evolution by pure trial and error* [i.e., by mutation and selection] and that their functional distribution invariably conforms to an improbable discontinuum *comes, in my opinion, very close to a formal disproof of the whole Darwinian paradigm of nature.* By what strange capacity do living organisms *defy the laws of chance* which are apparently obeyed by all analogous complex systems? [emphasis added]

Most gratifyingly, Denton seems to look beyond the merely negative insufficiency of chance to glimpse a solution to "The Puzzle of Perfection," as he calls it, in the "design hypothesis":

> It is the sheer universality of perfection, the fact that everywhere we look, we find an elegance and ingenuity of an absolutely transcending quality, which so mitigates against the idea of chance. . . . In practically every field of fundamental biological research ever-increasing levels of design and complexity are being revealed at an ever-accelerating rate. The credibility of natural selection is weakened, therefore, not only by the perfection we have already glimpsed but by the expectation of further as yet undreampt of depths of ingenuity and complexity (p. 342).

Mutations Going the Wrong Way

In God's handiwork, unlike man's, the closer we look, the more marvelous is the perfection we see. Unfortunately, we also have evidence that the transcendent ingenuity and design Denton sees has been

2. Michael Denton, Evolution: *Theory in Crisis* (Bethesda, MD; Adler & Adler, 1986).

Queen Victoria

marred and scarred. Even more serious than the mathematical problems with mutations is the fact that mutations are "going the wrong way" as far as evolution is concerned.

Upward or downward? Almost every mutation we know is identified by the disease or abnormality that it causes. Creationists use mutations to explain the *origin of parasites and disease*, the *origin of hereditary defects*, and the *loss of traits*. In other words, time, chance, and random changes do just what we normally expect: tear things down and make matters worse. Using mutations to explain the breakdown of existing genetic order (creation-corruption) is quite the opposite of using mutations to explain the buildup of genetic order (evolution). Clearly, creation-corruption is the most direct inference from the effects of mutations that scientists actually observe.

By producing defects or blocking the normal function of certain genes, mutations have introduced numerous genetic abnormalities into the human population. The hemophilia (bleeders' disease) that afflicted the royal houses of Europe may have arisen as a mutation of a clotting-factor gene in Queen Victoria. The dreaded Tay-Sach disease may have arisen in Czechoslovakia in the 1920s as a mutation in the gene for producing an enzyme crucial to brain function.

Mutations may not help explain the origin of species, but they do a great job of explaining the origin of diseases and disease organisms. Our intestines are full of helpful bacteria, for example, including one kind that makes vitamin K to assist in blood clotting. Imagine a mutation occurs in just one of the genes in a helpful bacterium. A series of reactions that depend on the product of that gene gets blocked, and an incomplete product that is harmful may be released, absorbed by the body, and cause illness. One mutation can change a helpful bacterium into a harmful germ! (Praise God — 97 percent of known bacterial species are still helpful, even in a corrupted creation.)

Some people like to call mutations "the means of creation." But mutations don't create; they corrupt! Both logically and often observationally, as in the examples above, *the ordered state must come before mutations can disorder it.* Mutations are real, all right, but they point to a *corruption* of the created order by time and chance.

Birth defects, genetic diseases, parasites, and disease organisms like the AIDS virus are posed as strong challenges to the "Intelligent Design" (ID) movement. Why would an intelligence (especially an all-powerful, all-loving one) design such things? The Bible has the answer: God did NOT create defects, disease, or disease organisms; these things developed, largely as a result of mutations, after man's sin ruined God's perfect world.

As a matter of fact, human beings are now subject to over 5,000 mutational disorders. Fortunately, we don't show as many defects as we carry. The reason they don't show up is that we each have two sets of genes — one set of genes from our mother and another set from our father. The "bad genes" we inherit from our mother's side are usually covered up by our father's genes, and vice versa. We can see what is likely to happen when an animal is born with only one set of genes. Based on a description in a genetics textbook, the drawing below represents the rare case of a turkey that was hatched from an unfertilized egg, so it had just one set of chromosomes. The poor bird couldn't hold its head up; instead, it bobbed up and down

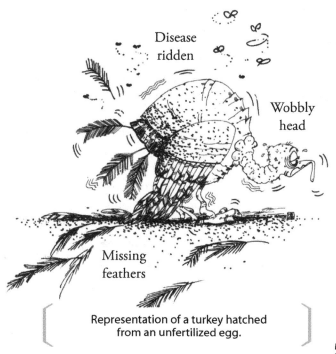

Disease ridden

Wobbly head

Missing feathers

Representation of a turkey hatched from an unfertilized egg.

from a neurological disorder. The feathers were missing in patches, and it finally had to be transferred to a germ-free chamber because its resistance to disease was so low.

Now here's the basis for a good horror story. Picture a mirror at the end of a dark hall. You claw your way through the spider webs to reach the mirror, and then you press a button. The mirror then splits you into halves, so you can see what you would look like if you had only your mother's genes or only your father's genes. In the next scene, you're writhing there in agony, your hair turning white as you fall over backward and die of fright! Unfortunately, that picture exaggerates only slightly what mutations have done to human beings and to the various kinds of plants and animals as well. If it weren't for having two sets of genes, few of us would be able to survive.

Evolutionists recognize, of course, the problem of trying to explain "onward and upward" evolution on the basis of mutations that are harmful at least 1,000 times more often than they are helpful. No evolutionist believes that standing in front of x-ray machines would eventually improve human beings. No evolutionist argues that destruction of the earth's ozone layer is good because it increases mutation rates and, therefore, speeds up evolution. Evolutionists know that a decrease in the ozone layer will increase mutation rates, but they, like everyone else, recognize that this will lead only to increased skin cancer and to other harmful changes. Perhaps a *helpful change might occur*, but it would be drowned in the sea of harmful changes.

Because harmful mutations so greatly outnumber any supposed helpful ones, it's considered unwise nowadays (and illegal in many states) to marry someone too closely related to you. Why? Because you greatly increase the odds that bad genes will show up in pairs and therefore come to visible expression. By the way, you also increase the odds of bringing out really excellent trait combinations. But did you ever hear anybody say, "Don't marry your first cousin or you'll have a genius for a child"? They don't usually say that, because the odds of something bad happening are far, far, FAR greater.

That would not have been a problem, by the way, shortly after creation. Cain had to marry his sister, for example, since that was initially the only possibility among the children of Adam and Eve. That posed no genetic problem, however. Until mutations had a chance to accumulate in the human population, no such risk of bad combinations existed. God did not write the law against close intermarriage until much later in human history, after mutations had increased to dangerous levels in the population.

Mutations are usually carried as "hidden genes" (recessives) that are difficult to eliminate by selection, so they tend to build up in populations. *The buildup of mutations with time poses a serious problem for plants and animals, as well as for human beings,* and time, evolution's "hero," only worsens the problem of mutational decay.

Geneticists, even evolutionary geneticists, refer to the problem as "genetic load" or "genetic burden." The term is meant to imply a burden that "weighs down" a species and lowers its genetic quality. In an article for the *Scientific American* book *Evolution,* paradoxically titled "The Mechanisms of Evolution," Francisco Ayala defines a mutation as "an error" in DNA. Then he explains that inbreeding has revealed that mutations in fruit flies have produced "extremely short wings, deformed bristles, blindness, and other serious defects."[3] Does that sound like "raw material for evolution"?

Even if good mutations were theoretically possible, the price would be too high. To explain evolution by the gradual selection of beneficial mutations, one must also put up with the millions of harmful mutations that would have to occur along the way. Even though he has been one of the "old guard" defenders of classic neo-Darwinian evolution, Ayala faces the problem squarely in his article in the *Scientific American* book *Evolution.* He is talking about variation within species (not kind, but species, the smallest possible unit). He says that variation within species is much greater than Darwin postulated. He speaks of such variation as "enormous" and "staggering." Yet when he gets to the actual figures, the variation is less than a creationist would have expected. (Ayala did say his figures *under*estimated the real variation.)

For creationists, all this variation poses no problem at all. If living things were created to multiply and fill the earth, then great variation within kind is simply good design. There

3. Francisco Ayala, "The Mechanisms of Evolution," *Scientific American,* Sept. 1978

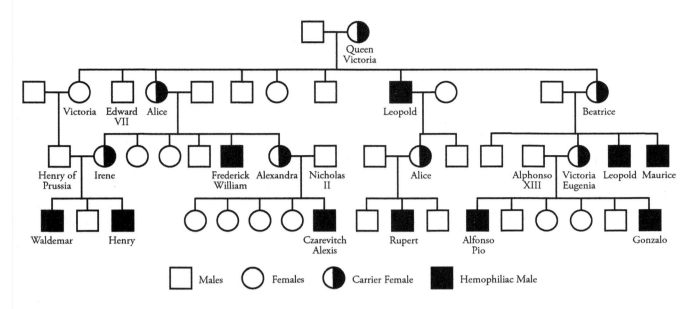

Figure 7.2. Even though Queen Victoria did not have "bleeder's disease" (hemophilia), she apparently carried a recessive gene for the condition on her X chromosome (X^h). Her female children would inherit a normal allele (X^H) from their father, Prince Albert, so they would have no bleeding problem. Sons would inherit a Y from their fathers, and the Y chromosome has no normal gene to cover up an X^H he may inherit from his mother, as Leopold did. In this manner, Queen Victoria's recessive gene quickly spread through Leopold's hemophilia and her daughters' recessives to royal families throughout Europe.

would be no price to pay for *created* variability, since it would result from creation, *not* from time, chance, and mutation. (Mutations have introduced further variability since creation was corrupted, but it's the kind of variability a bull introduces into a china shop!)

What problem does an evolutionist see with all this staggering variability? Just this: *for each beneficial mutant a species accumulated,* the price would be a thousand or more harmful mutations. When genetic burden gets too great, offspring are so likely to have serious hereditary defects that the ability of the species to survive is threatened.

Indeed, some evolutionists are now saying that mutational load or genetic burden limits the survival time for a species to about five million years. By that time (quite short, by evolutionary standards), accumulating mutations will reach such a high level that the chances become vanishingly small that two organisms can mate and produce offspring that can grow to maturity and reproduce. Mutations then become the *raw material for extinction, not evolution!*

Take the case of the Florida panther, which is considered an endangered species. What's it endangered by? Poachers? No. Traffic? No. Alligators? No. Polluters? No. It's endangered by mutations. The small population was riddled with so many mutations affecting its circulatory and reproductive systems that mating adults could not produce a cub that could survive even one year.

The problem is now being solved by crossing Florida panthers with western panthers that have different mutations, so recessives are less likely to pair up.

Thanks to our accumulated genetic burden, serious hereditary defects are present in perhaps 5 percent of all human births, and that percentage greatly increases among the children of closely related parents. An evolutionist even suggested that one day parents may have to get a license to have children — *not* a marriage license, but a separate license granted *if and only if* genetic tests show their DNA has few defects to pass on to the next generation! All of us have some genetic shortcomings, and it's really only by common consent that most of us agree to call each other "normal."

Natural selection cannot save us from this awful situation either. At the cost of a high death rate, selection can and does eliminate or reduce the worst mutations — but only when these mutants come to visible (phenotypic) expression. Most mutations "hide" as recessives, "invisible" to selection, and continue to build up in secret at multiple loci, somewhat like a "*genetic cancer*" slowly but steadily eating away at genetic quality.

Time cannot save us from mutational genetic decay, either. *The more time, the more the life-sucking genetic cancer grows.* As noted above, evolutionists are saying mutations may wipe out the average species in "five million years" — and that's using evolutionist assumptions about time. Mutation rates measured in

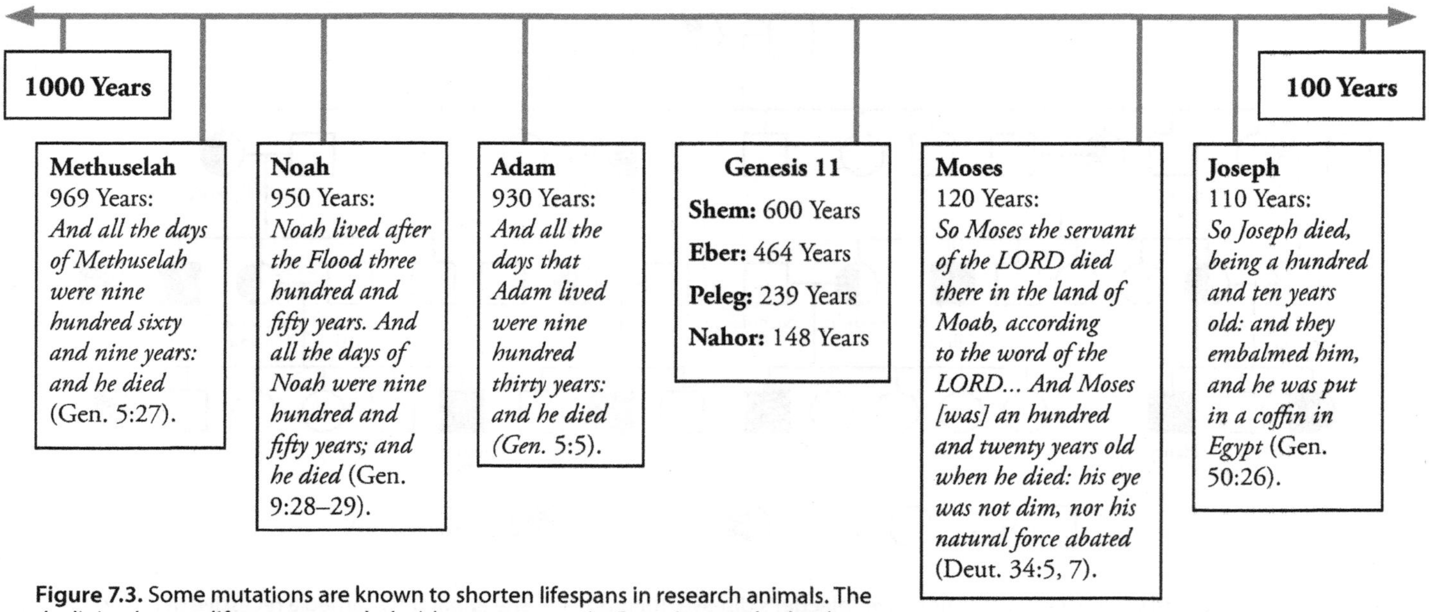

1000 Years					100 Years

Methuselah
969 Years:
And all the days of Methuselah were nine hundred sixty and nine years: and he died (Gen. 5:27).

Noah
950 Years:
Noah lived after the Flood three hundred and fifty years. And all the days of Noah were nine hundred and fifty years; and he died (Gen. 9:28–29).

Adam
930 Years:
And all the days that Adam lived were nine hundred thirty years: and he died (Gen. 5:5).

Genesis 11
Shem: 600 Years
Eber: 464 Years
Peleg: 239 Years
Nahor: 148 Years

Moses
120 Years:
So Moses the servant of the LORD died there in the land of Moab, according to the word of the LORD... And Moses [was] an hundred and twenty years old when he died: his eye was not dim, nor his natural force abated (Deut. 34:5, 7).

Joseph
110 Years:
So Joseph died, being a hundred and ten years old: and they embalmed him, and he was put in a coffin in Egypt (Gen. 50:26).

Figure 7.3. Some mutations are known to shorten lifespans in research animals. The declining human lifespans recorded without comment in Genesis may also be the result (physically) of accumulating mutational load.

the laboratory suggest mutational burden may build up far faster than that. Some creationist scientists are now beginning to research accumulating genetic burden as a potential indicator of the maximum time life has been on earth!

Using the best in 21st century supercomputer calculations, John Sanford documents that the genetic burden of mutational decay and selectional death is far, far worse than all but a few research evolutionists have realized, and he outlines a research program relating genetic decay to species survival times. The universal tendency for physical and chemical systems to lose order, useful energy, and/or information is called the law of entropy, so Sanford titled his book on the relentless decline in genetic quality *Genetic Entropy*.[4]

It's likely that the genetic information in Noah's family contained only a few mutations when they first stepped off the ark. But mutations built up rapidly in microbes, plants, animals, and people following the Flood. The number of mutational defects and diseases among human beings is about what would be predicted for a population growing from eight to six billion over the last 4,500–5,000 years — and new mutations are continuing to produce new defects and diseases. Since the parts of the body interact in such close harmony, it's not surprising that one mutation may

produce several harmful side effects, including decrease in life span. The Bible records that human life span dropped from 950 for Noah into the 600s, 400s, and 200s, until Moses writes of "three score and ten, or by reason of strength fourscore" (Ps. 90:10), the 70–80-year life span typical in today's world.

If evolutionists had known what scientists know now about mutations, it's most unlikely that mutations would have even been proposed as the pathway for evolutionary progress! Instead of "upward, onward" evolution, mutations leave a trail of shortened life spans, disease-ridden populations from princes to panthers, and early extinction.

Form your foundation.

Darwin's followers tout mutations as the "raw material for evolutionary progress," but scientists call mutations "genetic burden," the decay of genetic quality. It's not the origin of species mutations explain, but the origin of defects and disease corrupting creation after sin.

4. John Sanford, *Genetic Entropy and the Mystery of the Genome* (Lima, NY: Ivan Press, 2005).

1. Evolutionists use **mutations** to explain (in Darwin's words) "the origin of _____";
creationists use mutations to explain the origin of _____.

2. "If the earth was created by a God of love and power, why is the world so full of struggle, death, disease, and disaster — what Darwin called the "**war of nature**."' Use science and scripture to answer this evolutionary challenge.

   _____
   _____
   _____
   _____

3. "Don't Christians believe God created everything? Doesn't that mean He created defects and disease?" Respond.

   _____
   _____
   _____
   _____

4. All of these are caused by mutations except (choose one): (a) sickle-cell hemoglobin, (b) endangered reproduction in the Florida panther, (c) hemophilia that spread through European royalty, (d) possibly the decline in human life span following the Flood, (e) an increase in the quantity and quality of genetic information in the human genome.

5. Scientists call the accumulation of mutations in a species (**genetic burden/genetic blessing**) _____ and suggest large numbers of mutations promote (**evolution/extinction**) _____.

6. John Sanford, creationist geneticist, shows that mutations cause decay in genetic quality ("genetic entropy") much (**faster/slower**) _____ than evolutionists thought. Darwinian "selection" (**can/cannot**) _____ save us from genetic decay because most mutations "hide" as (**dominant/recessive**) _____ genes. Lots of time (**can/cannot**) _____ save us from mutations, since more time produces (**more/less**) _____ genetic decay.

7. Cain could marry his sister and Abraham his half-sister, but later on God's Law (mirrored in most state laws) prohibits close intermarriage. Explain why close intermarriage was not a problem for Cain.

   _____
   _____
   _____
   _____

8. It's widely touted that resistance to antibiotics in bacteria "proves" mutations produce evolution. However, (choose one): (a) mutational resistance damages a normal function, making resistant forms less likely to survive in normal environments; (b) some resistant forms are so crippled they can only live in hospitals, etc.; (c) scientists gave up on mutations in asexual bacteria beating odds of 10^{28} (1 in 10 million billion trillion!), and that led to the discovery of "sexually" traded plasmids, rather than mutations, producing "super-bugs"; (d) scientists praised Darwinian "selection" for its power to beat unbelievable odds; (e) all but d.

9. Famous evolutionist T. H. Huxley believed the odds against horse evolution were 1 in $10^{3,000,000}$, suggesting that Darwin's followers (**do/don't**) _____ believe in miracles, even if they (**do/don't**) _____ believe in the Miracle Worker!

Chapter 7

Darwinian Change vs. Biblical Change

Are there ANY examples of "good mutations" that evolutionists can point to with pride? That depends in part, of course, on what a person is willing to define or accept as a "good mutation."

An early mutation attracting evolutionists' attention was the appearance of short-legged sheep. That was "good" for farmers who did not have to build their stone fences so high, but NOT so good for the sheep trying to run away from a wolf while dragging its belly on the ground! Likewise, mutations producing seedless fruits are good for people, but no good for plants competing in a natural environment. Mutations producing a "biological monstrosity" like corn or a "hypoallergenic" hairless cat are good for people, but all are harmful to the species in its own environment and, hence, harmful in evolutionary perspective.

So-called back mutations really are beneficial to an organism in its native habitat. By changing one letter in its genetic code, a mutation can cause a bacterium to lose its ability to digest a certain sugar. If other foods are available, the bacterium and its asexual descendants (its

"clone") may survive until a mutation affects that same letter in the genetic code, changing it back to its original form. Back mutations are good for the organism, but no good for evolution because they only allow the organism to get back where it started.

While taking a graduate course in evolution on his way to a master of science degree in biology, a student asked his professor a simple question during a lecture on mutations as the raw material for evolution: "Would you please give us some examples of beneficial mutations?" After an uncomfortably long pause, the professor finally replied, "I can't think of any right now, but there must be hundreds of them." He did not come back to the next class with a list.

If there were any merit at all in using mutations to help explain evolution, the professor should have been able to say something like, "Yes, I'd be glad to. My favorite example of a good mutation is . . . A couple of other great examples are . . . Here's a handout that lists several more. For a more complete list of hundreds of good mutations, check pages 1024–1048 in the *Handbook of Biological Data*." Actually, the *Handbook of Biological Data*[1] lists

---

1. William S. Spector, *Handbook of Biological Data* (Philadelphia, PA: Saunders, 1956).

hundreds of harmful mutations. There's not even a single page listing beneficial mutations. You might think they would put in a blank page entitled "Good Mutations" so you could write it in, in case one were ever found!

The one example of a good mutation used over and over again in textbooks and museum displays is the change from normal to sickle-cell hemoglobin that's involved in sickle-cell anemia. Hemoglobin is the protein in red blood cells that carries oxygen. Why would anyone call a mutation beneficial that, in homozygous recessive form (ss) causes a serious blood disease? It's because heterozygous Ss people with one gene for normal hemoglobin (S) are resistant to malaria. Malaria is a deadly disease caused by a tiny protozoan that eats hemoglobin. It acts as if it doesn't like the taste of sickle-cell hemoglobin. So, Ss "carriers" or hybrids with "sicklecell trait" die of neither malaria nor sickle-cell anemia. But the price is high: 25 percent of the children of Ss parents are ss and can die of sickle-cell anemia, and another 25 percent (SS) can still die of malaria. If evolutionists want to call that a "good mutation" (and they do), they're welcome to it!

The sickle cell example brings us back to the problem of defining a "good mutation." If "goodness" is defined in terms of fitness (net relative reproductive efficiency), then, paradoxically, many harmful mutations could be called "good." Carriers of the sickle-cell gene survive in greater numbers — in and only in areas infected with the malaria parasite — because the harm they do to oxygen transport is less than the harm done by malaria. That is, sickle cell is a "good" mutation (in terms of fitness or survival value) because it's the lesser of two evils. Similarly, a mutation that makes bacteria resistant to penicillin by interfering with its cell wall production is "good" in the fitness sense, because it will out-reproduce competing bacteria in an environment rich in antibiotics, such as a hospital.

If "good" is defined in terms of adaptation, however, neither sickle-cell nor penicillin resistance mutations are good. Sickle-cell hemoglobin does not carry oxygen anywhere near as well as normal hemoglobin does, and bacteria resistant to penicillin by mutation produce faulty cell walls. If mutations like these were the raw materials for evolution, then the world should be full of defects, disease, and disease organisms.

Hmmmmm. The living world IS abundantly supplied with defects, disease, and disease organisms. There's no evidence mutations produce "upward" evolutionary changes, but there's lots of evidence that mutations produce harmful "downward" change. Even worse, natural selection often favors survival of defective and parasitic forms that feed off the hard metabolic work of free living forms — and that's so even if that short-term advantage for the exploiter means long-term decline for both parasite and host. Evolution (mutation-selection) cannot explain progressive upward change, but it does a great job of explaining bad changes in a fallen world, the corruption of creation following men's sin.

Again, it's not just that few if any truly good mutations have ever been observed; it's that any such mutation would occur in an organism riddled with harmful mutations. Moving up the evolutionary ladder by mutation would be like taking one small step up on the down escalator — an escalator moving down over a thousand times faster than anyone can step up.

Mutations: Evidence of Corruption and Creation

The mathematical challenges and the fact that mutations are going the wrong way for evolution should be sufficient reason to say "mutations, yes; evolution, no." But the simplest, most profound *reason mutations cannot produce evolution* is that mutations only produce changes — allelic changes — in genes that already exist. The most change mutations could ever produce are only allelic changes that make a gene pool wider, not deeper. (Review page 23.) Harmful, neutral, or perhaps even beneficial mutations can never produce more than variation in their kind. In that sense, *mutations point back to prior acts of creation.*

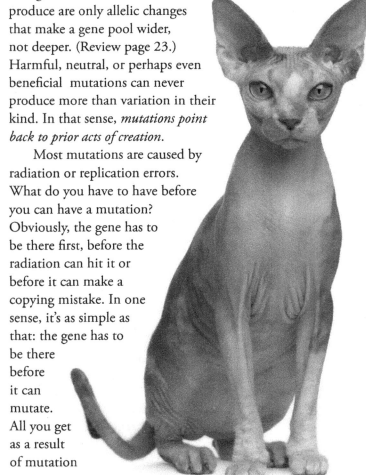

Most mutations are caused by radiation or replication errors. What do you have to have before you can have a mutation? Obviously, the gene has to be there first, before the radiation can hit it or before it can make a copying mistake. In one sense, it's as simple as that: the gene has to be there before it can mutate. All you get as a result of mutation is just a varied form of an already-existing gene, i.e., variation within kind (see below and Figure 8.1).

Uncritical acceptance of *evolution has so stunted scientific thinking* that people give mutations god-like qualities. They act as if a cosmic ray striking a cell can cause a "mutation" that somehow assembles over 1,200 DNA bases into a brand-new gene, regulators and all, that suddenly begins producing a brand-new protein responsible for a brand-new trait, raising the lucky mutated organism to the next higher rung on the evolutionary ladder! NOTHING remotely like that has ever happened, or ever could!

Mutations are NOT genetic "script writers"; they are merely "typographic errors" in a genetic script that has already been written. Typically, a mutation changes only one letter in a genetic sentence averaging 1,200 letters long.

To make evolution happen — or even to make evolution a theory fit for scientific discussion — evolutionists desperately need some kind of "genetic scriptwriter" to increase the quantity and quality of genetic INFORMATION. *Mutations have no ability to compose genetic sentences, no ability to produce genetic information, and, hence, no ability to make evolution happen at all (see below).*

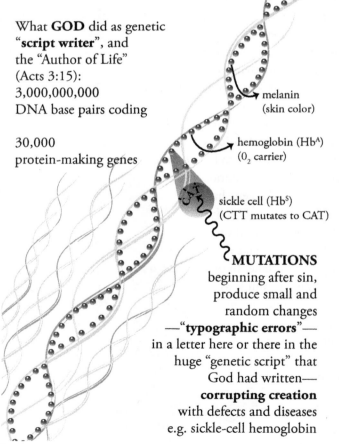

What **GOD** did as genetic "**script writer**", and the "Author of Life" (Acts 3:15):
3,000,000,000 DNA base pairs coding

30,000 protein-making genes

melanin (skin color)

hemoglobin (Hb^A) (0₂ carrier)

sickle cell (Hb^S) (CTT mutates to CAT)

MUTATIONS
beginning after sin, produce small and random changes —"**typographic errors**"— in a letter here or there in the huge "genetic script" that God had written— **corrupting creation** with defects and diseases e.g. sickle-cell hemoglobin

That simple, absolutely foundational fact completely stumped Richard Dawkins, the world's leading spokesman for evolution as of this writing. In a video production featuring several evolutionist and creationist leaders and skeptics, Dawkins argued eloquently that millions of years of mutation and natural selection would serve as a "blind watchmaker," producing all appearance of design among living things without any help from some supernatural Designer. Then in a quiet, non-threatening voice, not knowing what the answer would be, the narrator asked Dawkins to give an example of a mutation that adds information.

The usually effusive Dawkins gestured, opened his mouth, but stopped before he spoke. With his eyes shifting back and forth as if searching for some answer, he started to speak several times but always checked himself. Finally, after a long, embarrassing silence, the program resumed with Dawkins speaking on a different subject — leaving unanswered the ultimate question, the origin of genetic information.[2]

Yet molecules-to-man evolution is all about phenomenal expansion of genetic information. It would take billions of information-adding mutations to change "simple cells" into invertebrates, vertebrates, and mankind. *If there were any scientific merit at all to mutation-selection as a mechanism for evolution, Dawkins' reply should have been enthusiastic and overwhelming:* "My three favorite examples of mutations adding information are . . . Excellent examples among plants are . . . among insects are . . . among bacteria are . . ." His answer, instead, was silence, and with no mechanism to add genetic information, the "evolutionary tree" can't grow.

The problem with evolution is not some shortcoming in Dawkins, however. The problem is with the fundamental nature of information itself. The information in a book, for example, cannot be reduced to, nor derived from, the properties of the ink and paper used to write it. Similarly, the information in the genetic code cannot be reduced to, nor derived from, the properties of matter nor the mistakes of mutations; its message and meaning originated instead in the mind of its Maker.

As cogently presented by two of the world's leading information theorists, information comes only from pre-existing information. Information systems have the "exherent," created kind of design, which can be logically inferred from our scientific observations as explained in great detail in the section on DNA. Although mutations

2. Gillian Brown, *Biological Evidence from Creation: From a Frog to a Prince* (video), Keziah Productions, January 1998.

may corrupt it and selection may sort variations into different environments, *it was not a "blind watchmaker" that composed the genetic script for each kind of organism,* but a Creator with a plan and purpose and eyes wide open.

Mutation-Selection in Biblical Perspective

Let's look now at mutation-selection in biblical perspective. That may sound like a contradiction in terms, but it's not at all. Thousands of scientists, including many evolutionists, think the scientific evidence is abundantly clear: evolution requires an increase in the quantity and quality of genetic information, and neo-Darwinian mutation-selection — no matter how much time it's given — cannot provide it. But both mutation and selection are very real, observable processes going on around us every day. Evolution, no; mutation-selection, yes!

Mutation and selection don't produce evolutionary changes ("macroevolution"), but they do indeed produce changes. Mutations are no help at all in explaining the origin of "new and improved" species or even the origin of a single really new gene (genon), but mutations are great for explaining the origin of disease, disease organisms, and birth defects. Natural selection is no real help in explaining the origin of species, but it's great for explaining how and where different specialized subtypes of the various created kinds "multiplied and filled the earth" after struggle and death (Darwin's "war of nature") corrupted God's creation. Subspeciation (specialization), yes; evolution, no.

When we look at the world around us, what do we see: evidence of Darwinian evolution, or biblical creation? Perhaps you can see why some people might be honestly confused. Every day the evening news describes the latest murders, rapes, robberies, and drunk driver deaths; magazine articles detail the AIDS epidemic, wars and rumors of wars, the latest school shootings, and impending environmental doom; nature programs show a lion ripping the guts out of a zebra and a black widow spider devouring her mate. It looks like Darwin's war is everywhere. But we also revel in the beauty of a sunset and opening of a rosebud, feel overwhelmed by newlywed love and the miracle of birth, stand in awe of the awesome intricacy (and "transcendent simplicity") of integrated molecular machinery in living cells, and visualize (and hope for) peace and harmony restored in a never-ending relationship with our risen Lord. There's far, FAR too much beauty and elegant design to be the product of time, chance, and Darwinian evolution. But why would

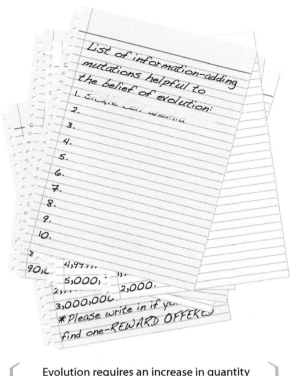

Evolution requires an increase in quantity and quality of genetic information that no amount of time could provide.

an all-loving, all-powerful caring Creator make a world with so much pain, suffering, struggle, and death?

The Bible Has the Answer

God's world reflects the "4C gospel theme" of God's word: Creation, Corruption, Catastrophe, Christ. The elegant design in DNA genes, the beauty and the love we find around us, is the result of plan, purpose, and God's creative acts (Creation). The horror, brokenness, and hate we also see the result of man's sin corrupting God's creation, bringing on mutational mistakes and Darwin's war (Corruption / Catastrophe). Praise God, Darwin's war (time, chance, struggle, and death) ends when Jesus' sacrifice conquers sin and death and life wins — new life, rich and abundant forevermore, in a renewed relationship with our risen Lord (Christ)! Mutation and selection have major roles to play in the history of our planet — NOT in its origin, but during the Darwinian warfare (Corruption / Catastrophe) that precedes and its restoration in Christ!

We need to do a better job of teaching evolution. The more people understand the evidence and how evolution is supposed to work, *the less likely they are to believe evolution* produces upward, onward progress. Certainly there should be far, FAR fewer *Christians willing to compromise evolution's millions of years of struggle and death with the biblical message of new life in Christ!*

Change and Variation

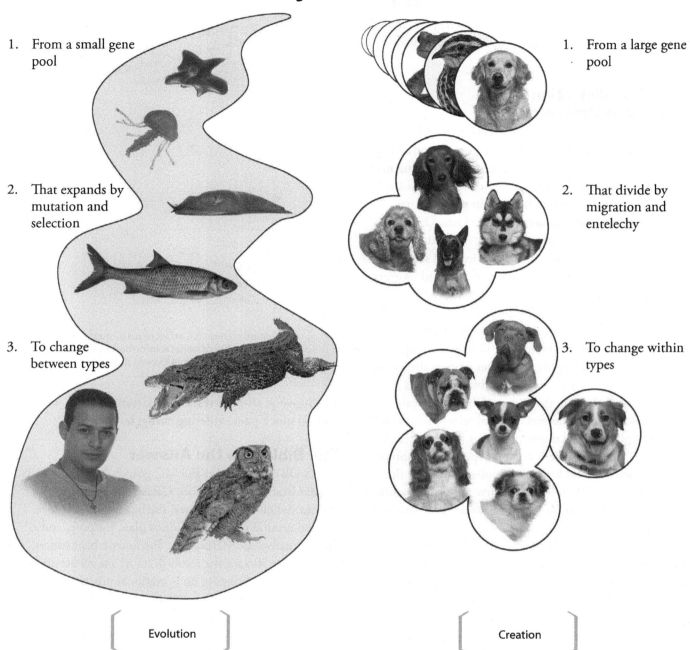

1. From a small gene pool

2. That expands by mutation and selection

3. To change between types

[Evolution]

1. From a large gene pool

2. That divide by migration and entelechy

3. To change within types

[Creation]

Figure 8.1. Change? Yes — but which kind of change? What is the more logical inference, or the more reasonable extrapolation, from our observations: unlimited change from one kind to others (evolution), or limited variation within kinds (creation)? Given the new knowledge of genetics and ecology, even Darwin, I believe, would be willing to "think about it."

Form your foundation.

Leading evolutionists like Dawkins can give NO examples of mutations composing new genetic information, but scientists can give thousands of examples of defects and diseases caused by simple letter changes ("typos") in DNA code, including sickle-cell hemoglobin. Chance mutations don't create; they corrupt!

1. Richard Dawkins is currently the world's leading spokesman for evolution. On a video about creation/evolution, he was asked to give an example of a mutation that added information. What did he say? _____
_____.

2. The author suggests schools should teach evolution much more thoroughly, since he believes the more someone knows about evolution the (**more/less**) _____ likely he or she is to believe it.

3. The sickle-cell hemoglobin gene (Hb^S) is the most widely hailed example of a "good" mutation leading to evolutionary progress. (a) Why do Darwin's followers call the sickle cell gene "good"? (b) Is the Hb^S mutation "good" for fitness or for adaptation, and what's the difference? (c) What's the "price" (the "bad part") of this "good" mutation? (d) Do you think sickle-cell anemia helps or hurts the evolutionists' cause? _____
_____
_____
_____

4. What does it mean (and why is it important) to note that mutations are "**genetic typos**," not at all "**genetic script** writers"? _____
_____
_____

5. All known mutations produce only (**alleles/genons**) _____, which are changes in genes that (**already exist/never existed before**) _____ pointing to creation. Any "good" mutations would "drown in a sea" of harmful ones, pointing to _____.

6. According to the world's leading information theorists, where does information (**including genetic information**) come from? _____. Making it more personal, the Bible expresses that thought as information comes from _____ (Genesis 1:1, John 1:1).

7. Do mutations and Darwin's "war of nature" fit among these 4 Cs of biblical history (fill in **yes or no**):
Creation _____, Corruption _____, Catastrophe _____, Christ _____?

8. To contrast the worldviews of creation and evolution, answer the following questions about mutations, Darwin's "war of nature" (selection), and "change through time":

   a. Both science and Scripture suggest that life on earth began with (**many/few**) _____ different kinds, each with a (**large/small**) _____ gene pool, whereas Darwin's followers believe life began with (**many/few**) _____ forms with (**large/small**) _____ gene pools.

   b. Evolutionists believe that mutations and Darwin's "war of nature" make things (**better/worse**) _____ by producing (**new species/defects and disease**) _____ and a tremendous (**increase/decrease**) _____ in both genetic quantity and quality. Using both science and Scripture, creationists suggest mutation and Darwin's war started (**at creation/after sin**) _____ and make things much (**better/worse**) _____ by producing (**new species/defects and disease**) _____ and a dramatic (**increase/decrease**) _____ in both genetic quality and quantity.

9. As they "multiplied and filled the earth," (**generalized/specialized**) _____ life forms tended to divide into (**generalized/specialized**) _____ subtypes (e.g., black, brown, and polar bears), illustrating (**creation/evolution**) _____ and (**variation within/changes between**) _____ kinds.

Chapter 8

Unit 2: Patterns in Structure and Development

If the laws of heredity had been known in Darwin's time, it's unlikely he would have published his Origin of Species (1859). Had Darwin published, it's likely his theory would have been picked up by some philosophers to use as a defense of atheism, but it's unlikely to have attracted any attention whatsoever from serious scientists. Indeed, Section 1 showed that discoveries about heredity fit so well with the principles of Scripture that genetics could be used in Christian witness as clear evidence that "the invisible things of him [God] . . . are clearly seen . . . through the things that are made" (Rom. 1:20).

"But," scoffs the evolutionist, "if God created each kind of life to multiply after its own separate kind, then why are so many parts the same in so many different kinds? Doesn't that prove that all living things descended from a common ancestor? Besides, even if we can't yet explain how it happened, we can trace lines of descent along branches of the evolutionary tree. Wouldn't a 'creative creator' be able to make each separate kind separate and special?"

"It is true," says the creationist, "that living things have many features in common — not because they descended from the same ancestor, but because they were designed by the same Creator. Genetics shows each kind of life and its variation reflects plan, purpose, and special acts of creation; patterns of similarity among different kinds show there is one Creator, not many. Furthermore, patterns of development from egg to adult (embryology) show evidence of working out a plan built in ahead of time (entelechy, not evolution), and studies of structural similarities (homology) among different kinds of living things (classification) contradict the evolution of incomplete traits distributed in branching patterns of descent and reveal instead complete traits in mosaic patterns reflecting creation!"

We've looked at genetics and reproduction in Section 1 (and will look more deeply at these and DNA in Section 3). Let's look now at structural similarities (homology) and stages in development (embryology) used in classification. What patterns do we find? Does a growing embryo retrace its evolutionary history, or does it reflect plan and purpose, showing how each creature was "fearfully and wonderfully made"? Are body parts among living things distributed in branching lines of descent from a common ancestor, or in mosaic patterns reflecting "theme and variation" in the mind of the One God in Christ, author of life?

As you dig into the science and compare two different worldviews, think about how the evidence you see in God's world fits with what you read in God's Word.

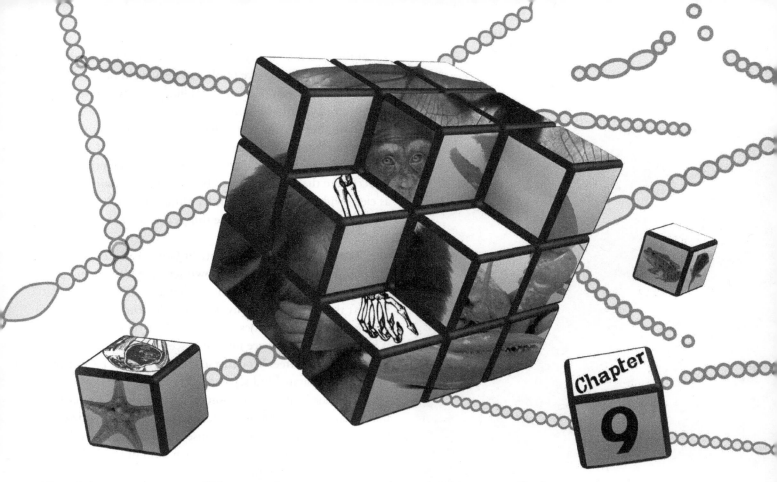

Patterns in Structure:
Descent or Design?

Scoffers may challenge: if God made people as people, why do we have so many parts like animals have? Look at your arm for a moment and try to picture the bones inside. There's one bone attached to the body, two bones in the forearm, a little group of wrist bones, and bones that extend out into the fingers. As it turns out, there are many other living things that have forelimbs with a similar pattern: the foreleg of a horse or dog, the wing of a bat, and the flipper of a penguin, for example, as shown in Figure 9.1. Biologists use the term *homology* for such similarities in basic structure.

Why should there be that kind of similarity? Why should a person's arm have the same kind of bone pattern as the leg of a dog and the wing of a bat? There are two basic ideas. One of these is the evolutionary idea of *descent from a common ancestor.* That idea seems to make sense, since that's the way we explain such similarities as brothers and sisters looking more alike than cousins do. They have parents closer in common.

Using descent from a common ancestor to explain similarities is probably the most logical and appealing idea that evolutionists have. Some think that our ability to classify plants and animals on a groups-within-groups

hierarchical basis virtually forces scientists to treat evolution as a "fact." However, we can classify kitchen utensils on a groups-within-groups basis, but that hardly forces anyone to believe that knives evolved into spoons, spoons into forks, or saucers into cups and plates.

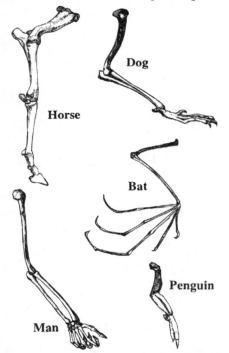

Figure 9.1. Similarities in structural pattern (homology) among bones in vertebrate forelimbs

After all, there's another reason in our common experience why things look alike. It's *creation according to a common plan*. That's why Fords and Chevrolets have more in common than Fords and sailboats. They have more design features in common.

What's the more logical inference from our observation of bone patterns and other examples of homology: descent from a common ancestor, or creation according to a common plan? In many cases, either explanation will work, and we can't really tell which is more reasonable. But there seem to be times when the only thing that works is creation according to a common design.

Support for this claim comes from renowned secular scientist Michael Denton, in his revolutionary book, *Evolution: Theory in Crisis*[1]. 1 In his chapter titled "The Failure of Homology," he admits his desire to find naturalistic explanations for patterns of structural similarities (homology), but he also admits the failure of evolutionary explanations. Dr. Denton is not only a research scientist with a PhD in molecular biology, but also an MD with an intimate knowledge of comparative anatomy and embryology.

Like every other scientist, Denton recognizes the striking similarity in bone pattern evident between vertebrate fore- and hindlimbs. Yet no evolutionist, he says, claims that the hindlimb evolved from the forelimb, or that hindlimbs and forelimbs evolved from a common ancestor with one pair of limbs. It was once taught that corresponding parts of the male and female reproductive systems illustrated "sexual homology." Homology, in that case, could not possibly be explained by descent from a common ancestor; that would mean that males evolved from females, or vice versa, or that human beings evolved from some animal that had only one sex.

Worse yet for evolution, structures that appear homologous often develop under the control of genes that are not homologous. In such cases, the thesis that similar structures developed from genes modified during evolutionary descent is precisely falsified. In frogs, for example, the five digits on each limb grow out from buds on the embryonic paddle; in human embryos, the digits form as the tissue between them is reabsorbed. Here quite *different* gene-enzyme mechanisms produce *similar* (homologous) patterns. Structures in adult lobsters and

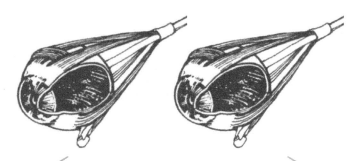

The squid and human eye show astonishing similarities in deep detail.

crayfish are so similar (homologous) that the same lab instructions can be used for dissecting either, yet the crayfish egg develops directly into the adult form while the lobster egg reaches the homologous pattern through a free-swimming larval stage.

Our observation of similarity or homology is real enough, but that's true, Denton points out, "whether the causal mechanism was Darwinian, Lamarckian, vitalistic, *or even creationist*"[2] (emphasis added). Although the evidence is not as spectacular and compelling as the DNA and embryological data soon to be discussed, the weight of our present knowledge of homology favors Denton's final alternative: creation according to a common design.

Perhaps the clearest anatomical evidence of creation is "*convergence*." The classic example is the similarity between the eyes of humans and vertebrates and the eyes of squids and octopuses. Evolutionists recognize the similarity between the eyes easily enough, but they've never been able to find or even imagine a common ancestor having eyes with traits that would explain these similarities. So instead of calling these eyes homologous organs, they call them examples of "convergent evolution." Rather than evolution, however, we have another example of similarity in structure that cannot be explained as evolutionary descent from a common ancestor.

Convergence, in the sense of similar structures designed to meet similar needs, would be expected, of course, on the basis of creation according to a common plan. As we'll see in the unit on fossils, both the octopus eye and the vertebrate eye are complete, complex, and totally distinct from one another right from their first appearance in the fossil sequence. Biologist Michael Land sounds

1. Michael Denton, *Evolution: Theory in Crisis* (Bethesda, MD: Adler & Adler, 1986) pp. 154–155.

2. Ibid. page 306.

like a creationist when he mentions in passing that the vertebrate eye "shares design features but not evolution"[3] with the eye of the cephalopod mollusks such as the squid and octopus.

The real focus of Land's article, however, is "*divergence*," the occurrence of quite distinct structures in plants and animals that otherwise are supposed to be close evolutionary relatives. Certain shrimp-like animals that live in deep ocean darkness, he says, have compound eyes with lenses all arranged to focus light at a common point (rather than forming multiple images, as most compound eyes do). But, he continues, some members of the group have "lens cylinders" that smoothly bend the incoming light, whereas others have square faces with a "mirror system" for focus (utilizing even a double-corner bounce). Ingenious use of physics and geometry should be evidence enough of creation — but there's more. Comparing the mirrors with the lens cylinder system, Land says, "Both are successful and very sophisticated image-forming devices, but I cannot imagine an intermediate form [or common ancestral type] that would work at all." The kind of design in these eyes, he says, seems impossible to explain as a result of evolutionary relationship. So Land goes on to suggest that the shrimp-like animals with different systems should not be classified as evolutionary relatives, even though they are otherwise quite similar.

Even more interesting is Land's statement about how he felt when he was trying to figure out the mirror system. He said he was "trying not to come to the conclusion that these eyes had been put there by God to confuse scientists." They may confuse evolutionists, but it seems instead that these eyes were put there by God to *inform* scientists. As such cases show, a mind open to examples of created order can hasten and enrich the scientific search for understanding. *National Geographic* for April 2008 featured attempts by various scientists to copy designs in nature (e.g., gecko's feet, fly's wing, shark's skin, etc.), yet as ingenious as they were, none came close to the elegance of God's original design.

Some of Darwin's followers admit they have failed to find good evidence of evolution in comparing large structures, so they are looking instead for homology among molecules. In a foundational book basically describing the three-dimensional structures first known for proteins, Dickerson and Geis state that "from the perfection of protein sequence and structure analysis... we can pin down with great precision the relationships between the species and how proteins evolved."[4] Then, with every example they give, they proceed to *disprove* that evolutionary prediction. Consider hemoglobin, for example, the protein that carries oxygen in red blood cells. Dickerson says that hemoglobins pose "a puzzling problem. Hemoglobins occur sporadically among the invertebrate phyla [the animals without backbones] in no obvious pattern." That is, they don't occur in an evolutionary branching pattern; they do occur in a creationist mosaic pattern, like bits of blue-colored stone in an artist's mosaic. We find hemoglobin in nearly all vertebrates, but we also find it in some annelids (the earthworm group), some echinoderms (the starfish group), some mollusks (the clam group), some arthropods (the insect group), and even in some bacteria! In all these cases, we find the same kind of molecule — complete and fully functional. As Dickerson observes, "It is hard to see a common line of descent snaking in so unsystematic a way through so many different phyla. . . ." (see page 26, Figure 3.4)

If evolution were true, we ought to be able to trace how hemoglobin evolved. But we can't. Could it be *repeated* evolution, the spontaneous appearance of hemoglobin in all these different groups independently asks Dickerson. He answers that repeated evolution seemed plausible only as long as hemoglobin was considered just red stuff that held oxygen. It does NOT seem possible, he says, that the entire eight-helix folded pattern appeared repeatedly by time and chance. As far as creationists are concerned, hemoglobin occurs, complete and fully functional, wherever it is appropriate in the Creator's plan, somewhat like a blue-colored tile in an artist's mosaic (e.g., in water, sky or flower).

Some are hoping that DNA comparisons and gene sequencing ("molecular homology") can somehow salvage evolutionary belief. Is there anyone who hasn't heard that DNA comparison suggests something like 98 percent similarity between man and chimpanzee? The evidence so convinced one evolutionist debater that he told the audience if a chimp asked to take his daughter out on

3. Michael Land, "Nature as an Optical Engineer," *New Scientist*, Oct. 4, 1979.

4. Richard E. Dickerson and Irving Geis, *The Structure and Action of Proteins*, Harper and Row, New York, 1969.

A 2 percent difference among three billion DNA base pairs would mean about *60 million* code letter differences between man and chimp.

Chimpanzees have 24 chromosomes in their genomes, and 20 percent more DNA per cell than humans.

Humans have 23 chromosomes in their genomes, or 46 in the diploid set present in most cells.

a date, he was not sure he could say "no." (I hope his daughter would be allowed to say no.) There are even some groups pushing for the extension of U.N. human rights protection to chimps and orangutans!

It only takes a trip to the zoo, of course, to convince us that man and ape share many features, and there are unseen similarities in bone, muscle, nerve and sense organs, circulatory and digestive systems, hair, milk, etc. It should be equally obvious, however, that creatures designed by the same Creator to move, eat, breathe, etc., in similar ways would have many molecular similarities in common.

An article on "The 2% Difference" (*Discover*, April 2006) praises evolution and puts down intelligent design, but the author (Robert Sapolsky) actually admits and describes key evidences noted by creation scientists over the past two decades. "Regulation is everything," he says. A sidewalk, fence, patio, and house may be made of bricks that are 100 percent identical, for example, but they are arranged in different ways to serve dramatically different purposes. Sapolsky points out that the brains of man and chimp operate using "the same basic building blocks" while they achieve "vastly different outcomes," so that in his opinion "there's not the tiniest bit of scientific evidence that chimps have aesthetics, spirituality, or a capacity for irony or poignancy." These awesome gaps or "qualitative distinctions" between the brains of chimps and people

Sapolsky credits to a "relatively few" genes that regulate the number of brain cells (neurons) produced. Sapolsky seems to forget, of course, that some dysfunctional or diseased brains have just as many neurons as the ones we call normal, and stuffing more chips into a computer does not automatically improve it. It's not just the number of parts that produce the great gulf between human and chimp; it's how the parts are connected. As creation scientists have long noted, and the Bible implies, living things (and their functioning parts) are not a product of substance, but of organization. At the atomic level ("dust of the ground"), all organisms are essentially 100 percent identical; if the 2 percent difference in DNA presumed for man and chimp told the other 98 percent how to organize, the differences would be at least as vast and unbridgeable as we observe.

And there's more. The April 2006 *Discover* article finally admitted what creation scientists have stressed for over 20 years: "a tiny 20/0 difference translates into tens of millions of AGCT [DNA base] differences." Indeed, a 2 percent difference among three billion DNA base pairs would mean about *60 million* code letter differences between man and chimp. So, as creationists pointed out long ago and Sapolsky admits, "There are likely to be nucleotide differences in every single gene." In fact, studies comparing chimp chromosome #22 with its presumed counterpart on human chromosome #21 had already shown by 2004 that a DNA difference of about 1.5 percent resulted in differences of more than 80 percent among the proteins produced by those genes. That did not surprise creation scientists, but shocked evolutionists.

Actually, studies of molecular homology have produced major controversies among Darwin's followers, since DNA trees frequently disagree with evolutionary trees based on fossils and/or on comparative anatomy. Even among those who prefer to base evolutionary belief on molecular data, there is a huge split when it comes to conflicting attempts (based on dubious, compounded assumptions) to use molecular homology as some sort of "evolutionary clock." "Selectionists" believe mutations are incorporated into populations at highly variable rates, since they assume some mutants will have much greater survival value than others. "Neutralists" believe the rate of incorporation of mutations, at least over the long haul, will average out to act like the steady, regular ticking of a "molecular clock." Neither side, by the way, bases its belief on actual rates of mutations observed by scientists; rather, the ticks of the clock are supposed to be PAMs (point accepted mutations). PAMs are the *unobserved* rates at which mutations are supposed to gradually win the struggle to the death within populations (natural selection), generally changing their percentage from 1 percent to 99 percent. After documenting the misfit of molecular data with *both* of the two competing evolutionary views, Michael Denton (reference 1, page 71) writes this summary (p. 306):

> The difficulties associated with attempting to explain how a family of homologous proteins could have evolved at constant rates have created chaos in evolutionary thought. *The evolutionary community has divided into two camps —* those still adhering to the *selectionist* position, and those rejecting it in favor of the *neutralist*. The devastating aspect of this controversy is that neither side can adequately account for the constancy of the rate of molecular evolution; yet *each side fatally weakens the other*. The selectionists wound the neutralists' position by pointing to the disparity in the rates of mutation per unit time, while the neutralists destroy the selectionists' position by showing how ludicrous it is to believe that selection would have caused equal rates of divergence in "junk" proteins or along phylogenetic lines so dissimilar as those of man and carp. Both sides win valid points, but in the process, the

credibility of the molecular clock hypothesis is severely strained and with it the whole paradigm [worldview] of evolution itself is endangered (emphasis added).

Denton doesn't stop with these devastating anti-evolutionary comments (and a comparison of belief in molecular clocks with belief in medieval astrology!). He also describes data from molecular homology as a "biochemical echo of typology," where typology is the pre-evolutionary view of classification developed by scientists on the basis of creationist thinking.

Although partial data fit too easily into conflicting branching patterns, comparative similarities and homologies don't fit well at all onto evolutionary trees. They fit instead into hierarchical (groups within groups) categories, perhaps suggesting a multidimensional matrix (a "cube of cubes" in more than three dimensions). When Mendeleev discovered the pattern God used in creating the chemical elements, he was able to predict the existence and properties of elements not then known to science. Using the mosaic/modular/matrix concept, creationists may one day discover predictive patterns of trait distribution among living things, and prediction is the real measure of merit among scientific theories.

Once again, God's Word has proven to be the surest guide to understanding God's world. Traits are complete and complex reflecting creation, not incomplete and transitional suggesting the "missing links" evolutionists had hoped to find. Furthermore, these complete traits are not distributed in branching patterns from common ancestors, but in mosaic patterns suggesting "theme and variation" in a created plan.

Form your foundation.

"Theme and variation" in music, art, architecture, etc., is recognized as evidence of creative genius, and "theme and variation" (homology) in the exquisite design of living creatures provides unmistakable evidence of the creative ingenuity of our awesome Creator God.

1. Different animals may have parts with a similar structural pattern, called _____. These similarities mean "descent from a common ancestry" say (**evolutionists/creationists**) _____, but they mean "design according to a common plan" to _____.

2. The detailed similarity (homology) of the human and squid eye is called "convergence." What problem does such convergence pose for evolutionists? How does it provide evidence of creation?

   _____
   _____
   _____
   _____
   _____

3. Two kinds of shrimp-like animals (krill) share a great many features in detail, but some have radically different eyes. What problem does this kind of "divergence" pose for Darwin's followers?

   _____
   _____
   _____
   _____
   _____

4. Hemoglobin, the protein that carries oxygen in most vertebrates, is also found scattered through many invertebrate groups (earthworms, sea starts, etc.) in a (**branching/mosaic**) _____ pattern that favors (**creation/evolution**) _____.

5. A "98% similarity" in the DNA of man and chimpanzee has been hailed by the media, museums, textbooks, and many teachers as "proof positive" that chimps evolved into people. However, that popularized belief has been challenged by these facts of science (circle all that are true):

   a. Chimps have 20% more DNA than humans, a difference 10 times larger than the 2% difference so widely touted.

   b. Even a 2% difference in the DNA of man and chimp means at least 60 million code letter differences, and that means differences in every gene are possible.

   c. Proteins produced by DNA on human and chimp chromosomes considered similar showed 86% difference, not 2%.

   d. The bricks used to build a house, fancy mailbox support, and fireplace are 100% the same, but creative organization gives the same parts quite different features — and even 2% "control gene" differences could create organisms as different as man and chimp.

   e. Human DNA was used as a guide to sequencing chimp DNA early on, introducing unreported and unfair bias (cheating) into the initial claim of 98% similarity.

6. Two groups of evolutionists (selectionists vs. neutralists) have tried to use DNA similarities as "molecular clocks" to "map" branching lines of descent. Famous molecular biologist Michael Denton (neither creationist nor evolutionist) says the two groups (**frequently agree/contradict each other**) _____ _____. Denton went on to say that molecular homology, like structural similarities, seems to suggest traits distributed in a ("M" word) _____ pattern supporting _____.

Chapter 9

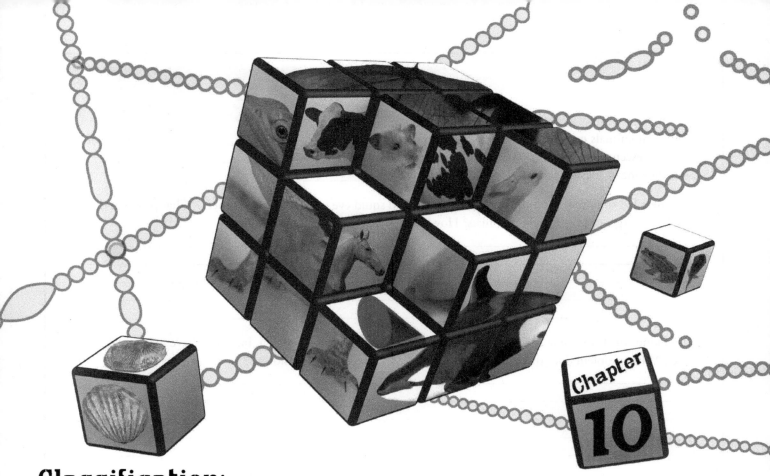

Classification: Mosaics or "Missing Links"?

Criteria for Classification

Scientists call structural similarity "homology," but people have been using similarities among body parts to identify and classify living things all the way back to the Garden of Eden. In fact, when He brought the animals before Adam to be named (Gen. 2:19–20), God made *Adam the first biologist* specializing in taxonomy (identification) and classification (systematics). Recognizing similarities and putting them into meaningful patterns is part of God's image in us, and it sets us far above animals and even most computers, though children do this gleefully to the *Sesame Street* song "One of These Things (Is Not Like the Others)."

No matter where or when they lived, for example, peoples in cultures worldwide have a word for "birds." The general category "bird" includes many different, much more specific created kinds/true species, each kind defined by objective criteria involving its reproduction and special adaptive features. But what defines the broader category "bird"? In this case, the answer seems to be easy: feathers. Birds are animals with feathers. Most birds have wings and use feathers for flight, but some can't fly and use feathers for warmth and for courtship (ostriches), others have feathers on flippers for swimming (penguins), and still other birds use feathers on forelimbs for both swimming and flying (puffins).

Should "birds" be defined instead as animals that fly? That would put buzzards with bats and butterflies, perhaps leaving running ostriches to be grouped with horses and swimming penguins with dolphins. Because it's so unfamiliar, that latter suggestion might sound silly, but is it more or less scientifically reasonable than defining birds as feathered animals? How would you know, and why?

Although evolutionists seem unaware of it, scientists recognize that biological classification involves two quite different types of grouping techniques. The first is recognizing and naming the true scientific species or created kinds (baramins). Even Darwin's followers still use the system devised by the creationist Carolus Linnaeus in the 1700s, which uses

Though both can fly, a bat (mammal) and
a gull (bird) cannot interbreed.

the biblical criterion of "multiplication after kind," or ability to interbreed, as the primary basis for assigning genus-species scientific names. Both appearance (size, color, adaptive features, etc.) and the ability to interbreed could have been affected by ecologic and geographic variation as living things "multiplied and filled the earth," of course, and also by mutational damage to genes and chromosomes after the Fall. Even then, however, laboratory tests for sperm-egg compatibility, chromosome structure, meiotic pairing, DNA sequencing, breeding experiments, statistics of variability, and other scientific tests can be used to identify created kinds or biological species on a purely objective, scientific basis.

The part of biological classification that emphasizes giving proper scientific names to organisms is called *taxonomy*. Apparently for reasons such as personal or political whim, fame or fortune, marketing or propaganda, *evolutionists have turned taxonomy into a sea of subjectivity.* Taxonomic naming, however, could and should be done on an objective, scientific basis (and creationists are leading the way!).

Unfortunately, the clear principles of Scripture and science that put taxonomy on an objective foundation are not so clear when it comes to *systematics*, the part of classification concerned with grouping specific, objective kinds/species into categories sharing more general, more subjective (at present) degrees of similarity. Even worse, the present subjectivity in systematics exists in two forms: (1) *What criteria can/should we use* (and why) to put objective kinds/species into groups, and (2) *which criteria are "more important,"* that is, which can/should be used for defining smaller versus larger groups, and why.

Consider, for example, how the many different kinds/species of algae ("pond scum" and "seaweed") are put into broader groups. Scientific classification often involves big words, so students have always been grateful that biologists put most algal kinds into broad groups based on their predominant color: greens, blue-greens, reds, browns, and goldens. These do have fancier, big names: Chlorophycophyta, Cyanophycophyta, Rhodophycophyta, Phaeophycophyta, and Chrysophycophyta. But the middle and end, "-phycophyta," translates as "algal plant," and the Greek prefixes mean, respectively, "green, blue-green, red, brown, and golden." (Even professional botanists regularly refer to the major algal groups as green, blue-green, red, brown, and golden algae.)

Although convenient for both students and professors, however, grouping algal kinds by color may have been a poor choice. The vital plant pigment responsible for capturing sunlight energy for the crucial food-making, oxygen-releasing process of *photosynthesis* is the same for all algal groups: it's the green pigment, *chlorophyll.* Among green algae, there is usually no other pigment to mask the green reflected by chlorophyll, so the algae look green. The other algal groups get their distinctive colors from "accessory pigments" that mask the green of chlorophyll: phycocyanin for the blue-greens, phycoerythrin for the reds, fucoxanthin for the browns, and xanthophylls for the goldens. These other pigments are not required for algal life like chlorophyll is, and serve mainly for "decoration." Decoration is important to God, who, as the Great Artist, made plants both "pleasant to the sight and good for food" (Gen. 2:9; RSV). But is "decoration" important enough scientifically to make it the most important criterion for putting algal kinds into the broadest groups?

Algal kinds differ from each other in at least two other major categories of traits that could be considered more important than decorating color when it comes to putting algal kinds together in broad groups: their structural complexity and their type of reproduction. When it comes to reproduction, some algae are only known to reproduce asexually (including the otherwise complex brown alga, *Sargassum*, that fills the Atlantic's "Sargasso Sea" and crowds some tidepools). Sexually reproducing algae include those whose sex cells (*gametes*) look alike (*isogamy*), those with gametes that differ somewhat (*heterogamy*), and those that produce large, non-motile egg and small, motile sperm cells — distinctively male and female gametes (*oogamy*). Since reproductive success is the ultimate value in evolutionary theory, one might have thought Darwin's followers would want to group algal kinds into major groups with names like Agamia, Isogamia, Heterogamia, and Oogamia (or Agamaphycophyta, Isogamaphycophyta, Heterogamaphycophyta, and Oogamaphycophyta!). Notice how much fun it is to make up big words — at least if you don't have to learn them for a test!

If algal kinds are grouped according to type of reproduction, however, the results conflict with the grouping based on type of pigment (color). Green algae, for example, include kinds with each of the four major reproductive patterns. Browns include asexual,

heterogamous, and oogamous forms, while reds are mostly oogamous and blue-greens only asexual.

Darwin's followers want to use biological classification to make "evolutionary trees" to show branching lines of descent from a "common ancestor," but the facts of God's world constantly frustrate them. Imagine a tree made up to show that some ancestral green algal kind branched out to produce, for example, blue-greens and browns, and that browns later evolved into reds and goldens. Such a tree would conflict with a tree based on the assumption that asexual forms evolved into isogamous sexual algal kinds that later produced heterogamous and oogamous branches. In a tree based on pigment (color), the oogamous reproductive pattern, for example, would have to evolve more than once from different ancestors; in a tree based on reproductive pattern, color would have to evolve more than once from different ancestors. *These contradictory branching patterns clearly contradict the concept that similarities reflect common ancestry.* In these cases, evolutionists really have nothing beyond personal preference to decide when similarities mean descent from common ancestry and when they don't.

What about structural complexity? Surely that's an important trait. Some algal kinds are one-celled (unicellular), while some are multicellular, consisting of several cells with different shapes and functions. Still other algal kinds are colonial; they include many cells arranged as balls, filaments, or blades, but all the cells in colonies The parts of blue-green cells are more like those of bacteria (procaryotic) than those of other algal kinds (eucaryotic), so they are now often called "Cyanobacteria" rather than "Blue-Green Algae" (Cyanophycophyta).

[Lampshells, or brachiopods, are bivalves like clams, but the animal inside is quite different.]

Are the blue-greens "*primitive*," prokaryotic forms whose descendants evolved more "*advanced*" eukaryotic cells — or are the blue-greens degenerated ("de-volved") from more complex algal kinds in which mutations produced loss of information and loss of structure? Similarly, did colonial algae "*evolve upward*" from unicellular forms, or "*de-volve downward*" from multicellular algae by harmful, information-losing mutations (the kinds actually observed by scientists)? Similarly, did evolution produce a chain of change from asexual to isogamous, heterogamous, then oogamous reproduction — or did corruption of creation and loss mutations *degenerate* oogamous forms into heterogamous and isogamous to asexual? *Or, were algal kinds created initially with different reproductive patterns, structural complexity, and color,* designed to play different roles in God's total plan for the web of life?

Scientists have discovered one thing for sure: *evolutionary theory is worse than worthless as a basis for biological classification.* Evolutionary trees based on structural complexity, reproductive pattern, and pigmentation differ radically from one another, necessitating numerous repeated evolutions of a given feature, which makes the whole concept of common ancestry completely meaningless. Although laymen think evolution is generally about simple-to-complex change, evolutionists call simpler features "primitive" in some cases and then reverse the trend to call it a "secondary reduction" from a more advanced state ("reverse evolution"?) — and many now say evolution has no direction at all, but only temporarily rewards those best at exploiting their environment.

While he was the internationally respected paleontologist at the British Museum, Colin Patterson stunned the scientific world by calling evolution an "antitheory" that generates "anti-knowledge" — a concept full of explanatory vocabulary that actually explains nothing and that even generates a false impression of what the facts really are. Admitting he had been duped all his life into taking evolutionism as "revealed truth," Patterson said that he finally awoke to find that evolutionary theory makes bad systematics (the science of classification). His research centered on fossil lampshells (brachiopods, facing page). Patterson had spent decades trying to come up with a tree reflecting branching patterns of evolution in this group. Lampshell fossils are abundant and have multiple features clearly preserved, so they should provide clear evidence of branching evolutionary descent — IF evolution were true. Since evolution is not true, Patterson's exceptional expertise and effort kept turning

up *anti-evolutionary results* with lampshells like those we see in algae: *mis-matching trees* requiring repeated origins of features, and *frequent reversals* of what were supposed to be evolutionary trends.

Frustrated with fossils, Patterson turned his attention to molecular data, only to become more frustrated. Finally, he asked his audience of prestigious evolutionists at the American Museum if they would permit him *to look at the classification evidence as a creationist would.* He was not claiming to be a creationist, but only a scientist willing to follow the evidence wherever it might lead. Patterson then proceeded to examine the data as a creationist would, in simple recognition that creationists produce testable hypotheses, and that he could understand and explain what inferences creationists would draw from the data, without either agreeing or disagreeing with them. What a superb example of *healthy scientific skepticism!* Patterson was able to see the data regarding classification in their wholeness, and experience the

CLASS: MAMMALS	
Nourish their young on milk and have at least some hair	
	Order: Chiroptera flyers with membranous wings
	Order: Cetacea swimmers with a blowhole
	Order: Perissodactyla ungulates (hoofed animals) with odd number of hooves (1 or 3)
	Order: Artiodactyla ungulates (hoofed animals) with even number of

unbridled freedom to wonder not only how *but whether* evolution occurred.

Patterns in Classification

A *garden, orchard,* or huge field of *small bushes* might be used to represent creationist classification: many separately created life forms, each showing variation within kind.

Evolutionary beliefs about classification are usually represented as a "tree of life." This evolutionary *tree* (quite different from the one in Genesis!) is meant to suggest *continuity* among all living things, with gradual, sequential changes progressing along *branching* lines of descent from ultimately one common ancestor to the multitude of separate species ("branch tips") we have today.

Winds can be classified in a continuous sequence of gradually increasing speeds (calm, breeze, gale, five categories of hurricane, etc.), and evolutionists hoped living things could also be classified arbitrarily along steadily increasing changes in degree.

Science revealed something radically different — a *hierarchical, "groups-within-groups" pattern* (like a big box with progressively smaller boxes inside). Think for a moment about triangles and four-sided shapes (quadrilaterals). Every triangle has three sides and three angles, and the three angles always add up to 180°. Some triangles have three equal sides and three equal angles (equilateral); some have two equal sides (isosceles); others are "long and skinny," others have a 90° right angle, and some right triangles have two 45° angles while others have 30° and 60° angles, or some other combination. Certainly triangles come in a wide variety of shapes and sizes, but all are "100 percent triangle," and each has all the defining characteristics of triangles (three sides with angles totaling 180°). So each triangle equally represents the "triangle idea"

(it's equirepresentative), and each is equally distinct (equidistant) from four-sided shapes.

Four-sided figures may be squares, rectangles, parallelograms, trapezoids, and a wide variety of other shapes in many sizes. Yet each is "100 percent quadrilateral," and each is equirepresentative of the "quadrilateral," and each is equidistant from all triangles. A "skinny" trapezoid with a tiny flat top may look superficially more like a triangle than a square does, but a closer look shows only the triangle has three sides and three angles totaling 180°. There is no "missing link" that's partly triangle and partly quadrilateral, and there is no evidence that these two shapes descended from a "common ancestral shape" with three and a half sides. Instead, geometric figures show discontinuity and reflect theme and variation in a created plan.

Living things are distributed in the *discontinuous, hierarchical, or mosaic pattern reflecting creation,* not *the continuous, sequential/branching pattern that evolutionists* had hoped to find. Take mammals, for example, a group defined as animals that nourish their young on milk (from mammary glands). Whether they run (horses), swim (whales), fly (bats), or burrow (moles), or whether they are large (elephants) or small (mice), each mammal is 100 percent mammal, "equirepresentative" of the group and the group and "equidistant" from other groups (reptiles, birds, or amphibians). Even evolutionists classify the egg-laying platypus as a mammal, since its

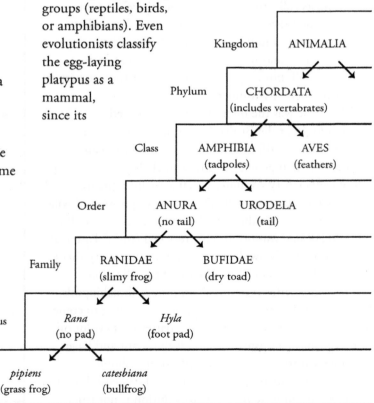

Figure 10.1. Taxonomic ranks, first suggested by Linnaeus (a Christian creationist) in the 1700s, are still used by scientists today.

[mammal] [bird]

[reptile] [amphibian]

defining milk and milk glands are 100 percent mammalian, and no traits in transition link it to reptiles (and neither do its fossils).

Within the mammalian class or "box" are smaller "boxes," mammalian subgroups separated from each other by features considered to have less significance than milk production: mammals with membranous wings (bats, order chiroptera), swimming mammals with blowholes (whales and dolphins, order cetacea), and hoofed animals (ungulates) with an odd number of toes (e.g., horses, order perissodactyla). Although subjectivity and bias have corrupted classification to varying degrees, the objectivity inherent in successive hierarchical "boxes" has produced an amazing consensus on classification that transcends time and culture.

Still, assigning groups of species to progressively broader groups involves much, much more subjectivity than assigning organisms to their true species or created kinds. Created kinds are defined biblically by reproductive criteria ("multiplication after kind"), and various scientific tests (breeding, egg and sperm union, chromosome pairing, DNA hybridization, etc.) can objectively identify variation within kind (fertilotypes, morphotypes, ecotypes).

The Bible mentions that "All flesh is not the same flesh: but there is one kind of flesh of men, another flesh of beasts, another of fishes, and another of birds" (1 Cor. 15:39; KJV). Earlier we described problems in picking traits for defining groups and ranking their importance, so we could wish the Bible said much more about the "higher categories."

The Christian creationist biologist *Carolus Linnaeus*, who gave us genus-species scientific naming based on biblical principles, also gave us a series of "*taxonomic ranks*" for grouping created kinds into a series of progressively broader categories: *family, order, class, phylum* (or *division* in plants), and *kingdom*. Examples illustrating Linnaeus' classification or taxonomic ranking system

are show in Figure 10.1. Evolutionists tried to pirate Linnaeus' system, substituting hypothetical common ancestors for the theme and variation in God's plan. In much more detail than the short summary in this section, Michael Denton, in his ground-breaking book, *Evolution: A Theory in Crisis*, documented the logical and scientific triumph of creationist systematics over evolutionary schemes. The triumph of creationist classification extends also to fossils, to be documented in Creation Foundations Volume 3, *Building Blocks in Earth Science*.

Still, much, much more work needs to be done on a creationist approach to higher taxonomic grouping. Are the higher ranks only categories of convenience for filing mountains of information? Or are there "real" groups reflecting God's design, a pattern that would be full of useful information or concepts if only we could grasp it? Is it even possible that the mosaic/matrix/modular concept can be applied to the higher categories in a way analogous to its use in identifying created kinds? Could this "second level" mosaic concept also be predictive, the real measure of merit in science?

Earlier we treated created kinds as "genetic mosaics," unique combinations of non-unique "genetic elements," somewhat like chemical compounds are unique combinations of a small set of non-unique chemical elements. Since God designed the various created kinds to interact as parts in an ecological whole (the "web of life"), the kinds may have been created to fill all ecological roles as living things "multiplied and filled the earth." Furthermore, God may have "mixed and matched" various complex and complete traits (e.g., flying adaptations) with other complex and complete traits (e.g., body covering) in ways that would (1) rule out evolutionary branching patterns of descent, (2) reject concepts of both no gods and many gods, and (3) make sure His "eternal power and divine nature have been clearly seen, being understood from what has been made" (Rom. 1:20; NIV).

Four Groups of Air-breathing Vertebrates			
mammals	birds	reptiles	amphibians
hair	feathers	scales	skin
flyers bats	eagles	pterodactyls	flying frogs
swimmers dolphins	penguins	plesiosaurs	axolotls

Air-breathing vertebrates can be divided into four groups on the basis of body covering, for example: mammals (hair), birds (feathers), reptiles (scales), and amphibians (skin). Each of these groups include flyers (bats, eagles, pterodactyls, and steering-gliding "flying" frogs). Each includes swimmers (dolphins, penguins, pesiosaurs, and axolotls), and each includes runners and burrowers. As with algal groups, any branching evolutionary tree based on mode of locomotion (flying, swimming, etc.) would contradict a tree based on body covering — necessitating repeated evolution by chance of complex features, and contradicting the essence of evolution, that similar features imply descent from common ancestry.

Identification of "genetic elements" may one day make identification of created kinds practical and even predictive. Identification of suites of ecological adaptations (wings, fins, feet, etc.) may likewise someday permit prediction of higher categories, perhaps based on filling a matrix of ecological roles. For further thoughts on the "biblical basis of classification," see the book with that title by Chard Berndt. There's much more to be discovered by the next generation of Christian, creationist scientists! God intends for us to use His Word to understand His world, and in science that means starting with God's Word, not stopping there.

Form your foundation.

Frustrating the faith of evolutionists who had hoped to find "missing links" with incomplete traits distributed in branching lines of descent, scientists found only complete traits distributed in "mosaic/ modular/matrix" patterns, suggesting plan, purpose, and special acts of creation.

Building Inspection

1. Two parts of the science of classification are **taxonomy** and **systematics**. Which deals mostly with practical identification? _____. Which with criteria for classifying groups? _____.

2. Which is based objectively on scientific tests? _____. Which is more subjectively based on opinion and persuasion? _____.

3. Which of these features has been used to separate algae (non-woody water plants) into major groups: color, type of reproduction, structural complexity? _____. Would most scientists today agree this is their most important feature? (**yes/no**) _____.

4. After years of research on lampshells (brachiopods), Colin Patterson of the British Museum (circle all that are correct):
   (a) found branching patterns for one trait often contracted those for another trait;
   (b) found numerous reversals, trends among fossils seeming to go from "advanced" to "primitive";
   (c) called evolution "anti-knowledge" and an "anti-theory," i.e., a false idea of what the facts are that leads to a false idea of what the facts mean;
   (d) showed a group of prominent evolutionists how molecular data fi t better with creationist than evolutionist thinking.

5. Classifi cation of wind speeds is (**sequential/hierarchical**) _____, i.e., one wind category gradually blends into the next one. Classifi cation of living things is (**sequential/hierarchical**) _____, i.e., a "boxes within boxes" system in which each category ("box") is separate and distinct. Separate and distinct kinds are predicted by (**creation/evolution**) _____, so the classifi cation of living things (**does/does not**) _____ support creation.

6. What Christian creationist biologist of the 1700s gave us our binomial system of scientifi c naming as well as our system of taxonomic ranks? _____.

   class   **family**   **genus**   **kingdom**   **order**   **phylum (division)**   **species**

7. Arrange the seven taxonomic ranks, alphabetized above, in order from largest to smallest group:
   _____, _____, _____,
   _____, _____, _____,
   _____.

8. Which two of the taxonomic ranks above make up a scientific name? _____ and _____. Which comes first in the scientific name? _____. Which is capitalized? _____.

9. "A unique combination of non-unique traits" describes the mosaic/modular/matrix concept that can be applied to defining (circle one):
   (a) species or created kind,
   (b) a higher taxonomic category,
   (c) both.

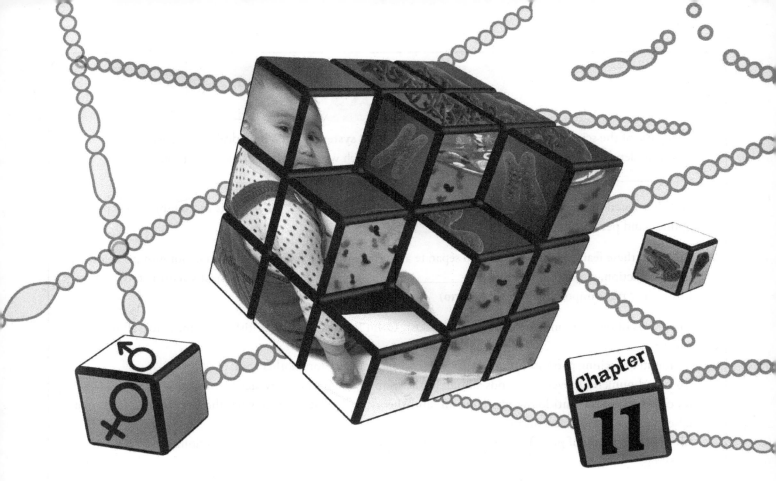

Development: Life Before Birth

Conception: A New Life Begins!

Even people who don't otherwise honor God may speak of the "miracle of birth." The incredible, awe-inspiring emergence of a baby from his or her mother is really just a visibly spectacular event that continues a series of incredible, awe-inspiring events that occur out of sight in the mother's womb and in the baby's developing body.

A new life begins with the miracle of conception, the union of a mother's egg cell and a father's sperm cell. Most human cells contain 23 pairs of chromosomes, 46 total, the "diploid number," or number in a "double set." Each chromosome is a long strand of DNA genetic information wrapped around proteins. A mother's egg cell is "just" a part of the mother's body and contains only her DNA, except that a mature egg cell contains only 23 single chromosomes (not 23 pairs) — *all* her genetic *information* (*genons*) but *only half* her *variation* (alleles, a "different half" in each egg cell). Likewise, the father's sperm cell contains only his genetic information, with half his DNA variation and half the chromosome number in adult human cells (23 versus 46).

New human life begins the moment sperm and egg successfully unite. The baby's first cell, called a fertilized baby's first cell 46 total chromosomes, the characteristic human number. All the baby's DNA is human, copied from parental DNA, which was copied from grandparental DNA . . . all the way back to the human DNA created in Adam and Eve.

Not only *fully human at the moment of conception,* the new baby is also a unique individual human being. God designed the first human beings (and the first of each sexually reproducing kind) with two sets of genetic instructions per cell. Genes for the same trait in two different sets may vary, like the genes ("alleles") for producing straight or curly hair ("c or C") or more or less melanin (A or a, for darker or lighter skin tone). The new baby gets half the genes of each parent, but the half may be mostly "capital letter" alleles (C or A), mostly "lower case" (c or a), or any mixed combination (C, a or c, A). The result is that each baby is fully human, but each will have combinations of human traits different from each of his or her parents, different from each brother or sister, and different from every other human being that ever was or ever will be born! *Each human being is a unique and special individual from conception onward.* WOW! The *number of trait combinations* in a fertilized egg cell or zygote are actually far, far, FAR greater than the number

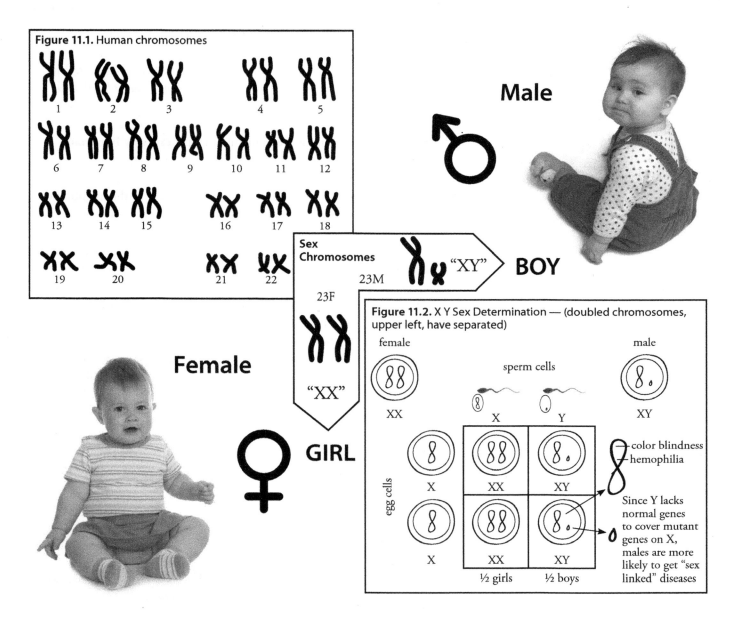

Figure 11.1. Human chromosomes

1 2 3 4 5
6 7 8 9 10 11 12
13 14 15 16 17 18
19 20 21 22

Sex Chromosomes

23M "XY" > BOY

Male

23F

"XX"

Female

GIRL

Figure 11.2. X Y Sex Determination — (doubled chromosomes, upper left, have separated)

female
XX

sperm cells

X Y

male
XY

egg cells

X
XX
XY

X
XX
XY

½ girls   ½ boys

color blindness
hemophilia

Since Y lacks normal genes to cover mutant genes on X, males are more likely to get "sex linked" diseases

of atoms in the known universe. *Each new human deserves to be respected and treasured right from the moment of conception!*

Abortionists often talk about a mother's right over her own body, but the baby inside her (unlike a wart!) is not part of her body. An egg cell is just part of the mother's body, but the fertilized egg cell definitely is not. The new human being produced by conception may have a blood type, hair and eye color, etc., different from the mother's, and about half of all children conceived are a different sex than their mothers!

As detailed above, the baby's genetic sex (or gender) is determined at conception by the father (although it's not his conscious choice!). Fathers produce two kinds of sperm cells, called X and Y. Most cells in the human male contain 22 "lookalike" pairs of chromosomes and one "odd pair," the XY "*sex chromosomes.*" When chromosome

pairs separate in the formation of sperm cells, half the sperm get an X chromosome and half the Y. Most cells in the female contain 23 "lookalike" chromosome pairs, including the sex chromosome pair called XX. When egg cells are formed by separation of chromosome pairs, all egg cells get one X. Whether a new baby is a boy (XY) or girl (XX), then, depends on whether the mother's egg, always X, is fertilized by an X or a Y sperm cell from the father. Although anatomical and behavioral differences between boys and girls develop in stages before and after birth, genetic sex is determined at the very beginning, the moment of conception.

Associated also with conception are *several proteins that "enforce" God's command that reproduction be only "after kind."* Most importantly, sperm and egg cells cannot unite unless they have compatible, interlocking recognition proteins on their surface membranes, often called *fertilizin and anti-fertilizin.* Many aquatic creatures shed egg and sperm cells into the same water, but potential chaos is averted because only those egg and sperm unite that have compatible recognition proteins, guaranteeing "multiplication after kind."

The preparation of egg and sperm cells for conception involves a special, intricate, elaborate kind of cell division called *meiosis.* Meiosis halves chromosome numbers by separating chromosome pairs; then fertilization (joining of egg and sperm) restores the pairing and the chromosome number characteristic of each kind (e.g., 46 for humans, 60 for horses, 8 for fruit flies, 16 for onions, etc.). Before chromosome pairs separate in meiotic division, however, they first line up gene-for-gene in a process called *synapsis.*

During synaptic pairing, segments of one chromosome can be exchanged for corresponding segments of another, a process called crossing over. The requirement for *meiotic pairing limits multiplication to "after kind,"* but crossing over during meiosis greatly increases *genetic variability within kind.*

The egg cell's membrane makes a very important contribution to conception. A human egg cell usually attracts millions of sperm cells, but the first sperm to penetrate the egg cell induces changes in the membrane that blocks the entry of all other sperm, so the new life begins with the correct number of chromosomes.

Although the small, motile sperm contributes half the genetic information (DNA genes) to the new baby's first cell, the large, non-motile egg cell provides stored food, energy-harvesting protein machinery, and the coordinated set of enzymes, hormones, and various regulators required to "read" DNA instructions in the proper sequence to convert a single human cell through the proper stages into a mature human adult with an average of 50 trillion cells of many specialized types. WOW!

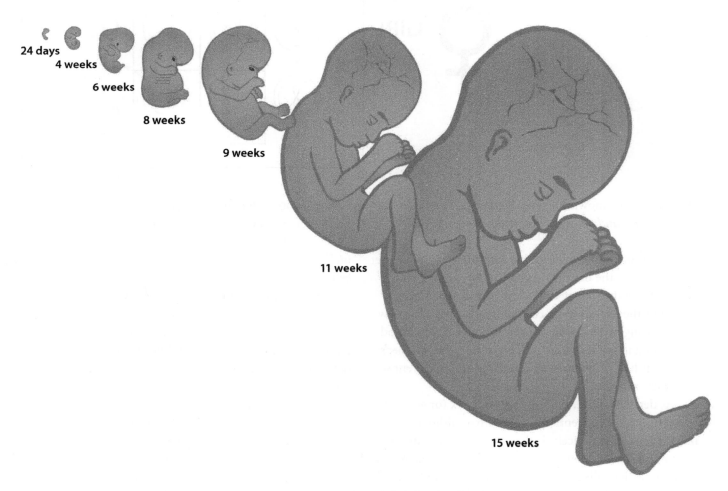

24 days
4 weeks
6 weeks
8 weeks
9 weeks
11 weeks
15 weeks

Figure 11.3. Babies before birth. ACTUAL LIFE-SIZE 3–15 weeks after conception!

Conception, then, accomplishes three major purposes: (1) it brings together the right kind and right amount of DNA for reproduction after kind; (2) it promotes individuality and a fantastic amount of variation within kind; and (3) it provides the complex and coordinated molecular machinery within the fertilized egg cell to properly read and implement the DNA instructions.

Cloning

The *Jurassic Park* movie left many with the impression that scientists could clone (make copies of) dinosaurs if only they could find dinosaur DNA. Not at all. Even perfect dinosaur DNA would be no help in producing dinosaurs — *unless* a dinosaur mother, or at least a living dinosaur egg cell, could be found that could "read" the DNA instructions in the proper sequence to produce an adult. Sheep DNA was used to clone sheep, because the sheep DNA was injected into a sheep egg cell that was implanted in the womb of a mother sheep!

Although cloning may sound like a scary new technique, amoebas and white blood cells do it naturally when they multiply after kind asexually. Propagating roses and grapes from cuttings is old-fashioned cloning with plants. *Twins* are natural clones, created when God gives one egg two spirits. Recent techniques, however, allow scientists and doctors to make multiple identical copies (clones) of some cell types. Such techniques could allow a burn victim to grow new sheets of skin from his or her own cells, thus avoiding problems of immune rejection. Using cloning to bring healing and restore a person to health would be following Christ's example as the Great Healer. But cloning people (including embryos) to provide "spare parts" for others, or trying to clone one or more asexual copies of a person, are vain attempts to play God, not to follow God. *We need God's Word to understand the science of God's world,* but we also desperately *need God's Word as a sure guide to applying scientific discoveries to help, not harm, God's world and those made in His image.*

Cleavage and Differentiation

The fertilized egg cell reflects two of the three major facets of human development described in Psalm 139. Inspired by God, the Psalmist David says that *his life (and each human life) really began before conception, as a plan in the mind of God the Creator,* who knew David's thoughts and words before any came to tangible expression. In a way, the DNA in a fertilized egg cell represents God's plan for each individual human life (including yours and mine) written out ahead of time. Further on, the Psalmist says that God beheld his "unformed substance" in his mother's womb (Ps. 139:16; NASB). In a way, the fertilized egg itself represents that "unformed substance." Like a lump of clay in the potter's hands (or the earth "without form and void" [Gen. 1:2; NKJV] on day 1), the egg cell has no arms, legs, eyes, ears, etc., although the instructions for forming all these things are already fully present in the formless egg cell.

As the plan (DNA) acts on the unformed substance (egg cell), we are each, in the words of Psalms 139:13 (NIV), "knit together" in our mothers' wombs. When a grandmother knits a sweater, she starts with a formless ball of yarn, then shapes it through an orderly sequence of stages to produce the design present in her mind from the very beginning. Similarly, the DNA plan acting on the formless egg cell develops a mature human individual through an orderly series of stages. As Psalm 139 declares in praise to our Creator, each of us is *"fearfully [awesomely] and wonderfully made"* (Ps. 139:14; NIV; emphasis added).

The first step in transforming a fertilized egg cell into a mature human being is *cleavage,* splitting the single large egg cell into many smaller cells each with its own copy of human DNA. Each of these early cells, now often called *stem cells,* has the ability to develop into any of the adult cell types — nerve, muscle, skin, bone, blood, glands, etc. As development continues, most of these stem cells *differentiate,* that is, become different from each other, specializing as cells with certain limited structures and functions (Figure 11.4). Actually, differentiated cells still have all the DNA to form all the cell types in an adult, but many of the genes in a cell are "turned off" as a cell specializes. Genes turned off in highly differentiated cells, such as nerve and muscle, often lose the ability to be reactivated, but cells of some tissues, like those lining the digestive tract, can be used to clone adults, because, under the right circumstances, all their genes can be reactivated.

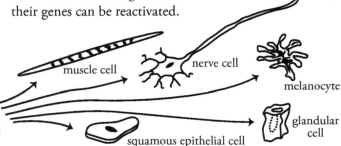

Figure 11.4. Unspecialized STEM CELLS can DIFFERENTIATE into all the body's different cell types. Medical advances so far have been made with umbilical and adult stem cells, which avoid both the moral and tumor problems posed by embryonic stem cells

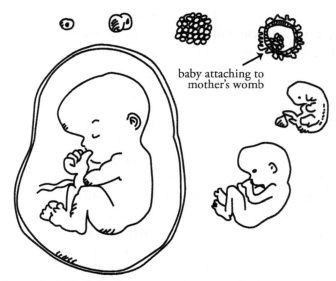

Figure 11.5. The baby from conception to practicing thumbsucking

baby attaching to mother's womb

In human beings, cleavage and early stages of differentiation occur hidden from sight in the mother's womb. But these processes can be observed in egg cells that develop in water, such as those of frogs and starfish. Frog egg cells are large enough to see easily with the naked eye or a hand lens. One hemisphere of the frog egg is colored black from cortical granules under the cell membrane, while the other end, full of yolk, is yellowish. When a sperm fertilizes the frog egg, the cortical granules shift, forming a "gray crescent" at the point of sperm entry. That point determines front-back and right-left in the future embryo, winding up where the tadpole's alimentary canal empties through the anus.

Although easy to see and describe in frog eggs, cellular and molecular motions during cleavage and differentiation are absolutely mind boggling. The first cleavage division that divides the frog egg in two occurs through the point of sperm entry, at right angles to the gray crescent. The second division also goes through the "poles" of the egg, at right angles to the first, producing a four-celled stage (like an orange with four big slices). The third division occurs at right angles to the first two, but parallel to the equatorial plane near the cortical pole, producing four smaller cells near the "top" and four larger, yolk-filled cells "below." Cleavage (division of the large egg cell into many smaller ones) continues until the egg cell develops into the "mulberry stage" (*morula*), a cluster of small, similar cells no bigger than the original egg. The solid ball morula forms a hollow ball *blastula* as cells use up some of their food supplies (Figure 11.6).

Cells up through the blastula stage are called *stem cells* because they can "branch out" to produce almost any

cell type — nerve, muscle, glandular, etc. Breaking up a blastula to harvest stem cells, however, means killing a very young child — and it's totally unnecessary as well as immoral. Stem cells are also found in a baby's umbilical cord, a mother's placenta, and in certain tissues in adults. As of this writing, all the *spectacular promise and results of stem cell research have been achieved with adult stem cells readily available without moral or scientific problems.* Nothing of scientific value is achieved by making and killing young innocents, and embryonic stem cells are also much more likely to produce tumors.

The easy-to-describe, difficult-to-explain miracle of embryonic development continues when astonishing cell movements convert the blastula into a gastrula with an embryonic gut (archenteron). The first cells to differentiate (become different) from the look-alike blastula "stem" cells are those that elongate and move inward (how?!) from the original point of sperm entry. The inwardly moving cells, the so-called dorsal lip of the blastopore, carve out an embryonic alimentary canal (archenteron) that encloses the yolk as food and leaves an opening, the blastopore or "future anus."

The outer, middle, and inner cell layers of the gastrula form the three basic embryonic germ (germinal) layers, respectively the *ecto-*, *meso-*, and *endoderms.* The outer ectoderm forms the skin, nervous system, and major sense organs such as eyes and ears. The middle mesoderm forms muscle, bone, and blood, and parts of other organs "budded off" from the endoderm. The endodermal tube forms mouth, esophagus, stomach, and intestine, and various organs develop (at least in part) from hollow "buds" outpouching from the gut: anterior pituitary gland, gills in tadpoles (lungs in adult), liver, pancreas, and, in adults, kidney and urinary bladder.

Once again, the stages are easy enough to describe. But how do the cells move? How do they know where and when to stop moving? What turns genes off in some cells and not others? Embryonic development definitely requires *intelligent design, planning ahead to accomplish a goal!* The *"miracle of birth"* is preceded by many, many other evidences of the miraculous!

Organ Formation

Many "miracles" of development occur out of sight among the molecules within cells or among the internal organs. But some of the miraculous formation of the nervous system, muscles, heart, and limbs can be viewed directly in the developing frog, through a "window" in the shell made for watching a chick embryo inside its shell, or by camera in the human womb.

Remember the "dorsal lip of the blastopore"? Those were the first cells moving into the ball-shaped frog embryo, and they "scooped out" the embryonic gut with the embryo's food (yolk) inside. The cells that followed the dorsal lip cells into the embryo form a stiff rod of cartilage, the *notochord* or "future backbone," along the top center or "roof" of the gut. The notochord, in turn, secretes chemicals that stimulate cells on the surface above it to develop into the brain and spinal cord.

Believe it or not, the nervous system starts off as ridges of surface (ectodermal) tissue that rise up to form a "mountain range" (the neural ridge) surrounding a "central valley" (the neural groove), which is wide at the front (future brain) and narrower down the length of the future spinal cord. Then the neural ridges do something ordinary mountains don't: they lean across the neural groove, touch, and grow together to form a neural tube! (Why do some cells form ridges and others grooves? How do the leaning ridges know which way to grow to reach the ridge on the other side?)

The neural ridges reach across to form the neural tube first in the middle, then the tube "zippers shut" toward each end, forming brain and spinal cord. Sometimes the zippering doesn't go far enough, and a baby can be born with an opening into the brain cavity or an open patch of nerve tissue at the end of the spine. Our hollow (but thick-walled) nervous system depends on careful regulation of the contents and pressure of the spinal fluid, so these birth defects can have consequences ranging from mild to severe. Notice how precisely cells have to "follow orders" and work together for the baby to be born healthy; a few cells that don't move far enough can disrupt normal nerve function — and all the other body processes that depend on nerve control! The more you know about stages in development, the more you appreciate the phrase, "the miracle of birth"!

The dorsal lip cells, differentiated at the point of sperm entry, triggered development of the notochord, which stimulated formation of the neural tube, which then induces production along its spinal length of segmental tissue blocks called *somites* (which are *nothing* like the body segments of earthworms!). The inner portions of each somite pair develop into a *vertebra*, one link in the chain of backbones — complete with processes that join it to other vertebrae to form a *spinal column* with the combination of strength and flexibility needed for *walking, running, swimming, climbing, lifting, dancing, sports,* etc.! The outer portions of the somites develop into muscles, and the spinal nerves extending between vertebrae follow (and/or lead) as the somite blocks develop into specific muscles. Parts of the developing brain stimulate development of eyes and ears. Like computers, the simple outside appearance of eyes, ears, and brain belies an incredibly complex "wiring" to accomplish phenomenal intellectual goals, integrating data input and effective output! (Evolutionists often try to fool people into believing brains evolved small to medium to large, without even trying to explain how even one nerve circuit was wired by time, chance, struggle, and death!)

Development of blood vessels and heart is dramatically visible when a thin glass cover slip is sealed over an opening cut into a chicken egg shell. Blood cells and vessels form in the yolk sac that stores food for the embryonic chick. Where vessels join, walls thicken with muscle and begin to contract rhythmically, forming the embryonic heart. In human beings, the heart begins to beat about 18–21 days after conception. In the context of God's instructions after the Flood about eating meat, the Bible says the life is in the blood (Gen. 9:4). Some say that means the baby is not alive until the heart begins to beat, but blood forms earlier, and "blood" in the sense of fluid flow appropriately distributing food and oxygen is present at conception.

Six weeks after conception (perhaps less than four weeks after the mother becomes aware of her pregnancy), the new baby is about ½-inch "tall" and all his or her

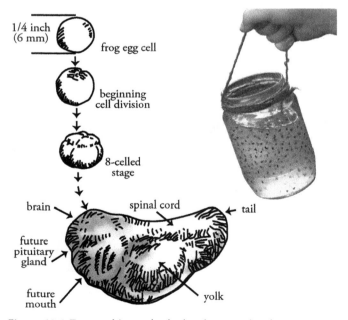

Figure 11.6. Try watching tadpole development in a jar or aquarium at home!

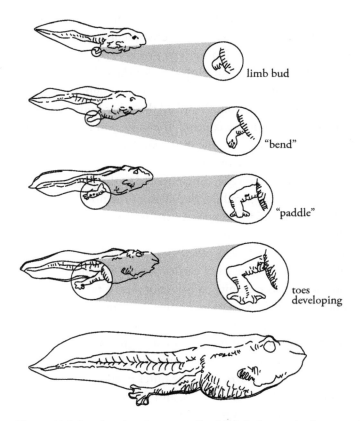

limb bud

"bend"

"paddle"

toes developing

Figure 11.7. Rear leg developent easily visible in frog tadpoles

major organs have already begun to form and function. The arms and legs are developing from "*limb buds*," with delicate muscle fibers and nerve wiring growing into the developing limbs in ways that make wiring super computers look like chipping with stone tools. The outwardly simple, inwardly mind-boggling development of limbs can be easily observed in frog tadpoles as they proceed along their pre-programmed change from tadpole to adult (*metamorphosis*). Limbs begin as buds or lumps of stem cells, which are undifferentiated or unspecialized, able to develop into (almost) any cell type. The bud lengthens, then forms a bend (the future elbow or knee). Acting out an amazing script involving DNA and on-off switches, a paddle reaches out from the end of the bud, and fingers develop, either by growing out from the paddle (frog) or by "webbing" between the future fingers dissolving from the paddle (human). During all this, multiple bones develop with joint surfaces, and muscle, nerve, and blood vessels all "organize themselves" according to God's plan. WOW!

Creation and Life Before Birth

Consider an orchestra playing a beautiful symphony. Every musician has a complete score

with all the notes, but each plays only a part of the whole. In like manner, all the cells in the human body have a complete set of DNA notes, but each expresses only some of them. In both cases, each part is coordinated with all the others to produce an inspiring symphonic melody, or unique human being, that is far greater than the sum of its parts. Imagine a marching band at the Super Bowl or the choreography opening the Olympics in Beijing. As each person follows his or her marching orders, it may look like chaos and danger as lines of performers pivot and march through and around one another, but then, as if by magic, each stops at a pre-planned position, producing an eye-popping pattern that was the goal from the beginning. Finally, picture a well-acted movie or stage play. It may seem that each actor is behaving individually, doing what comes naturally, following his or her own will. We don't see offstage the script, the director, the multitude of rehearsals that give a spontaneous look to the unfolding drama moving mysteriously to its predetermined climax.

Embryonic development has points in common with an orchestra, marching band, or stage play. Each is scripted from the beginning, with multiple parts working in intricate and elegant coordination to achieve an awe-inspiring goal. We honor the talents of musicians, marchers, and actors, sometimes offering the enthusiastic praise of a standing ovation. Perhaps doctors, nurses, family, and others ought to pause and applaud God for the birth of each child! That was the response of the Psalmist David, as he looked back (with greater knowledge than scientists would have until 3,000 years later) at his own development in his mother's womb: "I will praise thee; for I am fearfully [awesomely] and wonderfully made" (Ps. 139:14; KJV).

Form your foundation.

An egg cell is part of the mother's body with only her genes, but at the moment of conception the fertilized egg (zygote) becomes a new person who may have a sex, blood type, hair color different from his or her mother and who definitely has a unique new place in God's plan. Surely such a special person developing in his or her mother deserves as much care and protection as a baby eagle developing in its egg.

Building Inspection

1. How many chromosomes are in most human cells? _____. How many are found in a reproductive cell (egg or sperm)? _____.

2. Give the symbols used for "sex chromosomes" in girls: _____…in boys: _____. Is it the mother's egg or the father's sperm that determines whether their child will be boy or girl? _____.

3. An egg cell (**is/is not**) _____ a part of the mother's body and (**does/does not**) _____ have only her genes. A fertilized egg cell formed by union of egg and sperm (**is/is not**) _____ part of the mother's body and (**does/does not**) _____ have only her genes.

4. When does a baby inherit his or her sex, blood type, hair color, etc. (choose one): **conception, first heart beat, birth, adulthood**… _____

5. If perfect dinosaur DNA were found, would that be enough to clone a dinosaur? Explain why or why not.
   _____
   _____

6. Dividing a large egg cell into many small ones is a process called _____. These small, look-alike early embryonic cells can change into specialized adult cells (nerve, muscle, glands, etc.) by a process called _____, a process of "becoming different." Some cells in the umbilical cord and adult are called adult _____ cells because they can "branch out" to form all the specialized cell types. All the exciting medical advances as of this writing have been made with (**adult/embryonic**) _____ stem cells, and it seems to be only (**adult/embryonic**) _____ stem cells that can develop tumors.

   notochord **neural ridges** **neural tube** **somites** **backbones** **muscle**

7. Fill in the blanks in this amazing account of early life before birth with terms from the list above: When the baby is just a flat sheet of tissue, the "future backbone" or _____ stimulates tissue above it to form "mountains" called _____. Starting in the middle, the "mountains" lean across the "valley" and touch to form a hollow _____, which continues to "zipper shut" toward both the front (brain) and the back (tip of spinal cord). The developing nerve cord stimulates blocks of tissue called _____ to form along its length, and these develop into _____ and _____.

8. The change from a plant-eating, gill-breathing tadpole to insect-eating, air-breathing frog is called _____. Metamorphosis is guided by genes all built in ahead of time, so it is (**just like/nothing like**) _____ the hypothetical change from fish to amphibian, and is a good illustration of (**evolution/entelechy**) _____.

9. Human limbs develop somewhat like those of frogs do — but we can watch frog limbs develop in the tadpole from (**bend, bud, paddle, toes**—list in proper sequence): _____ to _____ to _____ to _____. Toes develop as tissue between them dissolves in (**frogs/people**) _____, but toes grow out from the paddle in (**frogs/humans**) _____.

10. T or F: All the organ systems of the baby have begun to develop by six weeks after conception, when the baby is only ½-inch long!

11. The best summary of life before birth was written 3,000 years ago by the shepherd-warrior King David: "I will praise thee, for I am _____ and _____ made" (Psalm 139:14; KJV).

Chapter 11

Creation, Evolution, and the Embryo

Many see the unfolding of pre-programmed human development as a miraculous gift of our Creator God — but others see the embryo as evidence of human evolution through millions of years of struggle and death (Darwin's "war of nature"). According to evolutionists, the human embryo about six weeks after conception has three major parts that reflect our animal ancestry: gill slits, yolk sac, and tail (below). Why, says the evolutionist, would God create a human with gill slits, unless our ancestors were

once fish swimming in the sea? Why would a human have a yolk sac with no yolk in it, unless our ancestors were once reptiles laying eggs on land? And why oh why, says the evolutionist, would a human embryo have a tail, except to remind us that our ancestors swung down from the trees? According to evolution, the developing embryo

was not following steps in a created plan; it was retracing stages in evolution.

The belief that embryonic development (ontogeny) was retracing (recapitulating) stages in the evolution of its group (phylogeny) was once summarized in the scientific-sounding phrase "*ontogeny recapitulates phylogeny.*"

It's almost as if students (and professors) who worked hard memorizing this intimidating phrase had no energy left to *ask if it were true or not.*

Ernst Haeckel

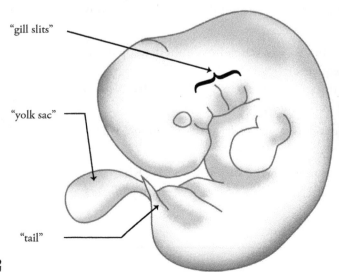

"gill slits"

"yolk sac"

"tail"

Early attempts to link embryology to evolution were led (or misled) by "Germany's Darwin," Ernst Haeckel. Haeckel made numerous diagrams of embryos from different animals at successive stages of development. Haeckel made his diagrams in the 1860s, yet — despite a superabundance of real photographs done in recent years, including those of the living embryo in the womb — a popular college biology laboratory manual published in 2006 still uses Haeckel's diagrams! Why would any modern science book use 140-year-old diagrams of embryos when exquisitely detailed photographs of real embryos are available? It may be this simple: *Haeckel's diagrams support evolution; real science does not.*

Long after it was scientifically disproven, however, the evolutionary view of human development was used to justify an unimaginably deadly tragedy — *abortion*, the taking of over 50 million innocent lives in America alone, far more than all the lives lost in all of America's wars. How could a mother be talked into taking the life of her own child? Too often she's *"counseled" (without being allowed to see the real evidence)* that the baby inside her is only at a fish or reptile stage, not yet human. *Politically correct or not, nothing could be further from the scientific truth.*

Actually, to support his belief in evolution, Haeckel had to "fudge" his diagrams, which are notoriously inaccurate. When Haeckel's scientific fraud was exposed (back in the 1860s), his only defense was that others also made their diagrams look more evolutionary than science would allow. Despite this shameful chapter in the history of "science falsely so-called" (1 Tim. 6:20; KJV), the author in his university debates has encountered several evolutionists who still try to support their belief with the *now defunct "biogenetic law: ontogeny recapitulates phylogeny."* Fortunately, knowledgeable evolutionists no longer believe that, and some have even agreed with

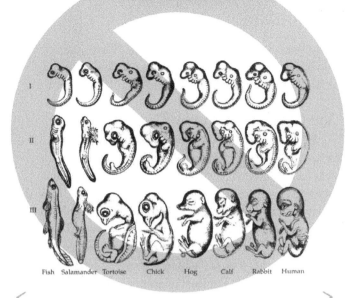

Romanes's 1892 copy of Ernst Haeckel's deceptive embryo drawings

creationists in debate settings that the concept was proven false decades ago.

Nevertheless, a month after conception, a baby really does have the features evolutionists like to call "yolk sac, gill slits, and a tail." Knowledgeable evolutionists no longer believe human embryonic development retraces stages in human evolution, but some assert that both the embryo and adult human being do have functionless parts, called *vestigial* structures, left over from structures that did function in our presumed evolutionary ancestors. Is that true? Does the human body contain useless vestiges of our evolutionary past? Darwin and Haeckel listed 180

Can you identify the eyes, nose, mouth, ears, elbow, thumb, fingers, and umbilical cord of this very young human being?

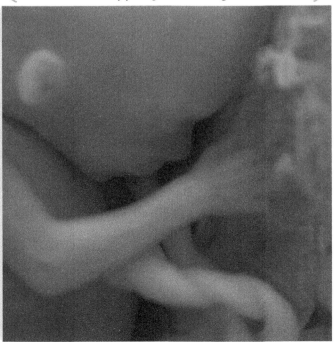

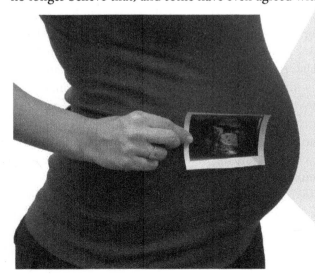

such useless vestiges in human beings. What does science tell us? Does scientific investigation support or refute belief in vestigial structures as leftovers of evolution?

"Vestigial Structures?"

Evolutionists consider the human embryo's yolk sac an obviously vestigial organ. It has no yolk in it, so what function could it possibly have? In our reptilian ancestors, evolutionists assert, the yolk sac stored food the embryo needed to develop within the egg. But a human embryo grows attached to the mother's body and receives nourishment from her bloodstream via the placenta, so in people the yolk sac is merely a useless leftover, evolutionists claim, a vestige of an organ that functioned in our evolutionary ancestors.

Does that mean the yolk sac can be cut off from the human embryo because it isn't needed? Not at all. *The so-called yolk sac is the source of the human embryo's first blood cells, and death would result without it!*

Now here's an engineering problem for you. In the adult, you want to have the blood cells formed inside the bone marrow. That makes good sense, because the blood cells are very sensitive to radiation damage, and bone would offer them some protection. But you need blood in order to form the bone marrow that later on is going to form blood. So, where do you get the blood first? Why not use a structure similar to the yolk sac in reptiles or chickens? The DNA and protein for making it are "common stock" building materials. Since it lies conveniently outside the embryo, it can easily be discarded after it has served its temporary — but vital — function.

Notice, this is exactly what we would expect as evidence of good creative design and engineering practice. Suppose you were in the bridge-building business, and you were interviewing a couple of engineers to determine whom you wanted to hire. One person says, "Each bridge I build will be entirely different from all others." Proudly he tells you, "Each bridge will be made using different materials and different processes so that no one will ever be able to see any similarity among the bridges I build." How does that sound?

Now the next person comes in and says, "Well, in your yard I saw a supply of I-beams and various sizes of heavy bolts and cables. We can use those to span either a river or the San Francisco Bay. I can adapt the same parts and processes to meet a wide variety of needs. You'll be able to see a theme and a variation in my bridge building, and others can see the stamp of authorship in our work." Whom would you hire?

As A. E. Wilder-Smith pointed out long ago, we normally admire in human engineers the principles of creative economy and variations on a theme. That's what we see in human embryonic development. The same kind of structure that can provide both food and blood cells to a reptile or chicken embryo can also be used to supply just blood cells (all that's needed) for a human embryo. Rather than reflecting time and chance, adapting similar structures to a variety of needs seems to reflect good principles of creative design.

The same is true of the *so-called gill slits*. In the human embryo at six weeks, there are wrinkles in the skin where the "throat pouches" grow out. Once in a while, one of these pouches will break through, and a child will be born with a small hole in the neck. That's when we find out for sure that these structures are *not* gill slits. If the opening were really part of a gill, if it really were a "throwback to the fish stage," then there would be blood vessels all around it, as if it were going to absorb oxygen from water as a gill does. But there is no such structure in humans of any age. We simply don't have the DNA instructions for forming gills.

Unfortunately, on rare occasions some babies are born with three eyes or one eye. That doesn't mean, of course, that we evolved from something with one eye or three eyes. It's simply a mistake in the normal program for human development, and it emphasizes how perfect our design features and operation must be for normal life to continue.

The throat (or pharyngeal) grooves and pouches, falsely called "gill slits," are not mistakes in human development. They develop into absolutely essential parts of human anatomy. The first pouches form the palatine tonsils that

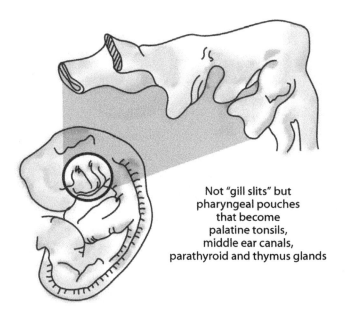

Not "gill slits" but pharyngeal pouches that become palatine tonsils, middle ear canals, parathyroid and thymus glands

a pouch or "lung bud" in a different location. Following DNA instructions in their respective egg cells, fish and human beings each use a similar process to develop their distinctive features.

What about the "*tail*"? You may have heard that man has a "tailbone" (also called the sacrum and coccyx), and that the only reason we have it is to remind us that our ancestors had tails. You can test this idea yourself, although I don't recommend it. If you think the "tailbone" is useless, fall down the stairs and land on it. (You may have actually done that — unintentionally, I'm sure!) What happens? You can't stand up; you can't sit down; you can't lie down; you can't roll over. You can hardly move without pain. In one sense, the sacrum and coccyx are among the most important bones in the whole body. They form a crucial point of muscle attachment required for our distinctive upright posture (and also for defecation, but enough said about that).

So, again, far from being a useless evolutionary leftover, the tailbone is quite important in human development. True, the end of the spine sticks out noticeably in a six-week embryo, but that's because muscles and limbs don't develop until stimulated by the spine. As the legs develop, they surround and envelop the tailbone, and it ends up inside the body.

Once in a great while there are reports of a child born with a "tail." Since the parents were quite pleased, one such child born in India was featured prominently on TV news in 2005. But was it really a tail? No, just a bit of skin and fat that tells us not about evolution, but about how our nervous systems develop. As described earlier, the nervous system starts stretched out open on the back. During development, it rises up in ridges and rolls shut. It

help fight disease. The middle ear canals come from the second pouches, and the parathyroid and thymus glands come from the third and fourth. The thymus prepares T cells, the immune cells destroyed by the AIDS virus, so you know how important the thymus is for human life. Without the parathyroids, we would be unable to regulate calcium balance and could not even survive. Another pouch, thought to be vestigial by evolutionists until just recently, becomes a gland that assists in calcium balance. Far from being useless evolutionary vestiges, then, these "gill slits," properly called *pharyngeal pouches*, are quite essential for distinctively human development.

As with the "yolk sac," "gill slit" formation represents an ingenious and adaptable solution to a difficult engineering problem. How can a small, round egg cell be turned into an animal or human being with a digestive tube and various organs inside a body cavity? The answer is to have the little ball (or flat sheet in some organisms) "swallow itself," forming a *tube, which then "buds off" other tubes and pouches*. The anterior pituitary, lungs, urinary bladder, and parts of the liver and pancreas develop in this way. In fish, gills develop from such processes, and in human beings, the ear canals, parathyroid, and thymus glands develop, while the lungs develop from

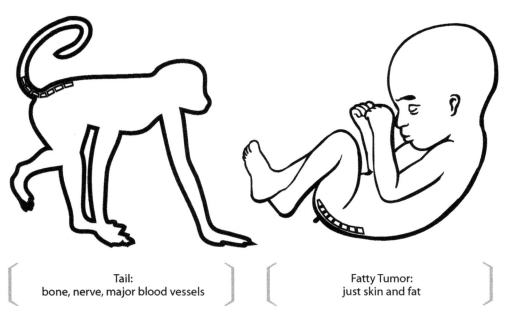

[Tail:
bone, nerve, major blood vessels] [Fatty Tumor:
just skin and fat]

starts to "zipper" shut in the middle first, then it zippers toward either end. Sometimes it doesn't go far enough down, and that produces a serious defect called *spina bifida*. Sometimes it rolls a little too far. Then the baby will be born, NOT with a tail, but with a fatty tumor. It's just skin and a little fatty tissue, so the doctor can just cut it off. It's not at all like the tail of a cat, dog, or monkey that has muscle, bone, and nerve, so cutting it off is not complicated. (So far as I know, no one claims that proves we evolved from an animal with a fatty tumor at the end of its spine.)

Unfortunately, evolution has such a hold on our thinking that doctors hate to tell a mother if she has a baby with a "tail." They can imagine the dismay: "Oh no; I've given birth to a throwback to the monkey stage in evolution!" Then the arguments begin: "It's your side of the family." "No, it's your side!" Fortunately, the extra skin and fat is not a tail at all. The details of human development are truly amazing. We really ought to stop, take a good look at each other, and congratulate each other that we turned out as well as we did.

There is an extremely rare but more serious defect in developmental regulation that can produce a "caudal appendage" with some muscle, nerve, blood, and cartilage or bone tissue. Defects in other embryonic regulator genes can result in too many or too few parts, failure of growth or of reabsorption, parts growing together that should remain separate, or parts remaining separate that should grow together, etc. *Hox gene errors* in insects can result in legs growing where antennae should be, and in flies with an extra but functionless set of wings. Such defects tell us nothing about evolutionary ancestry, but a lot about how normal development requires extreme precision in activating the right genes in the right places at the right times for the right duration.

There are a few famous cases of human beings with hair over most of their bodies (hypertrichosis universalis). Normal human beings have hair, of course, so all nucleated cells in the human body have the DNA instructions for producing hair. Regulators that turn genes on and off, therefore, may result in more or less hair than the normal amount in the usual places, but such people just have "people genes" and are NOT "throwbacks" to the supposed "ape stage" in evolution!

It was even once believed that the fertilized egg represented our one-celled ancestors, sort of the "amoeba stage." Sure enough, we start as small, round single cells, but notice how superficial that argument is. The evolutionists were just looking at the *outside appearance* of the egg cell. If we look just on the outside appearance,

Human Being

Mouse   Amoeba   Elephant

then maybe we're related to a marble, a BB pellet, or a ball bearing — they're small, round things! An evolutionist (or anyone else) would respond, of course, "That's crazy. Those things are totally different on the *inside* from a human egg cell." That's exactly the point. If you take a look on the inside, the "dot" from which we each start is totally different from the first cell of every other kind of life. A mouse, an elephant, and a human being are nearly identical in size and shape at the moment of conception.

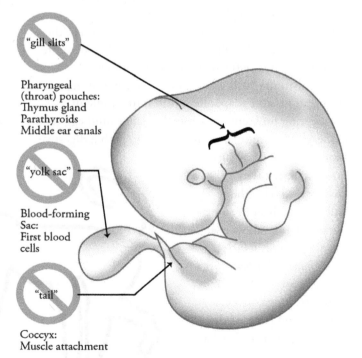

"gill slits"

Pharyngeal (throat) pouches:
Thymus gland
Parathyroids
Middle ear canals

"yolk sac"

Blood-forming Sac:
First blood cells

"tail"

Coccyx:
Muscle attachment

Yet in terms of DNA and protein, right at conception each of these types of life is as totally different chemically as each will ever be structurally. Even by mistake, a human being can't produce gills or a tail, because we just don't have and never had those DNA instructions.

Far from being "useless evolutionary leftovers," the misnamed structures above are absolutely essential for normal human development. Similar structures are used for different functions in other embryos — and we normally consider variation on a theme and multiple uses for a part as evidence of good creative design.

Creation

We are the clay; God is the potter.
John 1:1; Isaiah 64:8; Psalm 139

Embryonic development is not even analogous to evolution, which is meant to indicate a progressive increase in potential. The right Greek word instead would be *entelechy*, which means an unfolding of potential present right from the beginning. That's the kind of development that so clearly requires creative design. That's why evolutionists don't use the *metamorphosis* from tadpole to frog as an example of evolution. Unlike the *supposed* evolution of fish to frog, all the genes necessary to change a tadpole into a frog are present right from the very beginning.

Evolutionary Malpractice

Creationists believe God created human beings with human DNA right from the beginning. Evolutionists believe the DNA in human beings is a haphazard collection of bits and pieces from animal ancestry, with "vestigial DNA" continuing to produce some now useless, vestigial structures in our bodies. Unfortunately,

evolutionary belief generated nearly a century of "malpractice" in both science and medicine. Darwin and Haeckel listed 180 useless leftovers of evolution in the human body, so Darwin's and Haeckel's faithful followers didn't even try to find any function for these structures. That was the *scientific malpractice.* Even worse, doctors once removed organs like tonsils and the appendix, believing the body would be better off without those evolutionary vestiges "*falsely so-called.*"

Praise God, the medical sciences abandoned evolutionary assumptions in the mid-20th century and returned medicine to a *truly scientific (observational and experimental) basis.* Medical researchers following scientific evidence and procedure (instead of following Darwin and Haeckel) *discovered the human functions for all 180 structures Darwin's false belief predicted had no function* (other than making surgeons rich, as the bad joke went — before we found the bad "joke" was evolution itself!).

It was once common practice (or *malpractice!*) to remove healthy tonsils from healthy children (usually with the promise they would get lots of ice cream!). When tonsils get overwhelmed by infection, they can become reservoirs for germs and need to be removed, but that certainly does *not* mean tonsils are useless vestiges. The heart may become so damaged by disease that it must be removed and replaced, but that certainly does not mean the heart is a useless leftover of evolution! Only diseased hearts should be removed, and only diseased tonsils. Tonsils are actually frontline soldiers in the fight against disease. Like frontline soldiers, they may be wounded and need to be removed from the battlefield (but not while they are at fighting strength!). (The author's son has massive tonsils — but hardly ever a sore throat, for example.)

For far too many years the *appendix* was considered the best example of an evolutionary vestige. Then science proved *evolution wrong again.* The appendix is a small, hollow, finger-like (or worm-shaped, "vermiform") projection from the end of the large intestine, beyond

Frog metamorphosis is

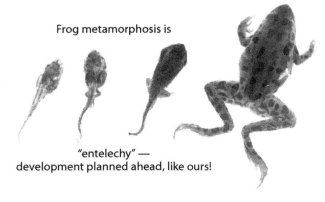

"entelechy" —
development planned ahead, like ours!

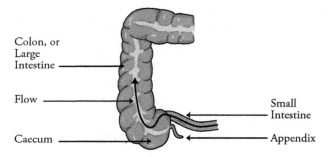

Colon, or
Large
Intestine

Flow

Caecum

Small
Intestine

Appendix

Figure 12.1. Lower right abdomen

the point where the small intestine joins the large at an angle. It does not fill up with food to digest, and nothing terrible happens when it's removed from an adult. But scientists looked beyond what the appendix does not do. Whether consciously or not, scientists acted like creationists, who were convinced the appendix was created for a purpose, and they went looking for it — and they found it! The appendix is an especially crucial part of our immune identification and defense system. It prepares certain blood cells, called B cells, to produce *antibodies*. The appendix completes most of its vital function before birth, so effects of removing it from adults are minimal. It does, however, perform immune system functions throughout life.

Like the appendix, the *thymus gland* completes its function early in life. The appendix prepares B cells to produce antibodies, proteins that circulate in the blood and lymph to protect us from foreign substances. The thymus prepares blood cells called *T cells*, which act as whole cells in immune defense, especially against cancer. T cells are destroyed by the HIV (AIDS) virus, so you know how crucial they are to human health and life. The thymus may also play a role in the developmental changes from childhood through adolescence to adulthood. This gland, which lies behind the sternum and extends into the neck, is large at birth then diminishes through adolescence until it disappears. The thymus may produce maturation hormones, although research in this area is ongoing.

At least *scientific research today is proceeding on a creationist basis*: if a structure or molecule exists, try to find out what it does and how it interacts with other parts of a living cell or body! Researchers are done with the godless and failed worldviews of Darwin and Haeckel, and scientists are no longer willing to leave a molecule or structure unstudied just because popular evolutionary "theory" says it should be useless. Increasingly, scientists are using engineering analyses to unravel and understand the awesome designs of the Master Designer!

Science and Scripture: Triumph over Evolution

Between the hemispheres of the brain is a bump of tissue now called the *pineal gland*. Darwin thought it was a vestigial remnant of a third eye in a presumed reptilian ancestor of human beings. Scientists discovered relatively recently, however, that the pineal is an endocrine gland secreting a *hormone, melatonin,* that gives us a sleepy feeling as part of the process that regulates cycles of sleepiness and wakefulness. Light is involved. Light penetrating the skin breaks down melatonin in surface blood vessels, normally allowing us to wake up during the day and encouraging us to sleep at night. Information about light conditions received by the eyes may also be communicated to the pineal along nerve pathways.

In pill form, melatonin now enjoys some popularity as a sleep aid and as a tool to reset "biological clocks" in travelers crossing multiple time zones. It is also involved in a mild to severely debilitating condition called *SAD, Seasonal Affective Disorder.* Some people (including the author!) have far above average difficulty in shaking off a sleepy, lethargic feeling on gray, cloudy days and/or during the short days and long nights of winter. "Winter depression" or "cabin fever" can prevent normal life in some people. Artificial lights producing the proper wavelengths can be used in treatment. (For the author, the best treatment, and his most wide-awake year on planet Earth, was the time he went from summer in America to summer in Australia and back to summer in America, skipping short days and gray skies altogether!)

The endocrine gland producing the hormone *calcitonin*, a part of the vital regulation of calcium balance in the body, was once written off by followers of Darwin and Haeckel as an incompletely developed gill slit.

Calling mankind the "naked ape," evolutionists often joke about how muscles that make our few body hairs "stand on end" are completely ineffective in insulating our bodies from heat loss. Scientists discovered, however, that the tiny muscles (arrector pili) attached to hairs are designed for other important functions. Anchored to hair shafts, these muscles put pressure on sebaceous glands in the skin, squeezing out oils that help prevent dehydration, keeping human skin moist and flexible. Rhythmic contraction of these muscles (shivering) releases tremendous amounts of heat in the skin, a process that helps keep us from getting too cold, even in the absence of insulating clothing (and there was no deep need for insulation in the mild climate of the earth originally created perfect). *Hairs "standing on end"* is an incidental consequence, neither the created purpose nor the vestigial function, of the arrector pili hair muscles.

Likewise, the ability of some people to "wiggle their ears" is an incidental consequence of muscle action designed for jaw movement and facial expression. Such muscles do not link some people more closely to their ear-wiggling ancestors any more than muscles some can use to roll their tongues link them more closely to some tongue-rolling ancestor (although it's possible that some evolutionist has made that claim).

What about *nipples* on men? Aren't they vestigial? Nipples in males are part of very incompletely developed organs that develop in females into milk-secreting breasts. Indeed, under the influence of their mothers' hormones, some newborn boys briefly ooze a secretion from their nipples crudely called "witches' milk." But nipples in males do NOT qualify as vestigial, even by evolutionists' own definition. According to evolution, a vestigial organ is one that performed a function with survival value in the ancestor of a species that currently possesses only a useless remnant of that structure. To an evolutionist, then, calling male nipples vestigial would mean that ancestral males had milk-producing breasts that lost function as males evolved into females!

Male nipples offer no support for evolution whatsoever (despite popular misconception), but they do point back to a profound part of the creation account. The biblical record tells us that God created woman (Eve) from a portion of man's side, eliciting from a joyous and grateful Adam the first poem in Scripture:

This at last is bone of my bones and flesh of my flesh:
she shall be called Woman,
because she was taken out of Man (Gen. 2:23; RSV).

Adam and all the other creatures were made from inanimate elements ("dirt and water"), but Eve was special, both as the only one whose creation was anticipated and as the only one made from living flesh. Although not a strictly necessary consequence, it seems that God may be indicating that Adam and Eve each fully

share mankind's complete genetic potential. In that sense, male nipples are simply testimony that the first people were created from the *same flesh*, each having all human traits, but differently accentuated in the two sexes.

Actually, it's not just nipples. Men have, in reduced form, traits amplified in females, and the female body contains, in reduced form, parts of male anatomy. Genetic sex is determined at conception. All egg cells have the X chromosome; fertilization by a sperm cell with a Y chromosome produces (or programs development

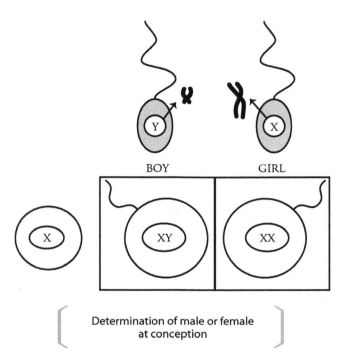

Determination of male or female at conception

for) an *XY boy*. An X sperm plus X egg develops into an *XX girl*. Both boys and girls, however, have all the genes on the X chromosome, and all the genes on other chromosomes, for forming either of the two sexes. The small Y chromosome contains only a few genes, which affect traits like those on the X, except that somehow the Y chromosome acts as if it triggers or favors production of the male hormone (testosterone), which is produced only in lesser amounts in females.

Early in development, the embryo passes through a so-called indifferent stage during which both male and female organs begin to develop. Then, according to the genetic program established at conception, the organs of only one sex develop fully. At any rate, corresponding parts developed to greater or lesser degree in the two genders do not qualify as vestigial organs; they tell us instead that both men and women are from Earth, created by God, not from Mars and Venus nor evolved by time and chance!

"Junk DNA"

Frustrated by scientific disproof of all their claims for anatomical vestiges, faithful followers of Darwin and Haeckel now claim to have found "*vestigial DNA*," useless remnants or "*junk DNA*," which they assert must be leftover from our evolutionary ancestors. Although *the gullible media loudly trumpeted the evolutionist's spin to their captive audiences, scientists didn't fall for it.* Whether or not they remembered the medical malpractice that followed the vestigial organ folly of Darwin and Haeckel, scientists acted like scientists and did research on the possible function of non-coding DNA before just dismissing it as "junk." Many scientists even acted like creationists, assuming the non-coding DNA had a purpose, and pressed forward with research to find its purpose or purposes — and they did.

Just like scientists discovered the functions of 180 structures dismissed as empty evolutionary baggage by Darwin and Haeckel, scientists have found, and are finding, numerous important roles for the sections of DNA that do not code for protein production: many serve as on-off switches or play other regulatory roles; others serve to line up chromosomes for gene-by-gene pairing in the meiotic divisions that produce sex cells; some serve in proofreading and code verification. More roles for non-coding DNA are still being discovered, and, despite intensive marketing by evolutionists, even the term "junk DNA" has lost almost all credibility with molecular biologists.

Biblical Perspective

Are there any valid examples of vestigial structures? Surprisingly, the answer may be yes — but the implications are creationist, not evolutionist. At the "upstream" end of the large intestine, for a few inches past its junction with the small intestine, is a blind pouch called the *caecum*. (The narrow vermiform appendix, discussed earlier extends from the end of the caecum.) Since the flow of digesting food can easily bypass the caecum, one might wonder what function it has. Many plant-eating (herbivorous) animals have large caecae (caecums) and/or other blind-ending digestive pouches where hard-to-digest plant parts are held for prolonged digestive action. Now, think about this: the biblical record tells us that God

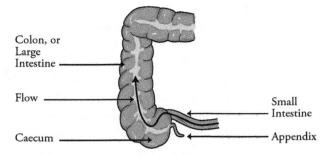

Figure 12.2. Lower right abdomen

originally created people to eat only plants, but following the Flood brought on by sin, God told Noah and his descendants that they may eat meat. Why?

Although the Bible doesn't say specifically, it seems possible that God allowed meat into the human diet in recognition that the Fall and the Flood had corrupted creation in many different ways, including such things as the following: decrease in fertility of post-Flood compared to pre-Flood soils; post-Flood rains leaching minerals from the soil that would have been brought up to plant roots by the pre-Flood watering system; decline and even extinction of nutritious pre-Flood plants; the changed post-Flood climate; mutations in genes for enzyme systems pre-Flood peoples had for digesting, absorbing, and/or processing nutritious foods; and *mutations producing loss or decline in function* of human digestive organs, possibly including the caecum.

It is likely that the earth's shielding from radiation decreased dramatically after the Flood, greatly increasing the mutation rate. Mutations affecting the

eight people surviving the Flood would affect practically all future generations. Many think the increasing genetic burden from accumulating mutations contributed to the decline in human life span. Mutations would also produce decline or loss of function in many body systems, including the digestive. Our present small caecum with minimal digestive function, then, might truly be a mere vestige of a more robust caecum enzymatically active in the breakdown of plant foods in our vegetarian ancestors.

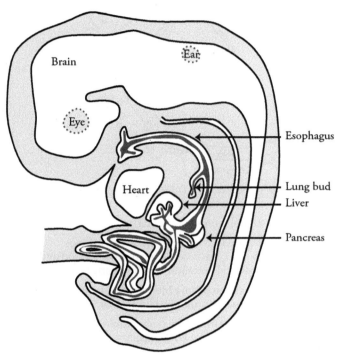

Figure 12.3. The digestive tube and its "buds" in the six-week embryo, with brain, eyes, ears developing and heart beating! Actual size: 1/2 inch or 12 mm

Note two major differences between creationist and evolutionist concepts of vestigial organs. First, our "vegetarian ancestors" with presumably more effective caecae were human, not animal, so vestigial organs might be used to trace patterns of human descent and migration, but could not be used at all to link us to some presumed animal ancestor. Indeed, evolutionists even frustrated themselves by trying to use the appendix to trace human

evolution from animal ancestry, since the appendix is absent in animals evolutionists think are our close relatives and present in animals presumably not related to us. As we saw in the homology section earlier, the evolutionary stories Darwin's followers make up about one organ very frequently contradict the evolutionary story based on some other organ.

The second major difference between creationist and evolutionist concepts of vestiges is also clear and straightforward: vestigial structures reflect *loss and decline, deterioration from a formerly better design and function — the exact opposite of the Darwinist's dream that the evolutionary processes of time, chance, struggle, and death would lead to a net increase in "new and improved" species.* To support the view of upward, onward evolutionary progress that Darwin's followers have been so aggressively marketing to politicians, lawyers, teachers, and school children, Darwin's followers need to find nascent organs — organs in the process of gaining new functions they did not have in the past. So far, the term and concept are barely mentioned in the scientific literature, and no detailed examples have been given.

As a marketing strategy (or propaganda ploy), evolution has been phenomenally successful; as a science, evolution has failed utterly. By abandoning the "faith-based" assumptions of Darwin and Haeckel, scientists discovered functions for all the structures once touted as useless leftovers of evolution. The evidence of decline and loss of function scientists did find pointed not to evolutionary progress but to the corruption of creation, just as creationists had predicted based on the biblical record of earth's history. If you see an apparent conflict between science and Scripture, just hang in there; science will catch up and find the Bible has been right all along!

Evolution could never and should never be the *"chief integrating principle"* in life science. *Only respect for scientific methodology can and should fill that role.* This respect for the scientific method should be coupled with a spirit searching for truth about nature (not merely "naturalistic explanations"), even if that *truth points toward Jesus, "the way, the truth, and the life"* (John 14:6; KJV).

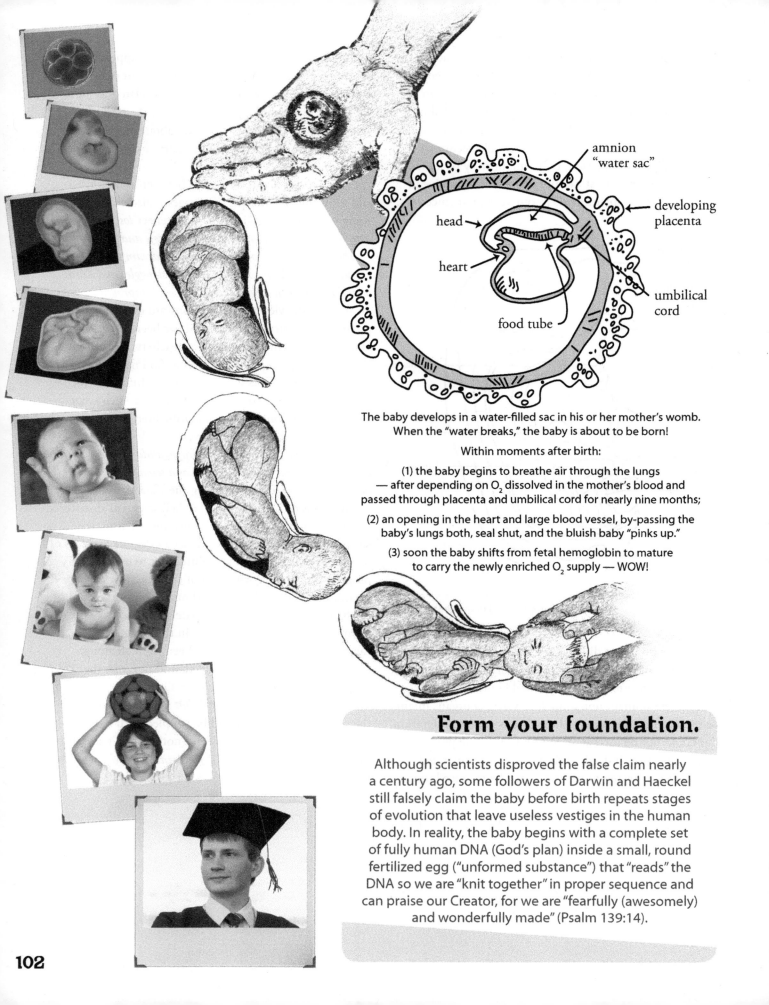

amnion "water sac"

developing placenta

head

heart

umbilical cord

food tube

The baby develops in a water-filled sac in his or her mother's womb. When the "water breaks," the baby is about to be born!

Within moments after birth:

(1) the baby begins to breathe air through the lungs — after depending on O_2 dissolved in the mother's blood and passed through placenta and umbilical cord for nearly nine months;

(2) an opening in the heart and large blood vessel, by-passing the baby's lungs both, seal shut, and the bluish baby "pinks up."

(3) soon the baby shifts from fetal hemoglobin to mature to carry the newly enriched O_2 supply — WOW!

Form your foundation.

Although scientists disproved the false claim nearly a century ago, some followers of Darwin and Haeckel still falsely claim the baby before birth repeats stages of evolution that leave useless vestiges in the human body. In reality, the baby begins with a complete set of fully human DNA (God's plan) inside a small, round fertilized egg ("unformed substance") that "reads" the DNA so we are "knit together" in proper sequence and can praise our Creator, for we are "fearfully (awesomely) and wonderfully made" (Psalm 139:14).

1. In the 1860s, Ernst _____ (the man called "Germany's Darwin") "fudged" his diagrams of embryos to support evolution, and his self-serving errors (**are/are not**) _____ still found in textbooks today.

2. Although disproven by scientists in the 1920s, the "biogenetic law" (falsely so-called) still claims in some modern textbooks that embryonic development ("ontogeny") retraces ("recapitulates") presumed evolutionary stages ("phylogeny"), falsely using so-called gill slits as "evidence" for the (**fish/reptile/monkey**) _____ stage, the so-called yolk sac for the _____ stage, and the so-called tail for the _____ stage. In reality, the human embryo goes through "stages of creation" like those described in Psalm 139, from (list in order: **"knit together"** / **"unformed substance"** / **plan in God's mind**): _____ to _____ to _____.

3. Darwin's followers once thought of the _____ as the "amoeba stage" in human evolution, but scientists found the DNA in our first cell is (**25%, 50%, 75%, 100%**) _____ human.

4. How do the stages in metamorphosis from tadpole to frog provide evidence against evolution and for creation?
    _____
    _____

5. Darwin and Haeckel once listed 180 "useless leftovers of evolution," called _____, in the human body. Scientists have since found the distinctive human function for (**30, 60, 90, 120, all 180**) _____ of these.

6. Below are several human structures once called useless evolutionary vestiges. Match each with its distinctive human function discovered by scientists:

    _____ a. tonsils   A. first blood cells and vessels for developing baby
    _____ b. appendix   B. form palatine tonsils, middle ear canals, thymus and parathyroid glands
    _____ c. thymus gland   C. attachment for muscles important for human posture (and for defecation)
    _____ d. pineal gland   D. help fight germs to prevent "sore throat"
    _____ e. "hair muscle"   E. part of immune system and helps people to make antibodies from B cells
    _____ f. "yolk sac"   F. makes T cells for immunity amd may function in change from adolescent to adult
    _____ g. "gill pouches"   G. makes the hormone melatonin to regulate sleep cycle
    _____ h. "tailbone"   H. squeezes out oil from glands in the skin

7. Explain why no knowledgeable evolutionist could use "nipples on men" as vestigial structures. Could they be used to support the Bible's record of Adam and Eve's creation? If so, how? _____
    _____

8. Can you offer a premise why God might choose an "empty yolk sac" as the source of the baby's first blood cells?
    _____

9. When it was first learned that most human DNA did not code for protein production, (**evolutionists/scientists**) _____ started calling it "junk DNA" and assumed it was useless. Remembering past "malpractice," however, (**evolutionists/scientists**) _____ assumed this new kind of DNA had important functions, went looking for them, and found this DNA (**was indeed junk/had many important functions**) _____.

10. It's possible that the _____, a pouch at the end of the human large intestine, really is a "vestige" of an organ that had a more important function in our (**animal/human**) _____ ancestors that God had created to eat (**everything/only plants**) _____.

11. Since Darwin's followers want to believe evolution produced "upward, onward" changes, the evidence they need is not (**vestigial/nascent**) _____ organs losing function but (**vestigial/nascent**) _____ organs gaining function, but so far (**many/only a few/none**) _____ have been found.

Unit 3: DNA and the Origin of Life

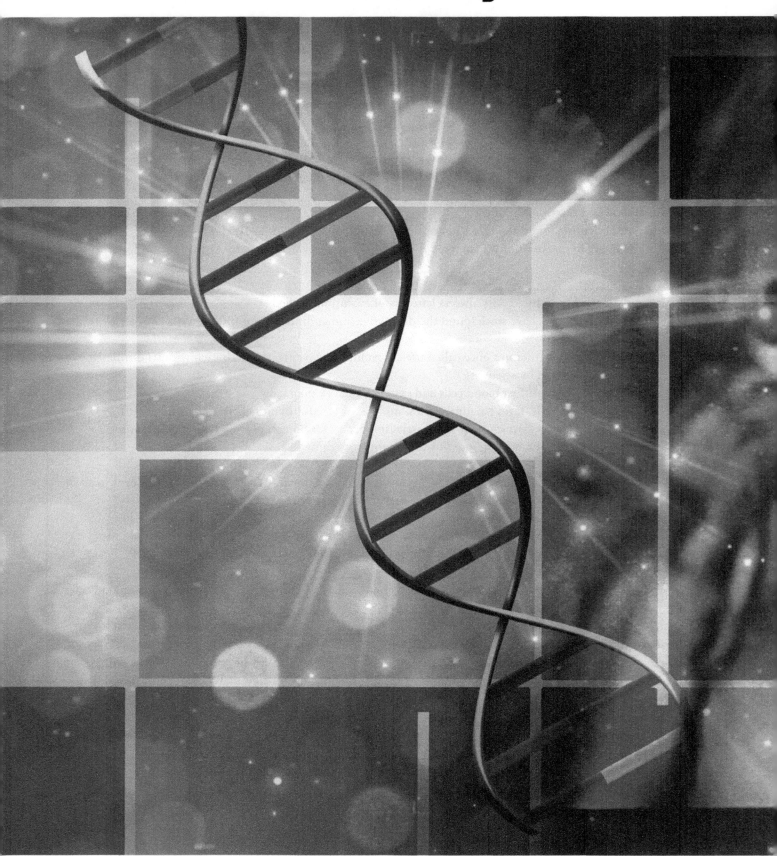

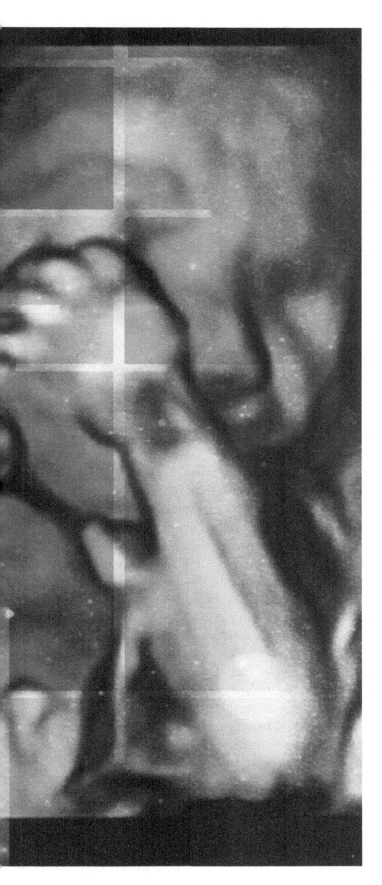

Perhaps you've wondered how the first life began. Your life came from your parents' life, their lives came from your grandparents, all the way back to . . . who, what, when, where, why, and how? Th e origin of life is the ultimate question in the evolution/creation debate in biology.

According to the Bible's book of beginnings (Genesis), all human lives came from the life in our first parents, Adam and Eve, and their life came from the life of God. The life of God is eternal, of course, infinitely older than the universe, since God's life existed before the universe began and will after it ends. WOW! The life eternal in God is the origin of all other origins. DOUBLE WOW!

Evolutionists hope you'll fall for a much simpler form of "logic." Since living things are made OF chemicals, they assert, life must have been made BY chemicals. But pencils are made OF graphite ("lead"), wood, and rubber, yet no one reaches the illogical conclusion that pencils were made BY those three things. Indeed, both scientists and ordinary people would logically conclude pencils were created — designed to organize graphite, wood, and rubber to accomplish the purpose of their creator.

Evolutionists have to accept the logic and evidence that shows pencils are the products of plan, purpose, and special acts of creation — human creation. Most evolutionists would have hailed a finding of pottery fragments on Mars as proof of intelligent design by Martians. Many are hoping to find coded (created) information in signals from outer space, eager to accept evidence of alien intelligence. Even the current "champion of evolution," Richard Dawkins, was willing to admit (in the Ben Stein film *Expelled*) that scientists could possibly find evidence of creation — but it would have to be creation by aliens, he insisted, never creation by God.

Seeming to put political correctness above science, some evolutionists have fought feverishly to censor any and all evidence pointing toward a transcendent Creator beyond the universe, and they have expelled numerous outstanding scientists for even suggesting the concept of Intelligent Design deserves open discussion in a spirit of academic freedom. Such mobster tactics by these evolutionists embarrass true scientists who are searching for the truth about nature, willing to follow the evidence wherever it might lead — even if it leads to God.

Scientists can discover evidence of transcendent creation using the ordinary tools of science: logic and observation. As we shall see in this section, the study of DNA and living cells provides the most direct and powerful evidence that *life is the gift of God and each of us is created with a special purpose and place in God's plan that no one else can take.* Let's help each other be all we can be in Christ!

Bio-Logical Molecules

You have no doubt noticed that living things (e.g., people, cats, and dogs) *grow*, *react*, and *reproduce* in ways quite different from non-living things (e.g., rocks, rivers, and stars). Why? What gives living things the ability to do so many things non-living things can't do? For centuries scientists thought there was some special, mysterious "vital force" within living things that made them different from non-living. Around Darwin's time, some scientists even put scales under the deathbeds of people, hoping to weigh this "vital force" as it left the body at death.

But the Bible had it right from the very beginning. The first person, Adam, was made from "dust of the ground," and other living things were likewise made from substances in the earth. Scripture and modern science agree: the differences between living (*biotic*) and nonliving (*abiotic*) worlds are based not on substance but on *organization*. Living and non-living things are made of the same simple substances (atoms or elements) put together in quite different ways.

> **Question**
>
> Who or what put non-living atoms together in ways that formed living cells: time, chance, and chemical evolution, or plan, purpose, and special acts of creation?

Chemists recognize that all materials on earth, living or not, are made up of less than 100 naturally occurring *elements*, "pure" substances containing only one kind of *atom*. *Hydrogen*, the lightest element, has the smallest atom, which consists of one positively charged proton (p^+) encircled by a fast-moving, negatively charged electron (e^-) or "electron cloud." Next to hydrogen, the most common atom in living things is *carbon*. Its center, or nucleus, contains 6 protons ($6p^+$), and their positive charge is balanced by encircling "clouds" or "shells" containing 6 electrons ($6e^-$). The carbon nucleus also contains neutrons, neutral particles with no electric charge ($n°$). The importance of neutrons is discussed in other books, but it's the number of protons ("*atomic number*") that determines the number of electrons, and *chemistry is mostly about trading and sharing electrons.*

When atoms join together ("*bond*") by sharing electrons, they form *molecules*. Most biological molecules are built from just five different kinds of atoms, and their atomic symbols are conveniently the first letters of their names:

H — hydrogen   N — nitrogen   P — phosphorus
O — oxygen   C — carbon

Biochemists usually use a line between atomic symbols to represent a pair of electrons forming a bond.

Even more conveniently, the number of bonds typically formed by these five atoms ranges from one to five:

$$H- \qquad -O- \qquad -\overset{|}{N}- \qquad -\overset{|}{\underset{|}{C}}- \qquad -\overset{||}{\underset{|}{P}}-$$

Actually, one atom can bond with another through one pair of shared electrons (*a single bond*), two shared electron pairs (*a double bond*), or three (*triple bond*):

$$-O- \qquad -\overset{|}{\underset{|}{N}}- \qquad -\overset{|}{\underset{|}{C}}- \qquad -\overset{||}{\underset{|}{P}}-$$

$$O= \qquad -N= \qquad -\overset{|}{C}= \qquad =C=$$

$$N\equiv \qquad -C\equiv$$

Chemical formulas like H_2O, CO_2, NH_3, or HCN just tell the numbers and kinds of atoms in a molecule ("*empirical formulas*"). Atomic symbols with bond lines are used in *structural formulas*, two-dimensional diagrams that crudely represent the 3-D arrangement of atoms in molecules:

$$H_2O$$
water
$$\overset{O-H}{\underset{H}{|}}$$

$$CO_2$$
carbon dioxide
$$O=C=O$$

$$NH_3$$
ammonia
$$H-\overset{|}{\underset{H}{N}}-H$$

$$HCN$$
hydrogen cyanide
$$H-C\equiv N$$

It's astonishing how much biological complexity can be built up from just five kinds of atoms forming one to five bonds. It's as if God were making it simple enough so that we wouldn't miss seeing His creative hand! Perhaps that's why the function of even huge biological molecules is often focused on just a few atoms organized into functional groups. Since atoms in *functional groups* stick together and act together, bond lines are omitted from the "condensed" structural formulas for functional groups, as shown top right:

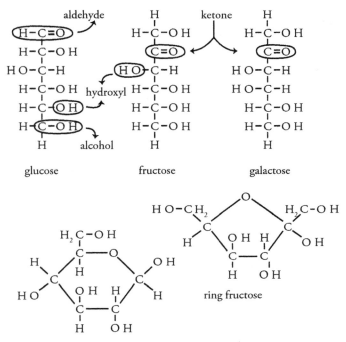

$-OH$ hydroxyl
(or $HO-$, $\overset{|}{O}H$, $H\overset{|}{O}$, etc.)

$H-C=O$ aldehyde
↘ carbonyl
$\overset{|}{C}=O$ ketone

$-\overset{|}{\underset{|}{C}}-OH$ alcohol

$-NH_2$ amine

$\begin{cases} -C\overset{\nearrow O}{\underset{\searrow OH}{}} \\ \text{or} \\ -COOH \end{cases}$ carboxylic acid

$-CH_3$ methyl

$-\overset{|}{\underset{|}{C}}H_2$ hydrocarbon

Structural formulas show that molecules with 6 C atoms, 12 H's, and 6 O's ($C_6H_{12}O_6$) can be arranged to form several different sugars like these:

glucose   fructose   galactose

ring glucose (glucopyranose)   ring fructose

Different arrangements of the same atoms, like the various $C_6H_{12}O_6$ sugars above, are called isomers (meaning "same segments"). Most amino acids, the building blocks of proteins, exist chemically as optical isomer pairs called left- and right-handed because they mirror each other like gloves. Each amino acid consists of a central carbon atom (C) bonded to four different groups. Three groups are the same for all amino acids: the amine ($-NH_2$) and the acid ($-COOH$) groups that give them their name, and a hydrogen atom ($-H$). The fourth group, labeled R, is one of 20 or so radically different groups that make each kind of amino acid different from all the other ones. Although 3-D images are better, the following represents a left- and right-handed mirror image pair of amino acids:

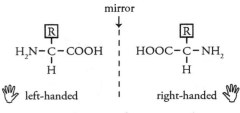

optical isomers of an amino acid

Chemical processes produce equal amounts of each amino acid isomer, but all proteins (except some poisons) in living things are built from left-handed isomers only, and even one right-handed form can destroy a protein's biological function. Wearing a right-handed glove on the left hand (or a right boot on the left foot) can be uncomfortable, but mixing up left- and right-handed amino acids is absolutely fatal to every single living thing! It's not the atoms that make the differences between living and non-living things; it's how those atoms are organized!

Some "simple" biological molecules contain so many atoms so precisely organized that "shorthand" diagrams are used to represent them:

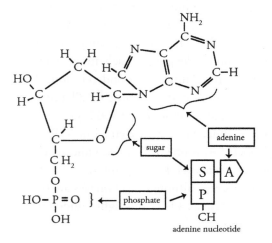

Adenine nucleotide, one link in a DNA chain (and a single human cell has 3 billion such links!), can be represented in a shorthand diagram like this:

Each DNA nucleotide consists of three parts: sugar, phosphate, and base. The sugar (S) and phosphate (P) groups join –SP-SP-SP- to form the sugar-phosphate "backbone" of a DNA chain. Four different kinds of bases, abbreviated GCAT, stick out to the side of the "backbone," somewhat like letters are held in place along an ink stamp. Interlocking shapes allow G to pair with C and A with T. These base pairs hold the DNA chains together, and twisting this double strand forms the famous DNA "double helix," the basis for life's reproduction. See Figure 13.1 below.

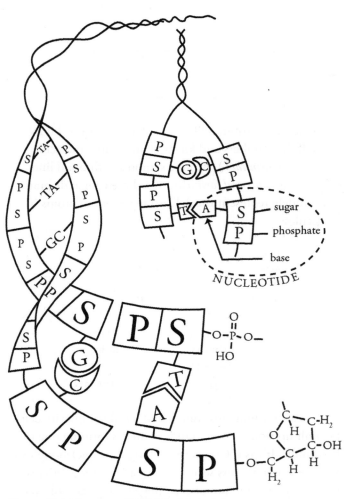

Figure 13.1. Diagram of DNA "double helix"

The four major groups of biological molecules are *carbohydrates, proteins, fats or lipids,* and *nucleic acids.* The first three are familiar as "food groups" (after all, living things eat things once living), and the last includes RNA and DNA, the famous molecule of heredity. All these groups include biologically distinctive long to very long chains. Fatty acids can include more than 20 carbon atoms in a row. Carbohydrates include starches and cellulose (wood) that can have more than 300 complex ring glucose molecules linked together to form *polymers* (*poly*, "many"; *mers*, "segments"). Protein polymers can include over 2,000 amino acid links in their chains, with an average of about 400. DNA is the runaway champion, however; its polymer chains may include millions of nucleotide links, many serving as letters in the "alphabet of heredity."

All polymer chains grow when subtraction of a water molecule forms a link between their monomers; addition of water molecules breaks polymers down into separate links:

SUBTRACTION of water ⇒ forms POLYMERS		
sugars	⇔ starches, wood	+HOH
amino acids	⇔ proteins	+HOH
nucleotides	⇔ DNA/RNA	+HOH
MONOMERS ⇐ ADDITION of HOH unlinks polymers		

That means life is like a "juggling act," intensely focused on balancing the "uphill" reactions putting together polymers and other molecular structures against the "downhill" reactions that tear down molecular order
— and these constructive and destructive relations both depend on the *motion of water molecules*.

Flowing rivers and crashing waves are obvious examples of water in motion, but even in a glass of water sitting calmly on a table, the water *molecules* inside it are in ceaseless violent motion: crashing into one another, banging on the walls of the glass, even jumping out of the glass and into the air (evaporation).

Water molecules are too small to see directly with an ordinary microscope, but you can see larger particles, called colloids, being knocked around by water molecules. Wow! Grind up a leaf or any biological material and put it in a drop of water under a microscope (or use India ink). Big particles (the kind that settle from suspensions) won't move, but soon your eye should catch dozens of smaller particles (colloids) vibrating, tumbling, or rolling around like a crook hit with a tazer. Their vibrations are caused by millions of much smaller water molecules smashing into them. More can hit momentarily from one side or the other or from above or below, producing the erratic dance call **Brownian motion**, a "jogging in place" motion that doesn't move the particle very far.

Colloids in warm solutions "dance faster" than those in cool ones, but the never-ending dance means colloidal particles never settle out (unlike suspensions). Many parts of living cells are colloidal in size or smaller. What makes

Colloidal particles vibrate or "dance in place," tracing zig-zag path.

Motion is faster and farther in warm solution, but colloid stays near starting point.

Figure 13.2. Brownian motion under microscope.

these molecules move? Bombardment by water molecules. What makes water molecules move? Heat. What causes heat? Molecular motion. Which came first, heat or the motion of particles that causes heat?! Answer: God came first! God created a universe in which small particles are in constant motion, and important consequences follow.

The spontaneous, God-ordained motion of small particles is called *random thermal motion — random* because each particle "dances" left or right, up or down in no special pattern or direction, and it's *thermal* because it's faster or slower depending on temperature. "Life temperature" (the biokinetic zone) is roughly the temperature range at which water is liquid and its molecules are in random thermal motion — but not so hot that the fastest-moving water molecules would break down biological structure (as they do when you cook food!), i.e., about 30–120° F (or a little less than 0–50° C).

Now comes the exciting part. Even though individual water molecules are moving at random, God designed living systems to take advantage of this "free" (spontaneous) *random* thermal motion to move groups of molecules in a *definite* direction at a *definite* rate to a *definite* end point. Thanks to the random thermal motion of air molecules, scent molecules from a delicious apple pie spread through the kitchen, into other rooms, and even out an open window. As the randomly moving scent molecules bang into one another, they tend to scatter out — so the net movement of the group of scent molecules is in a *definite direction* from a high concentration (where they are closely packed) to a low concentration (where there are few or none). Diffusion has a *definite rate* that depends so precisely on temperature and particle size that it can be used to calculate molecular weight! Finally, even though the random thermal motion of individual particles goes on "forever," diffusion of the group reaches a *definite end point* when the particles are evenly scattered (and that's why sugar diffused throughout coffee doesn't clump together along the side of the cup!).

In the lungs, diffusion "automatically" moves oxygen from air sacs into the blood at the same time carbon dioxide "automatically" diffuses in the opposite direction. Each is diffusing from its own high to low concentration. The system is so well-designed that diffusion can move a full charge of oxygen from lung to blood and carbon dioxide from blood and lung over a wide range of heart and breathing rates. Wow! And the body spends no energy and requires no "guidance system" to accomplish this life-giving gas exchange. Double wow! It's not the "chaos" of random thermal motion that gets the credit, of course; it's the God in Christ who *designed a system to "capitalize on chaos"*!

The design constraints are tight; diffusion is relatively slow since individual molecules are moving randomly and only the group is moving in a definite direction. Therefore, the distance between air sacs and blood in the lungs is very short. A lung infection that increases the air sac-to-blood distance (pneumonia) can cause death, since diffusion can no longer supply oxygen to the blood fast enough. Supplying extra oxygen, sometimes under pressure, can be life-saving by artificially boosting the difference between high and low concentration (diffusion gradient) and increasing the amounts of oxygen diffused — a way of escape from trial provided by God in a fallen world.

Within living cells, diffusion based on the motion of water molecules supplies "free transportation," moving molecules from the place where they are produced or supplied (high concentration) to places where they are used or secreted/excreted from the cell. If "blood" can be regarded as a "fluid transport system," then the Biblical phrase "the life is in the blood" (Gen. 9:4) might be understood to include water in living cells! The size and shapes of living cells and their distance from transport fluids is determined in part by design constraints related to diffusion rates. In designing living cells to use random (chance) thermal motion, *nothing is left to chance!*

Osmosis is a special kind of diffusion, the diffusion of water through a membrane that lets water through but not larger dissolved molecules (solutes). Like many cells, a red blood cell (rbc) is about 80 percent water and 20 percent solute. So, an rbc put in 100 percent pure distilled water will absorb water and swell up as water moves from its own high concentration (100%) to low (80%) — even though the water "forces" its way into an rbc already crowded with solutes (that the membrane keeps in). In fact, distilled water can cause an rbc to swell up and burst.

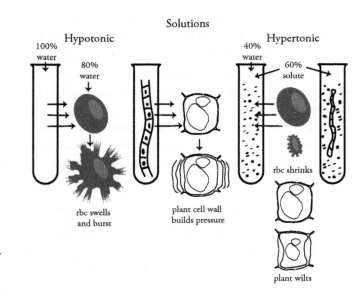

Solutions

Hypotonic

100% water

80% water

rbc swells and burst

plant cell wall builds pressure

Hypertonic

40% water

60% solute

rbc shrinks

plant wilts

Unlike an rbc surrounded by a thin membrane, a plant cell is surrounded by a thick, woody wall. Distilled water will cause a plant cell to swell, but the woody wall can stretch and exert tremendous back pressure, or turgor pressure. These osmotic and turgor pressures keep plants from wilting, but they can also reach pressures sufficient to lift sidewalks and crack house foundations (things even a strong man's muscle power can't do!)

Solutions causing cells to swell are called *hypotonic*. Solutions that cause cells to shrink, like jellies and brines, are called *hypertonic*, and they can be used as preservatives because they suck the water and the "life" out of contaminating cells, including bacteria. A solution that's "just right" is called *isotonic*; water molecules continue to move back and forth through the membrane but equally in both directions, so that no net change occurs to either swell or shrink the cell. Cells and living things have many features designed to maintain water balance within narrow limits, and life would be impossible without such design.

Form your foundation.

Centuries before scientists discovered it, the Bible revealed that living things are made of (not by) "dust," i.e., simple elements of the earth (e.g., H, O, N, C, P). In living cells, some simple substances are organized into long chains (polymers) whose build up and break down both depend on the actions of water molecules — making "life" a "juggling act" that requires a constant input of ordered energy and raw materials.
Wow!

Building Inspection

1. The Bible says living things are made of (not by) "dust," simple "earthly" substances like the hydrogen, oxygen, nitrogen, carbon, and phosphorus that make up over 95 percent of "living matter." Write the symbols for these five kinds of atoms: _____, _____, _____, _____, _____.

2. Bonds (shared electron pairs) can be represented by lines showing atoms joined to form molecules. How many bonds are usually formed by each of these atoms? H____, O____, N____, C____, P____. One line represents a single bond (H-), two a _____bond (O=), and three a _____ bond, such as _____. Using atomic symbols and bond lines, "draw" a molecule of water (H_2O), ammonia (NH_3), and carbon dioxide (CO_2):

3. Bond lines are often omitted between "functional groups" of atoms that act together. Label the functional groups below with one of these names: hydroxyl, alcohol, amine, acid: -OH_____ -COH _____-NH_2 _____ -COOH _____.

4. Molecules with different arrangements of the same kinds of atoms (like the $C_6H_{12}O_6$ sugars glucose and fructose) are called (**isomers, polymers/monomers**) _____, which means "same parts." Amino acids with the same parts often come as _____ and _____-handed forms, "mirror images" called optical _____-mers — but only the (**left/right**) _____-handed forms are helpful to life; _____ -handed forms cause (**evolution/death**) _____.

5. Key bio-logical molecules are long chains called (**iso-, poly-, mono-**) _____-mers made up of small, repeated links called _____. Protein _____ are made of _____ monomers; wood and starch _____ of _____ monomers, and DNA/RNA of nucleotide _____. What common molecule is subtracted (released on "split out") when monomers join to form polymers? _____. What molecule added to long chains (polymers) breaks them down or "digests" them into single links (monomers)? _____ _____.

6. What molecule adds "life" to living cells by moving other molecules around so they can interact? _____. Moving water molecules can "jump out of a glass," causing the familiar process called _____. Bombardment by water molecules causes small particles (colloids) visible under the microscope to "dance around" at random, a vibration called _____ motion, and the "random dance" goes faster if the water is (**hot/cold**) _____. Unfortunately, the motion of water molecules that makes life possible by bringing molecules together also makes (**life/death**) _____ occur as big molecules and structures (**evolve/are destroyed**) _____.

7. Heat causes individual water molecules and particles in Brownian motion to move at random ("random thermal motion"), going nowhere in particular. But God uses this "chaotic" motion of individual particles to move groups of molecules in a definite direction at a definite rate to a definite end point — a process called (**diffusion/osmosis/chaos**) _____. The direction of diffusion is from (**packed to scattered/scattered to packed**) _____, i.e., from (**high to low/low to high**) _____ concentration. The rate of diffusion is faster in (**warm/cool**) _____ water and for (**larger/smaller**) _____ particles. When particles are equally scattered out (like sugar in coffee), diffusion (movement of the group) (**ends/continues**) _____, but movement of the individual water molecules and Brownian particles (**ends/never ceases**) _____at "life temperatures."

8. The diffusion of water through a membrane that holds back dissolved particles (solutes) is called _____. A typical cell is about 80% water and 20% dissolved solutes, so a cell in distilled 100% water will (**swell/shrink**) _____, becoming (**firm/wilted**) _____ if it's a plant cell with a wall but possibly (**exploding/crinkling up**) _____ if it's human or animal.

Chapter 14

Living Cells

Although "bio-logical molecules" show dazzling evidence of design, they are not alive. What does it take to make a group of non-living molecules alive? For centuries, the answer was the mysterious "vital force." The answer suggested by Scripture and discovered by modern science is *organization*.

The fundamental unit of organization in living things is the *cell*. When the microscope was invented in the 1600s, scientists started looking at everything. The microscope revealed that living material, unlike nonliving, was divided up into tiny compartments (like the cells occupied by monks in a monastery). The obvious part of a *plant* cell is the thick, woody, non-living wall that surrounds the living protoplasm. Human and animal cells are much smaller, and the darkly staining nucleus in its center is much more obvious than its thin, living boundary, the *plasma membrane*.

By 1839, scientists accepted the cell theory, that all living things are made of cells. In 1858, scientists added the concept that all living cells come from previously existing living cells. Today, all scientists accept the cell as the fundamental unit of structure, function, and reproduction in living things.

In Darwin's time (the 1800s), cells were thought of as small sacks of liquid or gel with proteins, carbohydrates, and fats "floating" inside. By the 1950s, the vital role of DNA was recognized, and the incredibly powerful electron microscope (EM) revealed astonishing levels of structural and functional complexity within cells, even bacterial cells. Scientists now regularly refer to living cells as complex chemical factories run by "molecular machines" operating shipping and receiving departments, assembly lines, power plants, quality control centers, etc.! There is *no* cell known to modern science that can be called "simple"!

Although cells vary widely in size, shape, and specialized structures and functions, living cells share five basic kinds of "working parts":

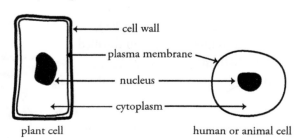

cell wall
plasma membrane
nucleus
cytoplasm

plant cell   human or animal cell

(1) *Membranes.* Th e living boundary of a living cell controls what goes in and out, so the right stuff gets in and the wrong stuff is let out or kept out. Internal membranes serve as assembly lines and form subcellular "workrooms" (*organelles*) to keep molecules for one function separate from those for another, thus providing the basic framework for organization. Membranes include proteins in a *phospholipid bilayer*, as shown at right.

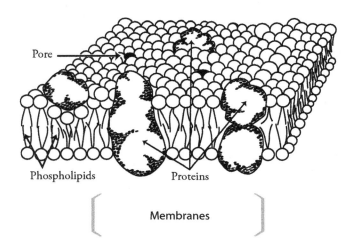

Pore

Phospholipids — Proteins

Membranes

(2) *Enzymes.* Enzymes are large protein molecules (see below) with specially shaped slots (*active sites*) that select and hold other molecules (their substrates) in proper position for speedy reaction. Enzymes are the "work horses" of living cells, and each cell has *hundreds* or *thousands* of different kinds of enzymes working together in harmony to organize the cell's multitude of chemical reactions that, taken together, are called *metabolism.*

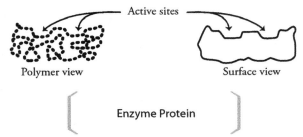

Active sites

Polymer view   Surface view

Enzyme Protein

(3) *ATP.* ATP, or an equivalent energy molecule, supplies the energy required to drive chemical reactions "uphill," toward increased order and complexity. Without ATP, enzymes would tear large molecules apart faster than they would put them together. Without enzymes, however, ATP could not energize the right molecules and might energize the wrong ones. Th e uphill reactions producing growth in living things require both ATP and enzymes (energy and order) working together in harmony! Energy from food and ultimately sunlight is needed to replace the millions of ATP energy molecules used up to "power life" in each cell each second of each day.

(4) *DNA.* The profound ability of living things, unlike non-living, to "multiply after kind" is based on the simple interlocking shapes of DNA bases, the letters in the genetic code. DNA's reproduction would be a trivial trick, however, if DNA could not be used to "tell" living cells how to make proteins, the molecules of structure and function. Enzymes wear out, but enzymes can't reproduce themselves. Using enzymes, ATP energy, and raw materials from food brought in by the membrane, however, DNA can "tell" the cell how to make specific proteins — and some of these specific proteins help DNA to make both specific proteins and more DNA for reproduction, the ultimate in *interdependence* — each molecular part depending on all the others.

(5) *Water.* If a cell consisted only of the four kinds of "working parts" above (membranes, enzymes, ATP, and DNA), it would be no more alive than a painting or photograph of a cell. It takes the *motion* imparted by molecules in liquid water to get the other parts moving and interacting. Removing liquid water from a cell removes its "life," something plants do to put "life on hold" in dormant seeds and scientists do when they freeze-dry bacteria, for example, to put them into "suspended

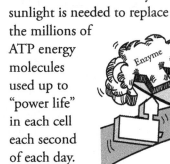

Enzyme now free to couple other molecules.

Enzyme   Enzyme   Enzyme

ATP and enzymes work together in harmony.

old child. Without losing your respect for the incredible human ingenuity that put the space shuttle together, you would recognize in living cells the handiwork of intelligence and creativity far surpassing mankind's — nothing short of the transcendent Lord God in Christ, Maker of heaven and earth and Author of life.

Matter and Life: Spontaneous Generation?

Scientists have discovered a great many amazing details about the organization and operation of living cells since Darwin's time. All this knowledge makes it surprising that some scientists still believe non-living matter can produce life without any plan, purpose, or creative intelligent design.

It was once thought, however, that people could actually see matter spontaneously generate life. Mud could be observed to generate frogs spontaneously, without supernatural intervention, and rotting meat could spontaneously generate flies . . . or so it was thought. An Italian scientist in the 1600s, Francisco Redi, showed that flies appeared in rotting meat *only if* flies could first get to the meat and lay eggs. Life came from life, not from matter. And the only mud that produced frogs contained cocoons of frogs formed as the mud dried before water returned. Again, it was life from life (*biogenesis*), not life from non-life (*abiogenesis* or *spontaneous generation*).

animation."

Adding water adds "life" back to dormant seeds or freeze-dried bacteria — but only because cells already have the four other kinds of "working parts." The motion imparted by water molecules is *necessary but not sufficient* to accomplish the harmoniously coordinated sets of chemical reactions we call life!

Somewhat paradoxically, the motion of water molecules *also destroys* the structures required for life, but a healthy cell with ample food (which supplies both energy and raw materials) can use the motion of water molecules to put the cell back together faster than the motion of water molecules can tear it apart. Wow!

Suppose you were selected to go on a detailed, behind-the-scenes tour of the space shuttle, even checking out the computer wiring and software programs. You would be overwhelmed by the fantastic intelligence and creativity that went into its design, the selection of different materials for different purposes, the tight interdependence of parts that allows one part to work in harmony with the others to accomplish a common goal. You couldn't help but admire the engineers and other scientists who dreamed up the space shuttle and made their dreams come true.

Now image you could shrink down and tour the living cells of the human body. By comparison, the space shuttle would be like a child's toy, like Lego® blocks put together by a six-year-

But if life comes only from pre-existing life, that implies *life came first, before matter, and life made matter, not the reverse.* That's what the Bible teaches. All life ultimately comes from the life of God, the eternal I AM (Exod. 3:14). It was the ever-living God who created matter (and time, energy, and space) from nothing beyond Himself (Gen. 1:1) by the word of His power, Jesus Christ (John 1:1–14).

Unfortunately, some people find an eternally existent Creator God personally unacceptable. They are *forced by that bias — not by science* — to believe either that nothing made everything, or that matter, not God, is eternal. In response to a talk show question, famous evolutionist Carl Sagan said that if someone asks where matter came from, just ask them where God came from. He said more than he meant to. Something must be eternal, either God or matter (mass-energy). Scientists have observed over and over again that matter loses order, information, and/or useful energy with time. Although mass-energy's quantity remains constant, its quality deteriorates. Eternal matter makes no scientific sense; eternal God does.

Those preferring *faith in matter* to *faith in God* accepted the evidence against matter producing complex life like frogs and flies, but they turned instead to belief in the spontaneous generation of microscopic organisms. Some scientists in the 1700s and 1800s conducted experiments to show that microbes would spontaneously appear in broths that initially had none. Belief in the spontaneous generation of microbes was popular among early evolutionists in the 1800s, and Charles Darwin, who published his *Origin of Species* in 1859, imagined that life might have started from a combination of chemicals in a "warm little pond."

Only a few years after Darwin's *Origin* was published, however, one of history's premier scientists and an outstanding creationist, Louis Pasteur, seemed to disprove once and for all that chemicals could spontaneously produce life — even so-called simple microscopic life. Scientists had already

Louis Pasteur

shown no microbes appeared in broths protected from airborne contamination, but early evolutionists argued that free contact with air was required for spontaneous generation. Pasteur simply made swan-necked flasks completely open to the air (below), but the sterile matter within never produced living microbes — and the flasks are still in France, maintaining continuous testimony that *living cells may be made OF chemicals, but they are not made BY chemicals.*

How do evolutionists respond to Pasteur's scientific demonstration that life comes only from pre-existing life? For many, strong personal bias prevents their even considering that life on earth comes from the life of God. With firm faith that matter must make life, the modern evolutionist argues that chemical evolution requires more time than Pasteur allowed — millions of years more — and perhaps even conditions as different as those on another planet! *Moving spontaneous generations so far back in time and so far out in space* that scientists could never disprove it or even test the idea. *Darwin's followers simply made chemical evolution an article of absolute faith beyond the reach of science.* It's certainly no wonder that evolutionists want to censor all criticism of evolutionary beliefs from science classrooms!

Ancient sun worshipers believed that matter energized by sunlight could turn into life. Adding much more time, modern evolutionists believe essentially the same thing. An influential college biology textbook claimed that anywhere there is a planetary surface (matter) and a flow through of energy (sunlight), life will inevitably emerge — adding that nothing supernatural appeared to be involved, but only time, chance, and the peculiarly suitable conditions on the ancient earth.

Mars should have gone through the right conditions to evolve life before Earth, so spacecraft sent to Mars tested the evolutionists' belief in the formula that matter + energy + time = life. Some evolutionists claimed living things would be looking back at the spacecraft's cameras, but tests on the soil failed to find microbial life or even a biological molecule. In the face of such crushing defeat, one famous evolutionist admitted that life must be harder to make than he thought! Perhaps it's not matter + energy + time that makes life, but *matter + energy + creative intelligent design*!

settled
contaminant

lifeless but
nutrient-rich
broth

Figure 14.1. Diagrammed below is a composite cell with major parts of different animal, plant, and human cells labeled so that you can identify the name and function of each key cell organelle. Memory challenge: try to learn the name of each cell structure then the function of each structure.

Structure

a. cilium or flagellum
b. lysosomes
c. vacuole
d. golgi (dietyosome)
e. endoplasmic reticulum (ER)
f. ribosomes
g. microvilli
h. microfilaments
i. desmosomes
j. microtubules
k. centrioles
l. plasmodesmata
m. nuceolus
n. chromosomes — DNA
o. nuclear envelope
p. peroxisomes
q. mitochondrion
r. chloroplast
s. cell wall

Function

a. move cell or move fluid
b. digestion
c. store, absorb, release substances
d. secretion
e. transportation, assembly line
f. protein production
g. absorption
h. cell shape and contraction
i. hold cells together
j. motion; chromosome separation
k. cell division
l. bridges between cells
m. store RNA; make ribosomes
n. heredity and cell control
o. active boundary nucleus/cytoplasm
p. break down peroxide
q. "power house of the cell"; respiration
r. photosynthesis
s. plant cell support; water flow

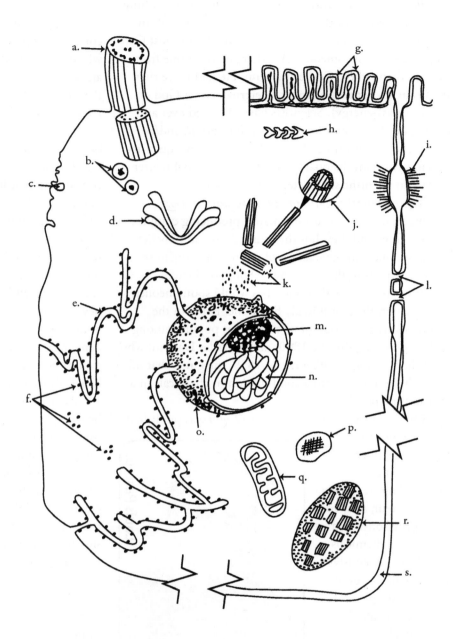

Form your foundation.

Airplanes are made of non-flying parts and cells of non-living molecules.What does it take to make non-flying parts become a flying airplane or non-living molecules become a living cell? Science and Scripture agree on the answer: *creative design and organization!*

Building Inspection

1. Bio-logical molecules can only interact to produce "life" when they are organized into special "compartments" called _____. Cells have a central, DNA-containing _____, cytoplasm, and plasma membrane, which, in plant cells is surrounded by a woody _____.

             membranes   **enzymes**   **ATP**   **DNA**   **water**

2. Above are five basic "working parts" of living cells. Using some more than once, relate the "cell parts" above to descriptions below:

    _____a. regulate what gets in and out of the cell

    _____b. large proteins with "active sites" that hold molecules with matching shapes for speedy reaction

    _____c. pass hereditary instructions from one generation to the next

    _____d. consist of proteins in a phospholipid bilayer

    _____e. used as a code to "tell" the cell how to make proteins, including enzymes

    _____f. provide energy to make "build up" reactions go faster than "break down"

    _____g. select which molecules get an "energy boost"

    _____h. provides the motion to molecules that make life possible

    _____i. provides the motion that destroys structure and can bring death

3. Describe how enzymes and ATP depend on each other.

_____

_____

_____

4. Describe how enzymes and DNA depend on each other.

_____

_____

_____

5. It takes creative design and organization to turn non-flying parts into a "flying machine" (airplane). What does it take to turn non-living parts into a living cell? _____.

6. When matter making life without "outside help" (spontaneous generation) was scientifically disproven by the famous creationist biologist _____, how did Darwin's followers respond? _____

_____

_____

7. Scientists have only observed life coming from life. Creationists agree, adding that the first life came from the life of _____. So life came (**before/after**) _____ matter (contrary to popular opinion!), and living things are made OF chemicals but NOT _____ chemicals.

Chapter 14

Chemical Evolution?

Chemical evolution is the belief that no Creator God or intelligent design was required to produce the first life on earth, but only time, chance, and the ordinary chemical properties of matter. The father of the modern concept of chemical evolution, A. I. Oparin, stated plainly and up-front that his belief started with Engles' materialistic philosophy, the assumption that matter is the only reality and there is no spiritual dimension to the universe.

Chemical evolution was born of belief in materialistic philosophy, *not science*, and its assertions about events in an assumed distant past cannot be tested by the methods of empirical science. But chemical evolutionists *do* make five predictions from their materialistic model of reality that can be tested by scientists, as shown in Figure 15.1:

	Popular beliefs of chemical evolutionists preached in science classrooms around the world
1	The early earth had a "reducing atmosphere" that included methane (CH_4), ammonia (NH_3), and water vapor (H_2O), but NO oxygen (O_2).
2	Simple energy sources such as lightning combined the molecules above to form simple biological molecules such as amino acids.
3	Conditions on the early earth combined amino acids to form proteins, and other small biological molecules joined in long chains to form other large polymers.
4	Membrane-bound droplets (coacervates) absorbed sets of interacting molecules, forming "proto-cells."
5	When time, chance, and chemistry finally produced DNA that could both reproduce itself and encode protein production, cellular life finally appeared on earth and began to evolve into all the forms we have today.

Figure 15.1. Popular chemical evolutionist concepts.

This oft-repeated story of chemical evolution is supported by numerous testimonials from famous people and vividly illustrated with computer graphics. But is the scenario supported, refuted, or left undecided by the scientific evidence? Classic experiments touted to support chemical evolution were done by Stanley Miller for steps 1 and 2 and by Sidney Fox for steps 3 and 4.

Miller's Spark Chamber

The most dramatic support for chemical evolution was an experiment done by Stanley Miller while he was working under Harold Urey in the 1950s. To simulate the presumed environment of the early earth, Miller put methane (CH_4), ammonia (NH_3), and liquid water (H_2O) into a small glass flask, carefully excluding oxygen (O_2). Then he introduced an electric spark to simulate lightning. After just a week, he harvested several kinds of biological molecules, including sugars and amino acids. WOW! Some newspapers of that time hailed the experiment as virtually "making life in a test tube." When he was an enthusiastic evolutionist, the author looked forward to sharing with his students this captivating and convincing "proof" for chemical evolution.

Miller's experiment, shown on page 121, was brilliant. But there are three small scientific problems:

1	He had the wrong starting molecules.
2	He used the wrong conditions.
3	He got the wrong results.

Wrong starting materials. Science has disproved the assumption the early earth had a reducing atmosphere. If methane (CH_4) had been present, it would have been found adsorbed to deep sedimentary clays, and it's not there. Ammonia is so soluble in water that it would be dissolved in the oceans, not present in large amounts in the atmosphere. That was no problem for Miller, since he used a very large tank of NH_3 to fill a very small flask with ammonia, but such a source would not be available to the early earth. CH_4 and NH_3 are found in the atmospheres of the outer, gassy, Jovian planets (Jupiter, Saturn, Uranus, Neptune), and that may have encouraged evolutionists. But the inner, rocky, terrestrial (Earth-like) planets with atmospheres contain oxidized carbon (CO_2, carbon dioxide), not reduced carbon (CH_4, methane), and hardly any ammonia.

In a *complete reversal* of evolutionary

expectations, the CH_4 and NH_3 were *absent* from the early earth's atmosphere, but oxygen (O_2) was *present*. Evolutionary theorists had deliberately left the oxygen out, because they knew atmospheric O_2 would destroy the molecules needed for chemical evolution. Somewhat paradoxically, oxygen is valuable to living cells because it's a powerful, even "corrosive," chemical that can "burn" (oxidize) biological molecules as food for energy. Living cells can handle O_2 because they have numerous built-in chemical protectants. During the presumed early stages in chemical evolution before such protections existed, however, oxygen would wipe out biological molecules, not help to make them.

It's easy to see why evolutionists want to imagine an early earth atmosphere without O_2, but the deepest rocks contain oxidized minerals that evidence the presence of oxygen as far back as we can go. Indeed, high energy radiation from the sun and space would produce some oxygen from the splitting of H_2O. It would take a "miracle" to keep O_2 out of Earth's atmosphere!

Note: there never was any scientific logic or evidence for assuming the early earth's atmosphere contained CH_4 and NH_3 but no O_2; that assumption was made to support the assumption of chemical evolution, and the scientific evidence contradicts both those assumptions.

Although the reducing atmosphere assumption is still featured in textbooks, television programs, museums, and magazines, research evolutionists (including Miller) have kept the assumption of chemical evolution but switched to new assumptions about the early earth. One "recipe" assumes chemical evolution began with gamma radiation acting on hydrogen cyanide (HCN) and carbon monoxide (CO). Those are all destructive of life today, and water interferes with the process, but faith in evolution remains.

Wrong conditions. Even if chemical evolutionists someday find scientifically reasonable starting materials, they still have a problem with conditions. Miller used an electric spark simulating lightning to put together biological molecules. But, as a good biochemist, Miller knew the same sparks that helped produce amino acids would also break them down — and the breakdown would occur much more easily and rapidly than the buildup. So Miller used a common chemist's trick to keep the reaction moving toward the buildup of amino acids: he siphoned off the amino acid products and trapped them out so the spark that put them together could not tear them apart. Problem: his experiment was supposed to show that no intelligence was needed to promote chemical evolution, yet he had to use his intelligence as a chemist familiar with the law of mass action (or principle of LeChatlier) to protect the products he wanted from chemical destruction.

Wrong results. Even if chemical evolutionists someday find some non-intelligent mechanism to protect amino acids from destruction in an early earth environment, they still must face the most serious problem of all: the kinds of amino acids and biological molecules Miller produced are the *wrong ones*. They would *prevent*, not promote, further steps in chemical evolution.

Miller wanted to make amino acids; he made amino acids. How can that be wrong? For one thing, biological proteins are composed of short (alpha) amino acids with only one C atom between the amine and acid groups. Many of Miller's amino acids were long (beta, gamma, delta), with two, three, four, or more C atoms between the amine and acid. Just one wrong "long" amino acid in a chain could destroy a protein's structure and function — preventing, not promoting, chemical evolution.

Furthermore, as discussed earlier (page 108), chemistry produces amino acids in left- and right-handed forms (optical isomers). Except for some poisons, biologically active proteins incorporate only the left-handed form. A sequence of left-handed amino acids can coil into a helical shape that's vital to protein structure and function. One right-handed amino acid in a chain can twist it in the opposite direction, producing a functionless or even harmful protein. All natural chemical processes, including those in Miller's flask, produce equal numbers of left- and right-handed isomers — the wrong ones to produce life. Miller's so-called primordial soup was really a flask full of *"primordial poisons"* that would destroy any hope for producing life. Indeed, no scientist has ever even tried to use the mix of chemicals from Miller's spark chamber as the basis for the next step in chemical evolution.

Evolutionists are very aware of the problem of handedness (chirality) in amino acids. Applying plan, purpose, and intelligent design, scientists can separate crystals of left- and right-handed amino acids under a microscope. But no one has ever discovered a mechanism in the non-living world that would select left-handed amino acids for making biological proteins. Asked about this problem, a prominent chemical evolutionist smiled, shrugged, and said, "Perhaps God is left-handed." He may have been closer to the truth than he knew; it takes the creative intelligence of human beings to select the proper parts to make a functioning computer, and it seems it

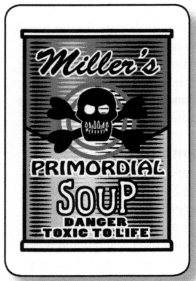

takes superhuman creative intelligence to select the proper parts to make a biologically beneficial proteins. The use of left-handed amino acids in building biological proteins does not seem to be the consequence of the chemical properties of matter, but rather the deliberate choice of a designer selecting materials to achieve a desired goal.

But let's suppose, quite generously, that chemical evolutionists someday offer scientifically plausible hypotheses for the right starting materials and right conditions for making the right amino acids for steps 1 and 2 in chemical evolution. Is there evidence that these could lead to steps 3 and 4, the first functional proteins and "proto-cells"?

Fox's Proteinoids and Microspheres

Admiringly described in textbooks, television programs, museums, and the media are the experiments in which Sidney Fox produced "proteins" under simulated early earth conditions, and then he showed how those molecules could be absorbed into lipid globules that could grow and reproduce. Awesome — except that Fox had the wrong starting materials, used the wrong conditions, and got the wrong results!

Wrong starting materials. You might have thought Fox started with Miller's "primordial soup," but he was too smart for that. He knew Miller's flask was full of all kinds of "poisonous" molecules that would react in life-destructive ways, including those "wrong" long, right-handed amino acids. Instead, Fox began with purified, short, left-handed amino acids he bought from a biological supply company that had extracted them from previously living things! That's an intelligent chemical choice, but it bears no relationship at all to any presumed chemical evolution occurring in a pre-biotic world with no intelligence! Fox was also smart enough to exclude sugars and the many other molecules in "Miller's soup," since these would have botched up the reactions among amino acids that he wanted.

Wrong conditions. In the classic experiment, Fox heated purified, short, left-handed, biologically derived amino acids to 175°C (347°F) in a drying apparatus that kept the humidity at 5 percent or below. Using such conditions, Fox did produce polymers of amino acids, protein-like molecules called *proteinoids*. The conditions were supposed to simulate warm tide pools and hot rocks along the flanks of seaside volcanoes in a lifeless, pre-biotic world. How realistic would 5 percent humidity be in such a setting? When the experiments were done in the presence of water and realistic humidity levels, instead of protein-like molecules only a black, tarry, non-biological gunk was produced.

Wrong results. When the proteinoids produced under dry conditions were mixed into a watery broth later, droplets called *microspheres* or *coacervates* formed. Small droplets could "grow" into big ones by absorbing other proteinoids, and larger droplets could "reproduce" by breaking into two! Is that growth and reproduction so much like that of a living cell that we should call these droplets "proto-cells"? If so, you had better be careful the next time you have a bowl of chicken noodle soup. Those little droplets floating on the top "grow" and "reproduce" just like Fox's microspheres, so they might "evolve" into something that crawls out of the bowl! Of course not!

Without a living membrane to separate helpful and harmful molecules, microspheres, coacervates, or "protocells" would inevitably absorb harmful molecules — and one "bad" one could undo the work of many "good" ones. Droplets that absorb molecules based on chemical properties instead of biological purpose would prevent not promote chemical evolution.

What about the "reproduction" of Fox's droplets? Is the splitting (fission) of droplets atop noodle soup like the fission (asexual reproduction) of an amoeba or a white blood cell? Of course not. The droplets are random collections of molecules, not coordinated interacting sets, and their random breakage produced smaller droplets that are not like each other or their "parent." When a living cell divides, a coordinated set of interacting molecules produces a faithful copy of the code (DNA) for duplicating the whole coordinated set of interacting molecules so the identical split cells can each grow

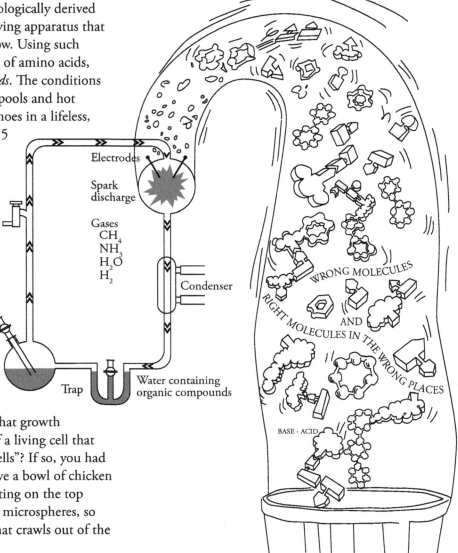

Figure 15.2. Representation of Stanley Miller's spark chamber

into exact copies of their parent — what the Bible calls "multiplication after kind"!

The ability of droplets to fuse, split, and absorb other molecules is a property shared by living and non-living things, not a step in chemical evolution. Although Fox's experiments have been popularized in textbooks and the media, they never earned respect from serious researchers interested in life's origin.

Chemistry and Coordination

Let's be generous and assume that someday evolutionists offer a scientifically possible scenario by which chemicals progress from simple gases through small to large biological molecules to droplets filled with the right molecules for life and none of the wrong ones.

Would mindless matter spontaneously (with no "outside help") turn such droplets into living cells?

We don't have to guess. We know. Where have you seen all the right molecules for life in the right place at the right time, exposed to the energizing rays of the sun? Answer: freshly dead road kill. How many times have you seen chemical reactions bring the dead animal back to life? Billions of cans of sardines each packed with a far greater number of molecules required for life than evolutionists have produced in a century represent billions of tests to see if chemistry can make life. It can't.

Chemistry is not our ancestor; chemistry is our problem. Living cells are *constantly juggling* chemical reactions that build up life against those reactions that tear it down. *Death is the triumph of chemistry over biology.* It takes a lot of cowboys working together to keep a herd of wayward steers moving toward spring pasture; if the cowboys lose control, each steer goes its own way and the herd is lost. It takes a lot of biological control molecules to keep a "herd" of chemicals moving toward "life"; loss of coordination lets each molecule go its own way, and life is lost.

Coordination is the key to life, **not** *chemistry* — *organization*, not *substance*. Imagine a chemical evolutionist could someday produce a cup full of beneficial biological molecules (like you could find in a fresh cup of road kill). They would win a Nobel prize for sure — but be no closer to making life than if they had made a cup of dirt. In fact, chemical processes (the properties of matter) would turn such a cup of biological molecules (or a cup of road kill) into a cup of "dirt," *not* into a living cell — the opposite of evolution.

In the well-known *Scientific American* book *Evolution*, a leading chemical evolutionist, Richard Dickerson, inadvertently seems to support this point. After describing problems (like those discussed above) in producing the right kinds of molecules for living systems, he says that those droplets that by "sheer chance" contained the right molecules survived longer. He continues, "This is not life, but it is getting close to it. The missing ingredient is. . . ."

What will he say here? The "missing ingredient is" . . . one more protein? . . . a little more DNA? . . . an energy supply? . . . the right acid-base balance? No, he says. "The missing ingredient is an orderly mechanism. . ." *An orderly mechanism!* That's what's missing — but that's what life is all about! Life is not a property of *substance*; it's a property of *organization*. The same kind of reasoning applies to the pyramids in Egypt, for example. The pyramids are made of stone, but

studying the stone does not even begin to explain how the pyramids were built. Similarly, until evolutionists begin to explain the origin of the "orderly mechanism," they have not even *begun* to talk about the origin of *life*.

When it comes to the evolutionary origin of that orderly mechanism, Dickerson adds, we have "no laboratory models; hence, one can speculate endlessly, unfettered by inconvenient facts." With "no laboratory models" to provide data, the case for the evolution of life must be based on imagination. But, as Dickerson admits, "We [evolutionists] can only imagine what probably existed, and our imagination so far has not been very helpful."

Notice: *the concept of chemical evolution was never based on science.* It's never been based on anything more than imagination, wishful thinking based on either personal bias or a philosophic preference for explaining the origin of life without any reference to creation or a Creator.

Actually, there is nothing unscientific about *imagination* as a *source* of ideas; many ingenious scientific breakthroughs began as dreams and hunches. If that imagination leads to predictions that can be tested by experiment and repeatable observations, then scientists can help us decide how likely those dreams are to be true. Numerous scientifically testable predictions have been made on the basis of faith in chemical evolution, and scientific tests have disproved or falsified every one of them.

To use the words of the famous researcher quoted above, Dickerson, chemical evolutionists today are left to "speculate endlessly, unfettered by inconvenient facts." As of this writing, there are "no laboratory models," as he said, or any other scientific evidence to encourage faith in chemical evolution. The next chapter will look at the scientific evidence that might encourage faith instead in creation.

Form your foundation.

When chemicals start "doing what comes naturally" in living cells, the result is death. Chemistry is not our ancestor, it's our problem! Natural reactions prevent rather than promote chemical evolution, so "life" was not made by chemicals but imposed on chemicals by God's creative design and organization.

1. The belief that time, chance, and the properties of matter produced life grew out of (**scientific discoveries/ materialistic philosophy**) _____, and the growing belief that chemical evolution occurred way out in space and way back in time ("in a galaxy far, far away long, long ago") is currently based on (**good science/good story telling**) _____. However, belief that chemicals made life through five stages (simple molecules — monomers — polymers — droplets — cells) is firmly supported by all these except (choose one): (**textbooks, television specials, testimonials of famous people, computer graphics, scientific evidence**) _____.

2. Miller's spark chamber has been used since the 1950s to indoctrinate millions of students worldwide that chemicals could make life (**only with/without any**) _____ "outside help" from God or intelligent design.
   (a) What's wrong with his starting materials (CH_4, NH_3, H_2, no O_2)?
   _____
   (b) What's wrong with his conditions (spark and trap)?
   _____
   (c) What's wrong with his results (amino acids)?
   _____

3. Long ago Miller accepted the evidence that his spark chamber experiment (**did/did not**) _____ support chemical evolution. He tried other starting materials and conditions: these also seemed to (**prevent/ promote**) _____ belief that chemicals produced life.

4. Fox heated a mixture of amino acids to 175° C or 357° F and produced protein-like molecules.
   a. Did he start with (choose one): (1) Miller's "primordial soup," or (2) purified, left-handed amino acids extracted from living things? _____
   b. Do the extremely dry and hot conditions he used sound like conditions he claimed to mimic: hot rocks along a seashore? (**yes/no**) _____
   c. Could any of Fox's "proteinoids" take the place of a protein in a living cell, or work in series to build complex molecules like protein enzymes in a cell's metabolic pathways? (**yes/no**) _____

5. When Fox put his "proteinoids" in water, they formed droplets (microspheres, coacervates, or "proto-cells"). Fox's so-called proto-cell droplets (**T or F**)
   _____ a. could keep "good" molecules inside and "bad" molecules outside, much like a living cells do;
   _____ b. could divide like a living cell into two identical daughter cells with the same DNA code;
   _____ c. could fuse, two drops forming one, just like matching egg and sperm cells unite to "multiply after kind;"
   _____ d. actually resemble living cells far, FAR less than they resemble droplets atop noodle soup;
   _____ e. would prevent, not promote chemical evolution by absorbing "wrong" molecules and dividing and fusing at random.

6. A "cup of road kill" or can of sardines has the right molecules in the right place and right amount to form life, but, according to a famed chemical evolutionist, the "missing ingredient" needed to bring "road kill molecules" to life is (choose one: more energy, enzymes, DNA, chance, an orderly mechanism): _____. However, what separates a living cell from a droplet of even biological molecules is NOT substance (material things) but _____, and organization requires thought and goaldirected action, i.e., plan, purpose, and special acts of _____. When molecules start doing "what comes naturally," the result is (**evolution/death**) _____.

Chapter 15

Evidence of Creation?

Science is both a fabulous body of knowledge and a fantastic method of investigation. Most people just assume evolution can be studied scientifically — but not creation. According to a slogan popular these days, "Evolution is science, and creation is religion," and that's supposed to stop the discussion even before it starts.

Question	Is it really possible to talk honestly and fairly about scientific evidence of creation?

For many people, the question above is a major stumbling block. Some even use it as an excuse to throw creation out of the courtroom or classroom without even hearing the evidence. But nothing is really easier for scientists and just "ordinary people" than finding and recognizing evidence of creation.

To illustrate, imagine that you are walking along a creek on a lazy summer afternoon, idly kicking at the pebbles along the bank. Occasionally you reach down to pick up a pebble that has an unusual shape. One pebble reminds you of a ship (Figure 16.1). As you roll the pebble around in your hand, you notice that the softer parts of that lines of wear follow lines of weakness in the rock. Despite some appearance of design, the ship shape of the tumbled pebble is clearly the result of time, chance, and the natural processes of weathering and erosion.

But then your eye spots an arrowhead lying among the pebbles (Figure 16.1). Immediately it stands out as being different. In the arrowhead, chip marks cut through the hard and soft minerals equally, and chip lines go both with and across lines of weakness in the rock. In the arrowhead, we see matter shaped and molded according to a plan that gives the rocky material a special purpose.

Pebble Time and Chance: Properties of Matter	Arrowhead Plan and Purpose: Properties of Organization

Figure 16.1. Could a scientist using only logic and observation conclude one of the objects above was created with plan and purpose? Could you?

You have just done what many people dismiss as impossible. In comparing the pebble and arrowhead, you were easily able to recognize evidence of creation. Creation here is only of human creation, of course. The arrowhead might have been carved by one of my ancestors, a Native American, for example, but the same approach can be used even when we don't know who or what the creative agent might have been.

What does it take to recognize evidence of creation? Just the ordinary tools of science: logic and observation.

Using your knowledge of erosional processes and your observations of hard and soft rock, you were able to distinguish a result of time and chance (the tumbled pebble) from an object created with plan and purpose (the arrowhead). If we had found such objects as arrowheads on Mars, all scientists would have recognized them immediately as the products of creation, even though in that case we would have no idea who made them or how. The late Carl Sagan, the evolutionist of *Cosmos* television fame, spent millions of dollars listening for signals from outer space, because he knew full well that we can tell the difference between wave patterns produced by time and chance and those sent with plan and purpose.

The author was in a friendly mini-debate at a California college when the evolutionist interrupted: "But creation can't be scientific. Science deals only with things you can see and touch. Take gravity, for example. . . ." Then he stopped. "Whoops! Made a mistake, didn't I?" He and his students all knew that there are forms of energy, like gravity, that you can't see or touch or put in a bottle. Yet you know "gravity" is there (whatever it is!) *because you can see the effects it has on matter.* Similarly, God is a Spirit and can't be seen — but you can see His effects on matter. Even the Bible tells us that "Through everything God made, they can clearly see his invisible qualities" (Rom 1:20 NLT).

Note	You don't have to see the Creator and you don't have to see the creative act to recognize evidence of creation.

Even when we don't know who or what the creative agent is, there are cases where "creation" is simply the most logical inference from our scientific observations.

Although the pebble and the arrowhead are made of the same substance, they reflect *two* radically different *kinds of order.* The tumbled pebble has the kind of order that results from *time and chance* operating through natural processes on the *inherent properties of matter.* Those same natural processes (weathering and erosion, here) will eventually destroy not only the pebble, but also the arrowhead, which has the kind of order clearly brought into being by *plan and purpose, mind acting on matter.*

In a way, the tumbled pebble represents the idea of *evolution.* As I once believed and taught, evolutionists believe that life itself is the result, like the tumbled pebble, of *time, chance, and the inherent properties of matter.* The arrowhead represents the creation idea, that living systems have *irreducible properties of organization* that were produced, like the arrowhead, by *plan, purpose, and special acts of creation.*

In our daily experience, all of us can distinguish between these two kinds of order (inherent and "*exherent*"). On the basis of logic and observation, for example, we recognize that wind-worn rock formations are the products of time, chance, and the inherent properties of matter. But those same techniques (logical inference from scientific observations) convince us that pottery fragments and rock carvings (and the presidents' heads on Mount Rushmore) must be the products of plan, purpose, and acts of creation, giving matter *irreducible properties of organization.*

Let's suppose that *"creation" (the paradigm, the process, and the products) can be studied scientifically.* Does that mean creation is true and evolution is false? Not at all! Indeed, there were a couple of teachers at a California university convinced that creationist ideas can be tested scientifically — but they thought that scientific tests proved them false! So we can agree ahead of time that both classic models of origin, creation and evolution can be compared on the basis of scientific merit, but we still have to examine the data to see which concept the bulk of scientific evidence currently available supports.

So let's "reason together" and apply ordinary

scientific techniques to the study of living systems. When it comes to the origin of life, which view is the more logical inference from our scientific observations: time, chance, and the evolution of matter, or plan, purpose, and special acts of creation? *Open and respectful discussion of evidence related to these two concepts is good science and good education* — and a great way to have *two winners* in the creation-evolution debate!

The Origin of Life: DNA and Protein

Used above to illustrate patterns produced by evolution vs. creation, the tumbled pebble and arrowhead were made of two parts — hard and soft rock. Two basic parts of every living system are DNA and protein. Living cells require three other "working parts" discussed earlier (membranes, ATP, and water), but to compare evolution and creation we'll look at just the two most distinctive parts, DNA and protein.

DNA is the famous molecule of heredity. It's a focus of crime scene investigations, and we often hear news stories about it. This is the molecule that gets passed down from one generation to the next. Each of us starts off as a tiny little ball about the size of a period on a printed page. In that tiny ball, there are over six feet (2 m) of DNA all coiled up. All of our physical characteristics (height, skin color, gender, etc.) are "spelled out" in that DNA. DNA "spells" using a four-letter alphabet, GCAT, which represent the four different kinds of DNA bases. Interlocking shapes allow these four bases to form two kinds of base pairs, G-C and A-T, which is the basis of reproduction in DNA and all life (more on that later!). But in coding for protein production, DNA's unpaired base letters act in long sequences, like letters in a sentence.

What are proteins? Proteins are the molecules of structure and function. Hair is mostly protein; skin cells are packed full of proteins; the enzymes that break down food and build it up are proteins; the filaments that slide together to make muscles contract are proteins.

So DNA and protein are two basic "parts" of every living system: DNA for reproduction and proteins for structure and function. When you get down to viruses (to be discussed later), that's all you find — DNA (or RNA) and protein. The DNA molecules code for more DNA and for the protein molecules that make us what we are physically. That same principle applies to all life forms: viruses, bacteria, plants, and animals, as well as human beings.

Fortunately, DNA and protein molecules are really quite simple in their basic structure. If you can picture a string of pearls, you can picture DNA: it is a chain of

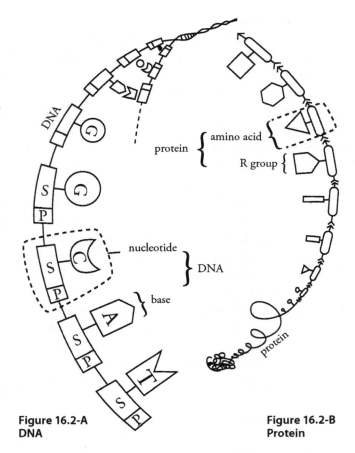

Figure 16.2-A
DNA

Figure 16.2-B
Protein

repeating units (a polymer). Figure 16.2-A is a diagram of a DNA molecule. The parts diagrammed as railroad boxcars are sugar and phosphate groups, and the parts that stick out from each boxcar in the chain are groups called bases.

RNA, the other familiar nucleic acid (NA) also consists of a *sugar-phosphate backbone* holding protruding *bases in a series*. In contrast to DNA, RNA usually (1) is shorter, (2) is single vs. double-stranded, (3) has base U instead of T to pair with A, and (4) contains the sugar ribose instead of deoxyribose, making it RiboNucleic Acid (RNA) instead of DeoxyriboNucleic Acid (DNA).

Like DNA and RNA, proteins are also chains of repeated units (polymers). As shown in Figure 16.2-B, the links in protein chains are called *amino acids*. In all living things, inherited chains of bases are used to line up chains of *amino acids*. These amino acid chains are the protein molecules responsible for structure and function. For example, chains of several hundred inherited DNA bases, acting through RNA, tell the cell how to make a protein called hemoglobin, and that protein functions as the oxygen carrier in red blood cells. There's more to the story, but in short form, *DNA ⇒ protein ⇒ trait*, and that relationship is the physical basis of all life on earth.

How did this life-distinctive relationship between DNA and protein get started? Evolutionists picture a time long ago when the earth might have been quite different. They imagine that fragments of DNA and RNA and fragments of protein are produced. These molecules are supposed to "do what comes naturally" over vast periods of time. What's going to happen? Will time, chance, and chemical reactions between bases in DNA/RNA and amino acids in proteins Rautomatically produce life?

At first, you might think so. After all, nothing is more natural than a reaction between acids and bases. Perhaps you've used soda (a base) to clean acid from a battery. The fizz is an acid-base reaction. So is using Tums to neutralize stomach acid. Nothing is more common than reactions between acids and bases. If you just wait long enough, acid-base reactions will get DNA and protein working together, and life will appear — right? Wrong! Exactly the opposite.

The problem is that the properties of bases and acids produce the *wrong* relationship for living systems. Acid-base reactions would "scramble up" DNA and protein units in all sorts of "deadly" combinations. These reactions would *prevent, not promote,* the use of DNA to code protein production. Since use of DNA to code protein production is the basis of all life on earth, these acid-base reactions would *prevent, not promote,* the evolution of life by chemical processes based on the inherent properties of matter (see Figure 16.3).

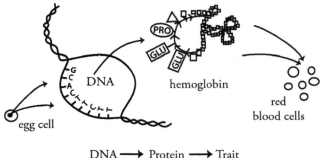

DNA $\longrightarrow$ Protein $\longrightarrow$ Trait

Time and chance are no help to the evolutionist either, since time and chance can only act on inherent chemical properties. *Trying to throw "life" on a roll of molecular dice is like trying to throw a "13" on a pair of gaming dice. It just won't work.* The possibility is not there, so the probability is just plain *zero* — not "nearly zero," but *absolutely zero.*

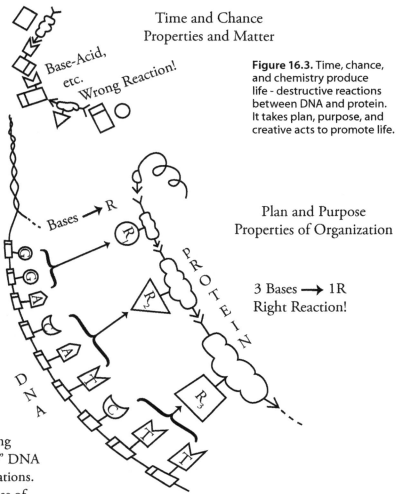

Time and Chance
Properties and Matter

Figure 16.3. Time, chance, and chemistry produce life - destructive reactions between DNA and protein. It takes plan, purpose, and creative acts to promote life.

Plan and Purpose
Properties of Organization

3 Bases $\longrightarrow$ 1R
Right Reaction!

The relationship between DNA and protein required for life is one that no chemist would ever suspect. It's using a series of *bases* (actually taken *three at a time*) to line up a series of *R-groups* (Figure 16.3). R-groups are the parts of each amino acid that "stick out" along the protein chain (like bases stick out along DNA chains). "R" stands for the "variable radical," and variable it is! An R-group can be acid, it can be a base, it can be a single hydrogen atom, a short chain, a long chain, a single ring, a double ring, fat-soluble, or water-soluble!

The point is this: there is no inherent chemical tendency for a series of bases (three at a time) to line up a series of R-groups in the orderly way required for life. The base/R-group relationship has to be *imposed* on matter; it has *no basis within* matter.

The relationship between hard and soft rock in the arrowhead in Figure 16.1 had to be imposed from the outside. All of us could recognize that matter had been shaped and molded according to a design that could not be produced by time, chance, and weathering processes acting on the hard and soft rock involved. In the same way, our *knowledge* of DNA, protein, and their chemical properties should lead us to infer that *life also is the result of plan, purpose, and special acts of creation.*

Consider a simpler example of the same kind of reasoning. Think about this question:

Question	
	Can aluminum fly?

That sounds like a trick question. By itself, of course, aluminum can't fly. Aluminum ore in rock just sits there. A volcano may throw it, but it doesn't fly. If you pour gasoline on it, does that make it fly? If you pour a little rubber on it, that doesn't make it fly, either. But suppose you take that aluminum, stretch it out in a nice long tube with wings, a tail, and a few other parts. Then it flies; we call it an airplane.

Did you ever wonder what makes an airplane fly? Try a few thought experiments. Take the wings off and study them; they don't fly. Take the engines off, study them; they don't fly. Take the pilot out of the cockpit; the pilot doesn't fly. Don't dwell on this the next time you're on

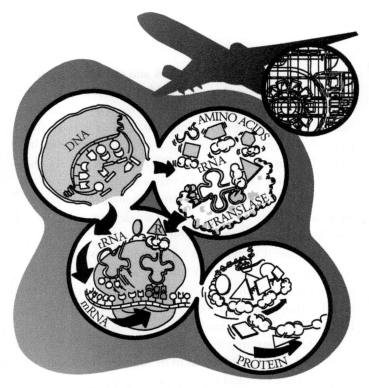

Figure 16.4. The airplane and the cell. It takes many parts working in close harmony to make an airplane fl y, and many molecules working in close harmony to make a cell live!

an airplane, but an airplane is a collection of non-flying parts! Not a single part of it flies!

What does it take to make an airplane fly? The answer is something every scientist can understand and appreciate, something every scientist can work with and use to frame hypotheses and conduct experiments. What does it take to make an airplane fly? *Creative design and organization.*

Take a look at the features of a living cell diagrammed in Figure 16.4. Notice the DNA molecule in the upper left circle and the protein in the lower right. What are all the rest of those strange-looking things diagrammed in the cell? Those represent just a few of the molecules that a cell needs to make just one protein according to the instructions of just one DNA molecule. A cell needs over 75 "helper molecules," all working together in harmony, to make one protein (R-group series) as instructed by one DNA or RNA (base series). A few of these molecules are RNA (messenger, transfer, and ribosomal RNA); most are highly specific proteins.

Contrary to popular impression, DNA does not even possess the genetic code for making protein, but only the genetic *alphabet.* The "alphabet letters" of DNA (the four bases, abbreviated GCAT) are used in groups of three (*triplet codons*) as code names for the 20 different amino acids of proteins. But bases are equally spaced along DNA; there's nothing in the structure or chemistry that even hints why or which bases should be grouped as triplet codons. Three letter groupings are *not inherent in* base sequences; they are *imposed on* the base series by huge cellular particles called *ribosomes.*

Ribosomes don't act directly on DNA, but on expendable "base pair copies" of DNA called messenger RNA, or *mRNA.* The production of mRNA, and more DNA for reproduction, is magnificently profound, but it's a simple consequence of interlocking base shapes and ordinary chemical attraction (mediated by enzymes). The way ribosomes establish the genetic coding system, however, completely transcends the inherent properties of DNA bases.

Ribosomes are "molecular machines" each consisting of about 50 specific proteins and three large RNA molecules (rRNA). Its overall 3-D shape gives a ribosome two adjacent slots each precisely shaped to hold three and only three bases, thus establishing the triplet coding system. This coding system is not based on time, chance, and the properties of the bases, but on plan, purpose, and intelligent design. In the structure of the ribosome, however, as in the arrowhead, nothing supernatural,

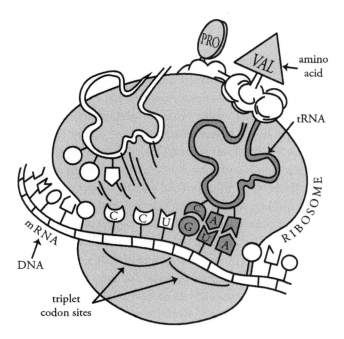

Figure 16.5. DNA and its base copy mRNA have only the genetic "alphabet." The genetic code is created when ribosomes take equally spaced bases and hold them in groups of three to make triplet codon names for amino acid links in protein chains.

amino acids and base triplets are possible, but these would destroy the code. It falls to transfer RNA (*tRNA*) molecules to pick up amino acids and base pair them with their codons in the ribosome slots. The base pairing of tRNA and mRNA triplets is based on interlocking shapes and ordinary chemical attraction (see Figure 16.5), but the proper pairing of tRNAs with amino acids requires *much more* than ordinary chemistry.

When it comes to "translating" DNA's instructions for making proteins, the real "heroes" are the *activating enzymes* that unite specific tRNA/amino acid pairs. Enzymes are proteins with special slots for selecting and holding other molecules for speedy reaction. As shown in Figure 16.6 below, each activating enzyme has five slots: two for chemical coupling (c, d), one (e) for energy (ATP), and, most importantly, two to establish a *non-chemical* three-base "code name" for each different amino acid R-group (a, b). Wow!

The living cell requires at least 20 of these activating enzymes, or aminoacyl synthetases, which might better be called "**translases**." At least one translase, or translating enzyme, is required for each of the specific

complex, or even unusual is involved, and the function of the ribosome is easy to understand and explain. In both the ribosome and the arrowhead, the *evidence of creation is not in what we can't see and don't know*; it's in the pattern of order (exherent) that *we do see and can explain*: matter shaped and molded to accomplish the purpose of its Creator, not to satisfy inherent chemical properties of the molecules involved.

Besides the above, the ribosomes that establish the amino acid code names for making proteins are themselves made of 50 or more specific proteins. *It takes specific proteins to establish the code for making specific proteins*, so how did the system get started? Evolutionists admit that's a problem for them because they insist evolution based on time, chance, and the properties of matter is a blind process that can't plan ahead or work toward a goal. On the other hand, creationists see the goal-oriented function of ribosomes as another evidence of creation. As batteries can be used to start car engines that then recharge the batteries, so proteins can be used to code for the production of proteins that can then "recharge" the coding proteins.

And there's more. Even after ribosomes establish triplet codon names for amino acids, the *protein building blocks (amino acids) have no chemical way to recognize their code names!* All sorts of wrong chemical reactions between

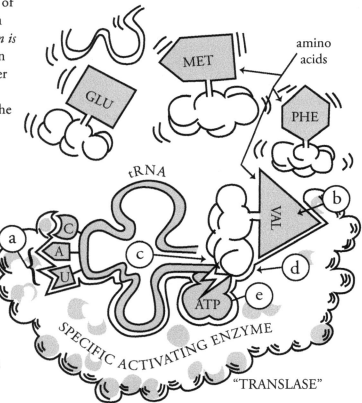

Figure 16.6. "Translases," activating enzymes that unite each amino acid with the tRNA carrying its proper triplet codon name, are the "heroes" that "translate" the DNA "base language" of heredity into the protein "R-group language" of structure and function.

R-group/base triplet code name (amino acid/tRNA) pairs. Even so, the whole set of translases (100 specific active sites) would be:

Worthless	without ribosomes (50 proteins plus rRNA) to break the base alphabet of heredity into three-letter code names;
Destructive	without a continuously renewed supply of ATP energy to keep the translases from tearing up the pairs they are supposed to form;
Vanishing	if it weren't for having translases and other specific proteins to remake the translase proteins that are continuously and rapidly wearing out because of the destructive effects of time and chance and water bombardment on protein structure!

Most enzymes are proteins that select and speed up chemical reactions that would occur slowly without them. Translases are an entirely *different category of enzymes*. They impose a relationship that transcends the chemistry of base triplets and amino acids, *a code that would not occur at all, slowly or otherwise, in their absence.*

When experimenters mixed amino acids with tRNAs, evolutionists hoped that chemical properties would spontaneously attract each amino acid to the tRNA bearing its code name. The results crushed their dreams of chemical evolution. Lots of reactions occurred between amino acids and tRNAs, but all these natural chemical reactions were *destructive* of the genetic code.

It's NOT that direct supernatural intervention is required to put together each specific amino acid-tRNA pair. What's required is a coordinated

set of "herding molecules" to keep other molecules moving toward a goal — a goal that the individual molecules on the "assembly line" have no "chemical desire" to reach. By analogy, no supernatural intervention is required to use a pencil to write on paper. But graphite (lead), wood, and rubber have no "natural desire" to shape themselves into a writing instrument — and writing a sentence like "In God we trust" is not a goal toward which graphite, wood, and rubber are striving! The supernatural creativity is NOT found in the way tRNAs and amino acids combine, nor in the way pencils make marks on paper; the creativity is *found* in the *organization* that put the parts together (either translases to combine tRNA-amino acid pairs or pencils) to accomplish a goal that transcends (a different dimension that goes far beyond) the natural tendencies of the individual parts.

The parts of a pencil work together to accomplish the purpose of its human creator, *not* the goals of graphite, wood, or rubber. The parts of a living cell work together to accomplish the purpose of its super-human Creator, not the chemical goals of tRNAs and amino acids. In the *non-living* world, chemical reactions wear things down until little or no further change occurs. In the *living* world, chemical reactions are channeled into building things up and promoting continuous growth and reproduction. The difference between "death" and life is not chemistry, it's creative design!

Form your foundation.

All it takes to recognize evidence of creation are the ordinary tools of science: logic and observation. Even if the creative agent or creative act is not directly observed, certain kinds of order imply plan, purpose, and special acts of creation so clearly that people are "without excuse" for not seeing it (Romans 1:18–20).

Which of these shows scientific evidence of creation?

1. The popular slogan "Evolution is science; creation is faith" is (**obviously the absolute truth/nearly exactly the opposite of the truth**) _____ and is meant to (**start/stop**) _____ discussion of scientific evidence.

2. Without seeing either the creator or the creative act, is there any way a scientist could tell whether an object were produced by time and chance or plan and purpose? Explain.
   _____
   _____

3. From viruses to people, living systems have _____ molecules for heredity and _____ for structure and function. Proteins are long chains of _____ and DNAs are long chains of _____ (GCAT) strung out along sugar-phosphate (SP) backbones. Darwin's followers hoped the natural reaction between acids and bases could produce life, but natural base-acid reactions would (**create/destroy**) _____ the genetic code and (**prevent/promote**) _____ chemical evolution.

4. DNA's genetic code uses (how many?) _____ of its GCAT bases to code for one of a protein's amino acids. All amino acids have the (**same/different**) _____ amine (-NH$_2$) and acid (-COOH) groups, so the DNA triplet codon specifically identifies the _____-group that makes each amino acid unique. But an R-group can be almost anything chemically (base or acid, short or long, single or double ring, etc.). There are (**lots of/absolutely no**) _____chemical reasons for a series of bases (taken 3 at a time) to line up a series of R-groups, so throwing "life" by chance is like trying to throw a (**6, 12, 13**) _____ on a pair of dice—the possibility is not there, so the chance is (**nearly zero/absolutely 0**) _____ and "zillions" of years make the chance (**much better/still absolutely zero**) _____. What we know about the laws of chemistry suggests life was (**made by/imposed on**) _____ matter by (**time, chance, and evolution/plan, purpose, and special acts of creation**) _____.

5. DNA and RNA both have the "genetic alphabet letters" (GCAT or GCAU), but (**neither/both**) _____ has the genetic code. The three letter code names for amino acid R-groups (**are/are NOT**) _____ found within the equally spaced bases of DNA or RNA; they are imposed on base sequences by large cellular particles called _____, each composed of 50 or so proteins and 3 huge ribosomal RNA (rRNA) molecules. Since it takes specific proteins to make the code to make specific proteins, which came first? (**time, chance, and evolution/plan, purpose, and God**) _____.

6. Which kind of RNA molecule brings the correct amino acid to its ribosomal coding slot? (**mRNA/rRNA/tRNA**) _____. What *astonishing molecule* — one that "translates" DNA "base language" and protein "R-group language" — is *absolutely required* to unite the tRNA having the proper triplet base code with the amino acid having the corresponding R-group? _____.
   Each of the sets of at least 20 *amazing* five-site "*translase*" enzymes has three chemical sites that, by themselves, would unite any amino acid with any tRNA, thus (**encouraging development of/absolutely destroying**) _____ the genetic code and (**preventing/promoting**) _____ chemical evolution. The other two sites on each "translase" impose a non-chemical coding relationship between the _____ of amino acids and the _____ of tRNAs, two groups that (**never/naturally**) _____ unite directly and their direct chemical union would (**evolve/destroy**) _____ the code.

7. If you saw a grocery list written in pencil on paper, would you assume the coded information (grocery list) (a) evolved by chance over millions of years due to the natural chemical attraction of pencil lead (graphite) and paper, or (b) was written with a purpose? ____ Is it more scientifically logical to conslude the DNA protein coding system (**evolved/was created**) _____?

Chapter
16

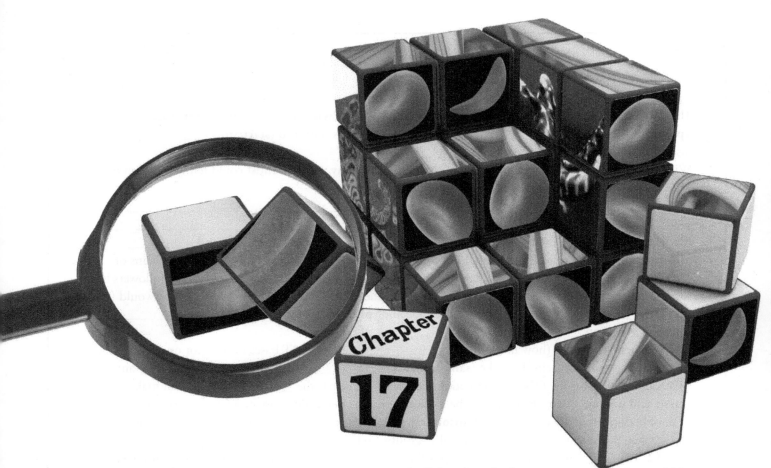

Origin and Operation:
God as Creator and Sustainer

Once the transcendent Creator organized the parts of the DNA-protein translation system into a coordinated whole, living cells use DNA base sequences to crank out proteins in ways scientists can describe quite well. Living cells *originated* by special, completed, supernatural acts in the past, but they *operate* by ordinary, continuous, natural processes in the present. God's power is clearly seen in *both* the *origin* and *operation* of living systems. The completed, supernatural acts in the past that brought into being the DNA-protein coding relationship in the first place (origin) reveal God's power as Creator; the continuing, "*natural*" (*repeating*) acts in the present by which cells use DNA's code to make protein (operation) reveal God as *Sustainer*, the One who daily faithfully takes care of what He created. Colossians 1:17 refers to Christ's work as Sustainer in these words: "In Him all things hold together" (NIV).

You may have heard the expression "The devil's in the details," which means nice-looking plans can get really messy when you try to work them out in practice. In living things, the opposite is true: God is in the details. The closer we look at man's handiwork, the more mistakes and sloppy craftsmanship we see; the closer we look

at God's handiwork, the more marvels and incredible precision we see! Some use "god" to explain the things scientists can't yet explain, but that false "god" just grows smaller with each new discovery. *The true God of the Bible is the One who is clearly seen in all the things He made* (see Rom 1:20). As the DVD *God of Wonders* stunningly illustrates, our appreciation of our awesome "God of wonders" only grows and deepens with each new detail discovered of His incredible ingenuity. It's not the things we don't know and can't explain that point to God; it's the things we *do know* and *can explain* that point to Jesus Christ, the Author of life, as both Creator and Sustainer.

We know a lot, for example, about how DNA information is used by living cells to make proteins. The laws of chemistry themselves tell us that something much more than chemistry is involved — creative design producing properties of organization that add purpose and direction to the properties of matter.

Consider, for example, how certain cells make hemoglobin (Hb), the protein that carries O_2 in the red blood cell (rbc). Human adult hemoglobin (Hb^A) consists of nearly 600 amino acids in two composite chains of nearly 300 amino acids each. Since *each* amino acid has a triplet codon name of *three* DNA bases, each of the two chains in the hemoglobin DNA has about 900 bases (300 x 3) in its coding sequence, and it has numerous other bases serving as start/stop signals and for on/off regulatory information. Let's follow the process whereby just nine DNA bases (three triplet codons) direct placement of just three of the 287 amino acids in half an Hb molecule.

In normal hemoglobin (Hb^A) amino acids numbers . . . 5-6-7 . . . of the beta chain are . . . proline-glutamic acid-glutamic acid . . . abbreviated as . . . pro-glu-glu. (Specific amino acids are often represented by three letters from their chemical names.) In the hemoglobin (Hb^S) associated with the blood disease sickle-cell anemia, amino acid number 6 is valine instead of glutamic acid, so the corresponding sequence is . . . pro-val-glu.

Obviously, the "translation" of a DNA base series into a protein amino acid series must be done with great attention to detail. A difference in one DNA letter out of nearly 900 can produce a difference in one amino acid out of nearly 300 in half a hemoglobin protein — and that tiny difference in one of the body's 30,000 proteins encoded by DNA can mean the difference between normal health and early death from a debilitating blood disease, sickle cell anemia.

Scientists have done a terrific job discovering the precise steps by which living cells use inherited DNA

information to make proteins for structure and function. To use a DNA *base series* to link up an *amino acid series* to form a protein like hemoglobin, for example, a living cell goes through seven major steps. As you read the summary of each step, follow the numbered steps in DNA ⇒ protein translation as diagrammed below (Figure 17.1).

1. **DNA.** Unlock the DNA base series (gene) for making a protein, here sickle-cell hemoglobin (Hb^S).
2. **mRNA.** Make messenger RNA (mRNA) as a "base copy" of DNA.
3. **Ribosome #1.** Use ribosomes (rRNA + proteins) first as *coding sites* to group mRNA bases as triplet codon "names" for amino acids.
4. **tRNA.** Let tRNA lock amino acids into place along mRNA (codon-anticodon base pairing).
5. **"Translase."** Let translase enzymes "translate" *DNA language* into *protein language* by pairing tRNAs having unique codons with amino acids having unique R-groups.
6. **Ribosome #2.** Use ribosomes secondly as linking sites with energy and enzymes to link amino acids.
7. **Protein.** Ribosomes "read" down mRNA, producing a protein like hemoglobin in about three minutes!

To keep the "big picture" of DNA-protein/translation in mind, refer to Figure 17.1 as needed. Now let's examine some of those seven steps in detail. We'll look for — and find — that indeed "God is in the details," God as both Creator and Sustainer.

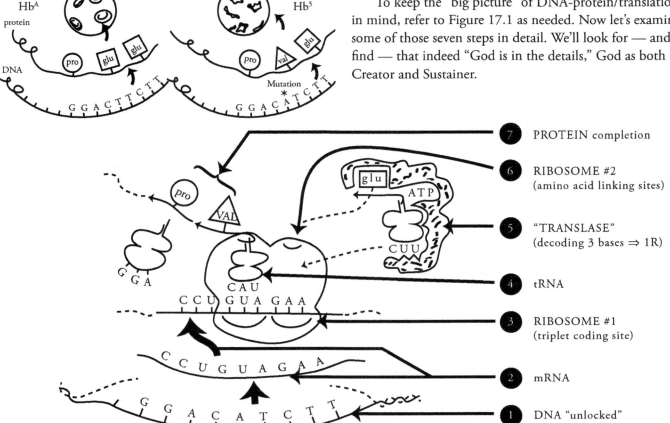

Figure 17.1 Summary of DNA ⇒ protein translation

(1) *Unlocking DNA.* When two strands of DNA are base paired to form a double helix, the DNA is protected from water bombardment and other dangers, but it's "locked" and its message is "turned off." Hormones and other factors can unlock or open up sections of the helix, and the DNA base sequence (gene) coding for hemoglobin production is "turned on" in bone marrow and other blood-forming tissues.

(2) *Making mRNA.* After appropriate regulatory factors open up the DNA double helix (unpair the two strands), the Hb gene makes a base-pair copy of itself called messenger RNA (mRNA). Both the reproduction of DNA (*replication*) and DNA's production of mRNA (*transcription*) are based in the *interlocking shapes of bases*, G-C and A-T (DNA) or A-U (RNA), a simple — but profound — bit of Nobel prize–winning chemistry

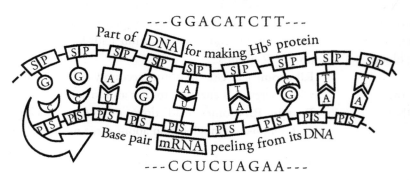

discovered with cardboard cutouts of base shapes!

Given the incredibly precise shapes and electric charges of DNA and RNA bases, their pairing results from natural chemical attraction. But pairing *also requires* an ample supply of unpaired and unlinked nucleotides (base-sugar-phosphate) units, and an abundant supply of energy! Although the pairing itself does not require protein enzymes, enzymes *are* required to link the nucleotides into polymers *and* to make the pairing process go faster than the tendency of water molecules to break nucleotide chains apart! Making mRNA also requires a stockpile of complex and highly energized RNA nucleotides — and a protein enzyme "machine" (RNA polymerase) to select RNA rather than DNA nucleotides for the pairing.

(3, 4) *Ribosomes, tRNA, and triplet base codes.* The manufacture of mRNA from DNA (*transcription*) just substitutes one base series (mRNA) for another (DNA), and brings us no closer to converting base series information into an amino acid series (a protein). Making mRNA has no de-coding or translation value, but it does have tremendous value in protecting DNA

for future generations. Coiled up as a base-paired double helix, DNA is quite resistant to destruction by water and chemical attack. The mRNA it makes is usually broken down or destroyed after perhaps a dozen uses.

Like DNA, mRNA possesses only the genetic alphabet, not the genetic code. The coding begins when mRNA is threaded into the ribosome, which acts as if it "knows" which end of the mRNA to begin "reading." As the ribosome "reads" down the mRNA, mRNA bases move through ribosome slots (the A and P sites) each with the right shape to hold three bases as the triplet code name for an amino acid. Each amino acid in sequence is locked into place along the ribosome-bound mRNA by its *tRNA.*

The tRNA with the three-base "anti-codon" GGA locks proline (pro) into place at mRNA codon position #5 (CCU), and that's true for both Hb^A and Hb^S. The codons at mRNA position #6 differ for normal adult and sickle-cell hemoglobin (GAA vs. GUA), so the interlocking tRNA anticodons are also different (CUU vs. CAU), as are the amino acids (glu vs. val). See Figure 17.1.

The pairing of mRNA and tRNA triplets is based on interlocking shapes and *ordinary* (God as Sustainer) chemical attraction. The pairing of tRNA with amino acids, however, requires something *much more than ordinary chemistry* (God as Creator)! Obviously, the amino acid cannot pair directly with its three base tRNA anti-codon, since that would block tRNA-mRNA pairing. Actually, tRNA molecules include about 70–90 bases, only three of which are the anti-codon triplet bases. Each tRNA is shaped like a three-leafed clover (Figure 17.1). The coding base triplet is on one "leaf," but the acid group of an amino acid molecule chemically combines with the sugar of the last nucleotide at the "stem" tip. All tRNA stem tips end with the A nucleotide, and all amino acids have the same acid group, so any amino acid can combine chemically with any tRNA — and that *natural* chemistry would absolutely *prevent or destroy* any genetic coding.

(5) *Translases!* "Natural" base pairing helps DNA to make mRNA and to bond mRNA with tRNA. But interlocking base shapes are completely unable to relate base sequences (the "language" of DNA and RNA) to amino acid R-group sequences (the "language" of proteins).

That's where those "hero activating enzymes," the *translases,* save the day! It's *translases and only translases* that establish the relationship between three distinctive coding bases (the tRNA anti-codon triplet) and a specific amino acid distinguished by its R group (Figure 17.1). As described earlier, each translase is a huge protein with five specially shaped active sites. Three of the active sites promote only ordinary chemical reactions that occur in the same way for all tRNA-amino acid pairs: (1) a sugar site on the stem tip adenine nucleotide that combines for chemical reasons with (2) the acid of an amino acid with the help of (3) energy supplied by ATP or its equivalent. This is complex, but it's just chemistry and does no coding (see below).

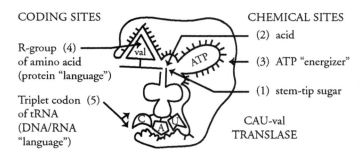

CODING SITES

R-group (4) of amino acid (protein "language")

Triplet codon (5) of tRNA (DNA/RNA "language")

CHEMICAL SITES

(2) acid

(3) ATP "energizer"

(1) stem-tip sugar

CAU-val TRANSLASE

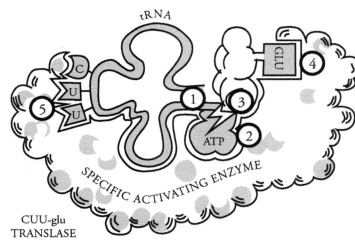

tRNA

SPECIFIC ACTIVATING ENZYME

CUU-glu TRANSLASE

Although required in the overall plan for DNA-protein translation, enzymes with only the three chemical sites above would combine any amino acid with any group of bases. For coding, sites 4 and 5 are needed to recognize (4) the R-group that makes each kind of amino acid different from all others, and (5) the tRNA triplet base group (anti-codon) coding for that particular amino acid. As diagrammed for *CUU-glu translase* and *CAU-val translase*, this awesomely fantastic genetic coding relationship that's so absolutely essential for all life on earth is just based on matching shapes! (See above.)

There is certainly *nothing mysterious, hard to understand*, or "*supernatural*" in how matching shapes lock together. Yet the way each translase forms a specific

tRNA-amino acid pair provides *direct and powerful scientific earth is a product of plan, purpose, and special acts of creation* (not chemical evolution)!

The interlocking base shapes that pair mRNA codons with tRNA anti-codons provide no such evidence of creation. Why not? What's the difference? *Base triplets of tRNA pair with mRNA triplets **because of** natural chemical forces* (+ and – charges) that attract and hold matching shapes together. *Base triplets of tRNA are paired with specific amino acid R-groups **in spite of** natural chemical forces* that attract and hold tRNAs and amino acids in all sorts of random, non-coding, life-destroying ways!

Imagine a plate with several small bar magnets scattered at random on it. Shake the plate, and the attracting N and S poles line up the magnets spontaneously, an "inherent" pattern of order based on each magnet "doing what comes naturally." That's the kind of order we see reflected in the pairing of tRNA and mRNA triplets.

Now, chew on a peppermint candy cane (in your imagination, not your mouth) and spit the sticky pieces of various sizes and shapes onto a plate with little bar magnets numbered from 1 to 20. Shake. Is there a natural tendency for sticky peppermint pieces with a certain shape to attach to bar magnets with a certain number . . . and for those magnets to line up in order from 1 to 20 with the correct peppermint piece? Of course not. What if we shake and shake again for millions and billions of years — will that produce the desired order? Of course not. In fact, *more time and more shaking (chance) makes matters worse*, not better. Some of the sticky candy pieces will stick to the N and S poles of the magnet, so the magnets can never line up properly ever again, and some of the candy pieces will stick to each other, making new sizes and shapes that eliminate the sizes and shapes needed! Time, chance, and random energy may "create," but they *create chaos*, destroying all hope of desired order, just as biological order is lost and death results when molecules start "doing their own thing," behaving naturally instead of acting as a coordinated set or part of a team.

Is there any way to use magnets to line up sticky candy pieces in a precise and repeatable order? Of course there is. Decide which candy shape should go with each numbered magnet; use tweezers to attach each sticky candy piece to the magnet with its code number; then line up the magnets so they will spontaneously join N-S poles in the proper sequence! You can repeat the process millions and billions of times and always get the same ordered result. Was the sticky property of the candy pieces used? Yes. Was the property of N-S magnetic attraction used? Yes. Was it the natural properties of stickiness and magnetic attraction that produced the ordered arrangement of magnets by number and candy pieces by size and shape? NO!

The properties of matter (stickiness and magnetism) were used, but the *order* was determined by plan, purpose, and special creative acts. It was by design to accomplish a purpose that different numbers were assigned to magnets that were otherwise alike. It was by design to accomplish the *designer's purpose* that different pieces of candy were assigned a code number *in spite of* the natural tendency of any candy to stick to any magnet in lots of wrong places.

But the designer needs more than a plan; to accomplish the purpose, the designer also needs tools to put the plan into action. When God designed the genetic code for living systems, He apparently decided to use triplets of DNA and RNA bases as code names for the amino acids in proteins. To implement His plan, God "invented" molecular machines (ribosomes) to break up the equally spaced bases of mRNA into proper groups of three and to "read" them in proper sequence from start to stop signals. To pair up tRNA and mRNA triplets for protein production (and to pair DNA bases for reproduction), God used the natural chemical attraction of interlocking base shapes (analogous to the natural attraction of N and S poles in magnets). Natural chemical attraction, however, would produce a host of catastrophic and code-destructive reactions between and among amino acids and tRNAs. So God "invented" five-site protein activating enzymes (translases) to unite each amino acid with the tRNA bearing its code name. In the magnet/candy analogy, the tweezers acted as translases, but in "real life" (literally) the reaction is so precise that each of the 20 different tRNA-amino acid combinations needs its own special tweezers or translase!

(6, 7) *Ribosomal linkage and protein completion.* Once the plan was designed and the tools created, living cells could use DNA to dictate protein production over and over again, in ways scientists have been able to describe in great detail. We left our hemoglobin example with amino acid numbers 5 and 6 attached to their tRNAs by their translases, then locked into place on the ribosome by base pairing of tRNA and mRNA triplets (Figure 17.1). When two amino acids are positioned side by side, enzymes and energy molecules on the ribosome linking sites separate one amino acid from its tRNA and then attach it to the next amino acid in the sequence. In our example, the

ribosome making Hb^A separates glu from its CUU-tRNA and attaches it to the pro amino acid, and the ribosome reading Hb^S mRNA joins val to pro. The growing protein in either case now has one more of the ultimately nearly 300 amino acids linked in one of two compound chains that together form the hemoglobin molecule.

Once the ribosome reading Hb^S mRNA has linked val to pro, it releases the pro-tRNA for re-use later on. Then it moves the val-tRNA into the forward of the two slots (A and P) holding mRNA codons. That motion brings the mRNA codon for glu, GAA, into the open site. The proper translase has already linked glu to the tRNA with anticodon CUU. The mRNA/tRNA triplets pair GAA with CUU, bringing glu amino acid into position on the ribosome behind val. Enzymes and energy molecules on the ribosome separate val from its tRNA and link it to glu, thus lengthening the growing protein from 6 to 7 links. The same process occurs in the ribosome reading the mRNA for Hb^A, except the amino acids linked at positions . . . 5-6-7 . . . are . . . pro-glu-glu.

Incredibly, the machinery of the living cell is so awesomely well designed that ribosomes can read mRNA and join the right amino acids in the right sequence at a rate of about two per second, completing the average protein in about three minutes! Wow! A sunset reflects God's artistry; DNA-protein translation illustrates His utterly awesome scientific and engineering design skills — and we've only looked at linking three amino acids in one of the human body's 30,000 proteins! Imagine the *intelligence* and *handiwork* involved in creating cooperating sets of DNA and proteins in cells of the eye or brain! God is indeed in the details, both as Creator and Sustainer. It's no wonder politically correct evolutionists don't want students to be allowed to ask questions about evolutionary beliefs!

Form your foundation.

It takes ribosomes with 50 specifics proteins to impose the protein coding system (three bases per amino acid) on a series of equally spaced bases, and it takes at least 20 fantastic five-site "translase" protein enzymes to pair each amino acid (R-group) with its proper tRNA triplet ("anticodon"). This goal-oriented process with complex prerequisites points to creation so clearly that evolutionists are left to "speculate endlessly, unfettered by inconvenient facts," a blind faith contradicted by science.

1. Looking at the operation of DNA protein translation in detail may provide clues to life's origin: Did the molecules put themselves together by time, chance, and natural chemical reactions, as (**creationists/ evolutionists**) _____ suggest, or were they organized by a plan giving them a coding purpose beyond anything chemicals can produce, as suggested by (**creationists/evolutionists**) _____?

   GGA-pro (proline)   **CAT-val (valine)**   **CTT-glu (glutamic acid)**

2. Above are DNA triplet code names for amino acids pro, val, and glu (each abbreviated by three letters from its chemical name). What DNA base sequence would code for pro-glu-glu, the amino acids at positions 5-6-7 in normal hemoglobin (Hb^A)? _____. What series of amino acids would be found in those positions in sickle-cell hemoglobin (HBS) produced by the mutant DNA sequence GGACATCTT? _____.

3. DNA bases have interlocking shapes forming base pairs G-C and __-__. In RNA, U pairs like T, so interlocking DNA-RNA bases are G-C and __-__. DNA makes "messenger RNA" (mRNA) by DNA-RNA base-pairing, so the DNA for HbA (GGACTTCTT) would make mRNA sequence _____; the DNA for disease-causing HBS (GGACATCTT) would make mRNA sequence _____.

4. Since the bases of both DNA and RNA are equally spaced, the triplet base coding system (**does/does not**) _____ come from natural chemical spacing. Coding is imposed on mRNA by _____, huge particles that have two sites side-by-side, each exactly the right size and shape to hold three and only three bases. Ribosomes include 50 specific proteins, meaning it takes specific _____ to establish the code for making specific _____—and that requires the goal-oriented planning ahead expected by (**creationists/evolutionists**) _____.

5. Amino acids are brought to their ribosome-bound triplet codons by _____. Triplet "anticodons" of tRNA unite with mRNA codons by _____, a natural chemical reaction based on interlocking base shapes. But tRNA (**can/cannot**) _____ pick up the amino acid matching its triplet anti-codon without the help of "code cracking" DNA/protein (base/R) protein "translating enzymes" called _____.

6. At right is the five-site activating enzyme or "*translase*" that unites glutamic amino acids having a "square" R-group (in this diagram!) with the clover-leaf-shaped tRNA having anti-codon CUU (for real!). The enzyme uses ATP energy (site #___) to pair the "stem tip" sugar of tRNA (site #___) with the acid part of the amino acid (site #___). (Use this diagram for #7 below also.)

7. These three sites are (**the same/different**) _____ for every tRNA-amino acid pair, and the natural chemical reactions they promote would, by themselves, (**establish/destroy**) _____ the genetic code. Coding depends on relating the CUU anti-codon of tRNA (site #___) to the (square here) R-group for the amino acid glu (site #___), but these coding sites (**naturally pair up/never touch**)_____, and if they did, their direct pairing would (**create/destroy**)_____ the genetic code. Most protein enzymes "just" speed up selected chemical reactions, but translase enzymes impose a coding relationship that, (**like/unlike**) _____ base pairing, has (**a simple/absolutely no**) _____ basis in natural chemical attraction. Furthermore, each tRNA/amino acid (triplet/R-group) pair uses (**the same/a different**) _____ translase, so using base sequences to line up amino acids requires (**only one/ at least 20**) _____ translase proteins and another 50 proteins in ribosomes to encode mRNA, i.e., it takes at least 70 highly specific, multi-site proteins to enable a cell to use one base sequence to make one protein, no problem for (**natural chemical reactions/goal-oriented plan and purpose**) _____ _____, starkly clear evidence that "(**the devil/God**) _____ is in the details" and life is the result of (**creation/evolution**) _____, a gift of _____ life.

8. The DNA-protein coding plan was established by completed, "supernatural" (non-repeating) acts in the past, evidence that God is (**Creator/Sustainer**) _____; details of the continuing, "natural" (repeating) process of DNA-protein translasion shows God as _____.

Chapter
17

"Transcendent Simplicity" and "Kind of Order"

Let's forget about all the complexity of the DNA-protein relationship and just remember two simple points. First, it takes *specific* proteins to make *specific* proteins. That may remind you of the chicken-and-egg problem: how can you get one without the other? That problem is solved if the molecules needed for "DNA-protein translation" are produced by purpose-driven creation.

Second, among all the molecules that translate DNA information into protein, there's not one molecule that's alive. There's not a single molecule in your body that's alive. There's not a single molecule in the living cell that's alive. A living cell is a collection of non-living molecules! What does it take to make a living cell alive? The answer is something every scientist recognizes and uses in a laboratory, something every scientist can logically infer from his observations of DNA and protein.

Creative design and organization!

Only creative acts could organize matter into the first living cells, *but once all the parts are in place, there is nothing "supernatural" or "mysterious" in the way cells make proteins.* If they are continually supplied with the right kind of energy and raw materials, and *if* all 75-plus of the RNA and protein molecules required for DNA-protein "translation" are present in the *right* places at the *right* times in the *right* amounts with the *right* structure, *then* cells make proteins by using coding programmed (created) into DNA's base series.

Scientists also understand how airplanes fly. For that very reason, no scientist believes that airplanes are the result of time, chance, and the properties of aluminum and other materials that make up the airplane. *Flying is a property of organization, not of substance.* A Boeing 747, for example, is a collection of over 4 million non-flying parts, but thanks to design and creation (and a pilot and a continuous supply of energy and of repair services!), it flies.

Similarly, life is a property of *organization*, not of *substance*. A living cell is a collection of several billion non-living molecules, and death results when a shortage of energy or a flaw in the operational or repair mechanisms allows inherent chemical processes to destroy its biological order.

It's what we *do know* and *can explain* about aluminum and the laws of physics that would convince us that airplanes are the products of creation, even if we never saw the acts of creation. In the same way, it's what we *do know* and *can explain* about DNA and protein and the laws of chemistry that suggests that *life itself is the result of special creation*.

The point is not based on probability or design *per se*, but on the *kind of design* we observe. As creationists point out, some kinds of design, such as snowflakes and wind-worn rock formations, *do* result from time and chance — *given* the properties of the materials involved. Even complex relationships, such as the oxygen-carbon dioxide balance in a sealed aquarium, can result from organisms "doing what comes naturally," *given* the properties of living things. But just as clearly, other kinds of design, for example, *arrowheads and airplanes*, are the direct result of *creative design and organization* giving matter properties it doesn't have and can't develop on its own. What we know about the DNA-protein relationship suggests that living cells have the *created kind* of design. It's not so much the molecular complexity as it is the *transcendent simplicity*.

Created origin is based on *logical inference* from our *scientific observations*, and on simple acknowledgment that everyone, scientists and laymen alike, realizes that certain kinds of order imply creation. Consider another example of the same sort of reasoning. Imagine that you have just finished reading a fabulous novel. Wanting to read another book like it, you exclaim to a friend, "Wow! That was quite a book. I wonder where I can get a bottle of that ink?" Of course you wouldn't say that! You wouldn't give the ink and paper credit for writing the book. You'd praise the author and look for another book by the same writer. By some twist of logic, though, many who read the fabulous DNA script want to give credit to the "ink" (DNA base code) and the "paper" (proteins) for composing the code of life.

In a novel, the ink and paper are merely the means the author uses to express his or her thoughts. In the genetic code, the DNA bases and proteins are merely the means God uses to express His thoughts. The real credit for the message in a novel goes to the author, not the ink and paper, and the real credit for the genetic message in DNA goes to the Author of life, Christ the Creator, not to the creature (Rom. 1:25).

The message conveyed by DNA is the kind called *specified complexity* in contrast to randomness or to "mere" order. It takes only a simple program or algorithm, for example, to generate a random sequence of letters: (1) print any letter; (2) repeat step 1. An ordered, repeat pattern, such as ABCABCABC, could be generated by an algorithm nearly as simple: (1) print ABC; (2) repeat step 1. A program ENORMOUSLY larger and more sophisticated would be required to specify, for example, the letter sequence in the first volume of an encyclopedia set! The letter sequence is complex and specific (specified complexity), like the base letter sequence in human DNA — except that the DNA contains more information than a thousand volumes of literary works!

Occasionally, naïve evolutionists argue that crystal formation demonstrates that order can appear spontaneously, without "supernatural" help. *Crystal order, yes; specified complexity, no.* A crystal is a beautiful but simple repeat pattern produced by the shape and charge of it constituents. At 32° F (0° C), for example, the areas of partial plus and minus charges on water molecules attract them with a force greater than the thermal motion that keeps them apart at higher temperatures. The exquisite shape of the ice crystal is an automatic, natural consequence of the shape and charge distribution (*design features*) of the water molecules. (Incidentally, ice crystal formation is driven by decreasing electrostatic potential, an illustration — not a contradiction — of the famed second law of thermodynamics.)

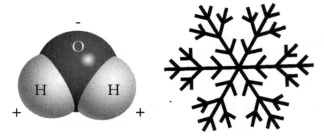

The "specified complexity" in a DNA sequence is nothing like the "ordered simplicity" or repeat pattern in the ice crystal. Breaking a big ice crystal produces little ice crystals, each with structures and properties like the original. Breaking a DNA chain produces fragments that are dissimilar in structure and lose their function entirely. A child at home can make ice crystals; it takes a team of chemists using expensive equipment to produce a specific DNA sequence from scratch.

The specified complexity in a DNA gene sequence has very *high information content*. Scientists know two things about information. First, *information is independent of the material that carries it*. Our national motto, "In God we trust," can be written in pen or pencil, typed onto paper or a computer screen, embroidered in lace, etched in stone, impressed on American coins, etc. The message is the same in any case, and it is obviously not produced by the material that conveys it. In other words, informational messages — including genetic messages — have the "exherent" kind of design, reflecting plan, purpose, and special acts of creation. Thus, *the meaning of a message lies with its creator, not its carrier*.

Second, information comes only from pre-existing information. Much more information on information can be found in the landmark book by internationally respected information theorist Werner Gitt, *In the Beginning Was Information*[1]. Biblically, that concept is expressed as "In the Beginning God . . ." (Gen. 1:1; KJV) and as "In the beginning was the Word" (John 1:1; KJV). The word "Word," identified as Jesus Christ in John 1:14, is the Greek word Logos. Logos is a grand word in Greek, connoting divine plan, reason for being, etc., and means "study of " as the suffix "-ology" attached to the various academic disciplines (biology, psychology, cosmology, etc.). Wow! Our DNA ties us back to God in Christ, the ultimate source of meaning and purpose for the whole universe!

In this sense, the Bible proved to be, as it often has, far ahead of its time. It's not the stuff (*dust*) we're made of that makes us special; it's the *way* we're put together. It's not the metal and glass that make an airplane fly, nor the ink and paper that write a novel. Similarly, it's not the "dust" that makes life, but the way it's put together with creative design and organization. When that organization is lost, we return to "dust," the simple elements that we are made of, just as other created objects break down into their simpler parts when left to the ravages of time, chance, and chemistry.

The *creationist*, then, recognizes the orderliness that the vitalist doesn't see, but he *doesn't limit himself* to only those kinds of order that result from time, chance, and the properties of matter, as the *evolutionist does*. Creation introduces levels of order and organization that greatly enrich the range of explorable hypotheses and turn the study of life into a *scientist's dream*. Science requires an orderliness in nature. One of the real emotional thrills creation scientists experience is realizing that there are many more levels of order than evolutionists imagine and that order in nature, and a mind in tune with it, are guaranteed by God Himself. It's no wonder that explicit biblical faith gave initial success to the founding fathers of modern experimental science (a couple of centuries before evolution came along to shift the emphasis toward time and chance).

If evidence for the creation of life is as clear as I say it is, then other scientists, even those who are evolutionists, ought to see it — and they do.

Francis Crick shared a Nobel Prize for the discovery of DNA's structure. After explaining why life could not and

1. Werner Gitt, *In the Beginning Was Information*, Master Books, Green Forest, AR, 2006.

did not evolve on earth, he argued instead for "directed panspermia," his belief that life reached earth in a rocket fired by intelligent life on some other planet. Crick admitted that his view only moved the creation-evolution question back to another time and place, but he argued that different conditions (which he did NOT specify) might have

Francis Crick

given life a chance to evolve that it did not have on earth. Similarly, in the film *Expelled: No Intelligence Allowed*, famous atheist and anti-creationist *Richard Dawkins expresses his blind but firm faith* that any evidence for creation on earth could only point to evolved intelligence on another planet, not to a transcendent God.

Creationists are pleased that Crick and Dawkins recognize the same potentially fatal flaws in earthly chemical evolution that they have cited for years, but creationists also point out that the differences between "chemical chemistry" and "biological chemistry" are wrapped up with the fundamental nature of matter and energy and would apply on other planets as well as on earth.

That opinion seems to be shared in part by famed astronomer Sir Fred Hoyle, who made the news under the heading: "There *must* be a God."[2] Hoyle and his colleague, Chandra Wickramasinghe, independently reached that conclusion after their mathematical analyses showed that believing life could result from time, chance, and the properties of matter was like believing that "a tornado sweeping through a junkyard might assemble a Boeing 747 from the material therein."

Drawing the logical inference from our scientific knowledge, both scientists concluded that "it becomes sensible to think that the favorable properties of physics on which life depends are in every respect *deliberate*" (emphasis Hoyle's). But both were surprised by their results. Hoyle called himself an agnostic, and, in the same article, Wickramasinghe said he was an atheistic Buddhist who "was very strongly brainwashed to believe that science cannot be consistent with any kind of deliberate creation."

2. Sir Fred Hoyle and Chandra Wickramasinghe, as quoted in "There Must be a God," *Daily Express*, August 14, 1981; and "Hoyle on Evolution," *Nature*, Nov. 12, 1981.

Quoting these scientists (and others later on) is simply to show that experts in the field, even when they have no preference for creationist thinking, at least agree with the creationists on the facts, and when people with different worldviews agree, we can be pretty sure what the facts are. It also shows that scientists who are not creationists are able to see that *creation is a legitimate scientific concept whose merits deserve to be compared with those of evolution*.

In that light, consider the revolutionary book *Evolution: A Theory in Crisis* by a prominent molecular biologist Michael Denton. Denton describes himself as a child of the secular age who desires naturalistic, materialistic explanations when he can find them. But when it comes to the origin of life, Denton explains with authority and stark clarity that evolutionists are nowhere near a *naturalistic* explanation at present. After comparing the genetic programs in living things to a library of a thousand volumes encoding billions of bits of information and all the mathematically intricate algorithms for coordinating them, Denton refers to the chemical evolution scenario as "simply an affront to reason," that is, an insult to the intelligence!

He openly and frankly states that the thesis of his book is "anti-evolutionary" (p. 353), but it seems that he is cautiously taking a step even further. The first chapter of his book is titled "Genesis Rejected," and while he would react very strongly against being called a creationist, in his honest analysis of the creation-evolution controversy through history, Denton freely admits that many of the scientific views of the early creationists have been vindicated by modern discoveries in science.

Take William Paley's classic argument that design in living things implies a Designer just as clearly as design in a watch implies a watchmaker. In *The Blind Watchmaker*, Richard Dawkins argues — incorrectly — that Paley was wrong. Denton states, "Paley was not only right in asserting an analogy between life and a machine, but also *remarkably prophetic* in guessing that the technological ingenuity realized in living systems is vastly in excess of anything yet accomplished by man" (emphasis added). Then Denton goes on to summarize his thinking on life's origin as follows (p. 341):

> The almost irresistible force of the analogy has completely undermined the complacent assumption, prevalent in biological circles over most of the past century, that the design hypothesis can be excluded on the grounds that the notion is fundamentally a metaphysical

a priori concept and therefore scientifically unsound. *On the contrary, the inference to design is a purely* a posteriori *induction based on a ruthlessly consistent application of the logic of analogy. The conclusion may have religious implications, but it does not depend on religious presuppositions* (emphasis added).[3]

Now that's quite an admission! Even though he would deny any leaning toward a Christian concept of creation, this leading molecular biologist sees quite plainly that a scientific concept of creation can be constructed (just as explained earlier in this text) using the ordinary tools of science: logic and observation. *In fact, Denton intimates that creation scientists have shown more respect than evolutionists for empirical evidence and a "ruthlessly consistent" application of logic!*

It's also true that creation may have religious implications, but, as Denton concludes, so does evolution, and that should not prevent our evaluating their scientific merits on the basis of logic and observation alone. In a short but thought-provoking article, British physicist H. S. Lipson reached the same conclusion. First he expressed his interest in life's origin, then his feeling — quite apart from any preference for creation — that, *"In fact, evolution became in a sense a scientific religion; almost all scientists have accepted it [sic] and many are prepared to 'bend' their observations to fit with it"*[4] (emphasis added).

After wondering how well evolution has stood up to scientific testing, Lipson continues: "To my mind, the theory [evolution] does not stand up at all." Then he comes to the heart of the issue: "If living matter is not, then, caused by the interplay of atoms, natural forces, and radiation [i.e., time, chance, and chemistry], how has it come into being?" After dismissing a sort of directed evolution, Lipson concludes: "I think, however, that we must go further than this and admit that the only acceptable explanation is *creation*" (emphasis his).

Like Hoyle and Wickramasinghe, Lipson is a bit surprised and unhappy with his own conclusion. He writes, "I know that this [creation] is anathema to physicists, as indeed it is to me," but his sense of honesty and scientific integrity forces him to conclude his sentence thus: "But we must not reject a theory that we do not like [creation]

Dr. Duane Gish

if the experimental evidence supports it."

By the way, not all who see the evidence of creation are unhappy about it! Witness Dr. Dean Kenyon. Kenyon is a molecular biologist whose area of research interest is specifically the origin of life. His book on life's origin, *Biochemical Predestination*, opened with praises for Darwinian evolution, and he taught evolution at San Francisco State University for many years.

A couple of students in Kenyon's class once asked him to read a book on life's origin by Dr. Duane Gish.[5] Dr. Gish, a highly qualified biochemist, lectured and debated very effectively for creation at universities on six continents. Dr. Kenyon didn't want to read Dr. Gish's book, but thanks to the students' polite persistence (see 1 Pet. 3:15), he resolved to read it and refute it. But he read it and *couldn't* refute it. Instead, Dr. Kenyon got interested in creation science and began a long re-evaluation of the scientific evidence, which finally led him to the *happy* conclusion that life, including his, is here as a result of creation, the deliberate plan and purpose of a personal Creator God!

Form your foundation.

Everybody, scientists included, knows that the arrangement of letters and words in a novel ("specified complexity") was produced by the author, not the ink and paper, and that "In God We Trust" was imposed on, not produced by, the material that carries it (whether coin, paper money, wall plaque, etc.). The same logic points to our transcendent Creator, not to DNA and protein, as author of the genetic code. Our life is a gift of God's Life!

3. Michael Denton, *Evolution: Theory in Crisis* (Bethesda, MD: Adler & Adler, 1986) p. 341.
4. H.S. Lipson, "A Physicist Looks at Evolution," *Physics Bulletin*, May, 1980, p. 138.

5. Duane Gish, *Creation Scientists Answer Their Critics*, Master Books, Green Forest, AR, 1993.

1. "IN GOD WE TRUST," America's national motto, can be pressed into coins, printed on paper money, written in pencil, typed on a computer, stitched into a pillowcase, etc. In any case, the "coded information" in this motto was (**produced by/imposed on**) _____ the material that carried it by (**time, chance, and the properties of matter—TCM/plan, purpose, and acts of creation—PPC**) _____. The differences between the two kinds of order (TCM v. PPC) are easily recognized every day by (**just scientists/everybody**) _____ on the basis of (**blind faith/logic and observation**) _____. Even evolutionists would accept all the following as examples of created codes imposed on matter except (choose one): a. Egyptian picture writing (human creation), b. deliberate signals from outer space (alien creation), c. DNA-protein coding as the basis for life (God's creation) _____.

2. Circle each item below that provides direct and positive scientific evidence that DNA-protein coding has the created kind of order that results from plan, purpose, and creative acts imposing patterns of order on matter that molecules could never make themselves:
   a. Base-acid and the many other natural reactions between DNA and protein destroy the coding relationship.
   b. Since DNA-protein coding is not based on anything molecules do naturally, waiting a loooong time for a very lucky chemical accident to make the code is like waiting to win the lottery *without buying a ticket* (or trying to throw 13 on a pair of dice).
   c. Unlike systems that must evolve one little step at a time, created systems can start with "complex prerequisites" — like DNA-protein coding requires ribosomes with 50 proteins to impose the triplet coding system on mRNA and 20 "translase" enzymes to relate those triplets to the proper amino acid R-group: specific proteins needed to make the first specific protein, then many more — and this requires (**no/lots of**) _____ energy and complex raw materials (**continuously/at the start**) _____.

3. Surprisingly, Darwin's followers often use the spontaneous formation of ordered ice crystals in freezing water to "prove" order in DNA and proteins could also occur without "God's help." But, (**T or F**)
   _____ a. Natural chemical attractions form ice but destroy DNA-protein coding.
   _____ b. An ice cube split in half still cools soda; a protein or DNA split in half loses all functions.
   _____ c. Ice is formed by cooling water; it takes a continuous stream of raw materials and energy to form DNA or proteins.
   _____ d. Ice has simple repeat pattern order; DNA and protein have "specified complexity" with high information content.
   _____ e. It takes deep scientific ignorance to claim the order in ice crystals is like that in DNA and protein.
   _____ f. DNA and protein have the created kind of order; ice crystals have the spontaneous kind produced by water molecules doing what comes naturally at freezing temperatures.

   Crick   Dawkins   Denton   Hoyle   Lipson

4. Well-known scientists above who do not claim to be creationists still recognize the evidence of creation in living cells. Match alphabetized names with statements (paraphrased) they made.
   _____ a. Evolution became a scientific religion, and many scientists will bend their observations to fit with it.
   _____ b. Chemical evolution on earth is impossible; life was seeded here from outer space.
   _____ c. I don't believe there's any evidence of creation, but if there were, the "creator" would be aliens, not God.
   _____ d. There must be a God; the odds of getting life by chance is like a tornado going through a junkyard assembling a Boeing 747 jumbo jet.
   _____ e. The inference to design is based on a ruthlessly consistent application of logic; Paley was right—design implies a Designer.

Chapter

18

DNA and Reproduction
DNA Duplication/Replication

The way living cells convert DNA base series into coded information that organizes several sets of RNA and proteins into molecular machinery for manufacturing millions of protein molecules is incredibly inspiring, carefully coordinated, clearly created, and (let's face it) more than a little brain boggling! Good news: the structure of the DNA double helix was discovered using cardboard cutouts, and its reproduction — the basis of reproduction for all living things — was so obvious and easy that Watson and Crick could walk with their Nobel Prize in the 1950s without even having to explain the details!

From the work of others, young Watson knew both that DNA molecules likely had a helical shape (like a spiral staircase) and that the amounts of DNA bases G and C were equal, as were A and T. He also knew atomic ring structures made each base like a jigsaw puzzle piece: flat with an edge having a special shape. When he made cardboard cutouts and played with them awhile, he noticed G and C had the right shape and charge to form a "plank" or stair step exactly the same length as one formed by an A-T base pair (and that would explain why amounts of G=C and A=T).

It's amazing how much of "life" depends on the "transcendent simplicity" of interlocking base shapes — and amazing, too, that the "God of details" arranged complex sets of atoms so that we could understand them with simple diagrams and cardboard cut-outs (Figure 19.1). It's as if God want us to see Him in the things He made.

Figure 19.1. Details and diagrams of base pairing

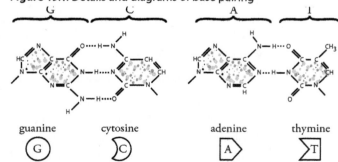

If two DNA chains lying side by side were linked by these interlocking base shapes, Watson imagined, the base pairs would be like rungs in a twisted ladder, the sugar and phosphate (S + P) parts of nucleotides acting like banister supports in a spiral staircase, with G-C and A-T base pairs forming steps in the famous "double helix"! Next step: Nobel Prize!

Figure 19.2 shows a base-paired DNA double helix "untwisted" from its spiral staircase shape into a straight ladder shape. In a well-fed living cell about to reproduce, the double-stranded DNA would be surrounded by numerous DNA nucleotides, each made of sugar-phosphate (S-P) groups with one of the four bases (GCAT) sticking out from the sugar, capable of forming interlocking pairs G-C and A-T. Think about a DNA double helix surrounded by nucleotides with interlocking

Figure 19.2. DNA duplication

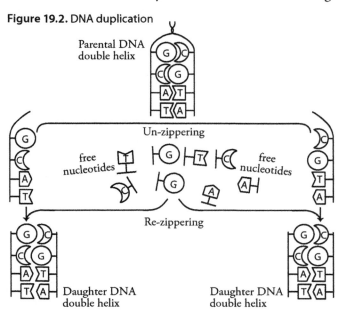

base shapes and S-P groups that "like" to form long chains. Can you imagine, like Watson, how one double helix could become two, each identical to the other and to the original DNA? . . . (Time to think) . . . (Think about zippers). . . . Imagine the original double-stranded DNA "un-zippered" as G-C and A-T base pairs each unhooked. Then imagine interlocking base shapes causing single nucleotides to pair with each base sticking out along the separated DNA chains. Then "zipper together" the S-P backbones of the newly forming DNA chains or strands. Study Figure 19.2, then circle yes or no to these questions:

Circle: yes or no	Questions
yes or no	Would the two new double strands be identical to each other?
yes or no	Would they be identical to the original double-stranded DNA?
yes or no	Would one DNA double helix have been successfully reproduced?

Wow! *Un-zippering, base pairing, re-zippering* — three easy steps based on interlocking shapes, and we have DNA replication, the basis for reproduction in all living things (viruses, microbes, plants, animals, and people)! Double WOW!

For centuries, reproduction had been a mystery. How did a baby wind up with arms, legs, eyes, and ears like his or her mom and dad? At one point, some thought parents had "little people" (homunculus) in either egg or sperm cells — and these miniatures must have had even tinier people in their reproductive organs! *God had a better, simpler, more ingenious plan.* Parents don't pass arms, legs, eyes, and ears to their children; they pass on the *DNA code for making* arms, legs, eyes, and ears (and grasshopper parents pass on the DNA code for antennae, wings, compound eyes, and an outside skeleton!).

It's astonishing that the awesome mystery of life's reproduction is based so simply on the interlocking shapes of two DNA base pairs. Enormous consequences have followed this landmark discovery from "DNA fingerprinting" in CSI work (crime scene investigation) to the promise of curing genetic diseases, resurrecting extinct species, growing spare body parts, or even cloning (making exact physical copies of) whole individuals. Yet in spite of all the hype in both science fact and science fiction, making copies of DNA would, by itself, be nothing more than a cheap magician's trick ("full of sound and fury signifying nothing").

When scientists make exact copies of a DNA double helix in the lab, they often refer to it as *replication* or *duplication* rather than reproduction. With the right conditions, energy, and starting materials, labs can use an automated PCR (polymerase chain reaction) to make millions of copies of DNA (even a tiny amount left at a crime scene!). DNA *replication* IS the *basis* for reproduction in all living things, but *full reproduction* requires the DNA code be passed on *in a living cell* (such as a fertilized egg cell) that has all the organization, energy, and molecular machinery (enzymes) to properly "read" and implement the coded/created DNA instructions. Perfect dinosaur DNA, for example, could NOT be used to make "Jurassic Park" dinosaurs *unless* it could be put into a mother cell capable of reading the dinosaur code in proper sequence while absorbing nutrients, etc., to support growth.

DNA is fantastically important and deserves enormous respect, most especially because *small* changes in DNA can have huge effects on all the other parts of a cell or living thing — and that's true whether the little changes are caused deliberately by experimenting scientists or accidentally by random changes ("mutations") occurring in nature. Nevertheless, DNA *by itself* does practically nothing for life; DNA can't digest food, contract muscles, sense light, conduct nerve impulses, etc. DNA doesn't even possess the genetic code, but only the genetic alphabet. A bar code on a store product means nothing, for example, apart from a scanner or reader that can give it meaning. Similarly, DNA base letters mean nothing and do nothing until ribosomes and translases in the living cell give them meaning. Replication processes copy any DNA helix, whether it's random nonsense or a crucial gene.

Question	Is DNA a self-reproducing molecule?

NO. It's not even close. When the un-zippering/ base pairing/re-zippering replication of DNA was first reported, DNA was widely touted as "self-reproducing," almost worshiped as if it were "alive" or at least a perfect "link" between non-life and life. Try a thought experiment. Put a DNA double helix in a glass of water and watch it for a million years. What would happen? Nothing. (Actually, the DNA would be not-so-gradually broken down by water into the small molecules of "dust" from which it came.) Now imagine the DNA helix un-zipped, and you could watch it another million years. What would happen? Nothing. (Actually, single stranded DNA breaks down much faster in water than the base-paired double strand.) Think back on the process of DNA reproduction/replication. *What had to be present with the DNA* for new base pairing and re-zippering to occur? Many, many single nucleotides with the four different types of bases. Where did the loose nucleotides come from? From food — and all that implies: a food source, mechanism for harvesting and processing food, and making some molecules (like nucleotides) by putting together parts of other food molecules.

Although they are "simply" small links (monomers) in very long DNA chains (polymers), nucleotides are quite complex themselves, each consisting of three groups: phosphate, sugar, and base. The phosphate is simple enough and comes from phosphate minerals in soil ultimately. The sugar (deoxyribose) is a five-sided ring with multiple C, H, and O atoms put together in a

multi-step reaction series requiring much ATP energy and a coordinated set of several enzymes. The bases include N as well as C, H, and O atoms, and come as single rings (C, T) or double rings (G, A) (see Figure 19.1.) They are manufactured from a multitude of parts, including amino acids, and the long series of coordinated steps (including ring closure), guided by numerous enzymes, have given nightmares to biochemistry students for a long time. Furthermore, the nucleotides for DNA re-zippering come "pre-energized," having extra phosphate groups necessary to supply energy for linking the base-paired nucleotides into a new chain.

In short, *DNA is NOT self-reproducing.* Its replication requires lots of raw materials and energy. Its continuing replication requires a continuously renewed supply of "expensive" raw materials and energy, the complex and pre-energized single nucleotides.

DNA-protein translation requires created enzyme systems (ribosomes and translases) to establish a code for DNA, but DNA replication (in the context of a living cell!) follows easily from natural chemical attraction of interlocking base shapes. Still, enzymes play a variety of important "supporting roles" in replication. It takes an enzyme (responding to various biological and environmental regulators) just to open ("pry apart") the double helix. One enzyme (RNA polymerase) opens a small section to make mRNA; DNA polymerases open the whole helix for replication. Enzymes speed up base pairing and zippering of the newly forming strand. Without these "speed up" enzymes (polymerases), it's likely replication would be too sloppy to support life, since single-stranded DNA is easily damaged by water. Multiple coordinated enzyme sets are also required to make the pre-energized single nucleotides used to zipper together new DNA strands. So enzymes are required to help make DNA, and DNA is required to help make the enzymes that are required to help make DNA, and . . . so on and on in a *kind of created "circle of life."*

DNA Repair. A special set of enzymes plays a vital role in repairing the damage done to DNA by UV (ultraviolet) radiation in sunshine. As shown in Figure 19.3, UV can act on two T's side-by-side in a DNA chain. The T's let go of the A's they were paired with on the opposite strand and pair instead with each other (a "thymine dimer"). That corrupts the DNA code. A base copy of the strand with the T-T damage might skip two letters in the DNA base series, changing all the triplet codon names for amino acids from that point on. The result? Cell death or — worse — cell malfunction that turns into skin cancer that may spread through the body.

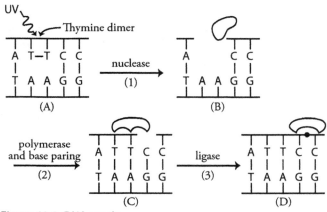

Figure 19.3. DNA repair

But praise God, a special enzyme, an *endonuclease*, is on patrol, and it can detect a sag in the DNA double helix where the T-T is. At that point, it cuts an opening into the damaged strand. A second enzyme, an *exonuclease*, then "chews out" a section of the damaged strand, including the T-T. A third enzyme, a DNA *polymerase*, splices in a repaired strand, using base pairing with the undamaged strand as a guide or *template*. The final enzyme, a *ligase*, ties the repaired sequence back into the main chain. Wow!

Actually, enzymes like those used in DNA repair also function in DNA replication. Un-zipping the two helically coiled strands of DNA would be like pulling apart twisted strands in a rope: the spin generated by untwisting the strands (rope or DNA) would produce a swiveling motion that would churn apart the living cell! So God designed a system much like repair to cut into the DNA strands and replicate them in sections ("Okazaki fragments"). Double wow!

Without DNA repair enzymes, a day at the beach would produce so many skin cancers, few people would survive. Unfortunately, some people are born with a defect in this repair system (sometimes called xeroderma pigmentosum). A movie was made about a family with such a genetic problem. The children couldn't even go outside to play because sunlight hurt their skin. The preference for activities at night generated suspicion among their neighbors — until they finally found a caring Christian community in northern California. Their problem was made worse because scientists and doctors were only just beginning to find out about these fantastic and helpful repair enzymes.

Before evolution's mutations corrupted God's creation, the repair enzymes enabled us to enjoy the sun's benefits (e.g., vitamin D synthesis) without harm. God even designed "proofreading" enzyme systems that, even in our fallen world (corrupted creation), give DNA

replication a far, far lower error rate than any comparable copying system ever designed by man. Evolution's hope is based on mutational mistakes, but with God, "quality control" reaches its ultimate expression.

Antibodies. "Planning ahead" is a characteristic of creation that sets it dramatically apart from the "blind" process of evolution (time, chance, struggle, and death, TCSD). An excellent illustration is provided by antibodies, a class of proteins famous as disease fighters.

A typical antibody is a huge, Y-shaped protein with a very specific shape at its Y-tips designed to interlock with a corresponding shape on a foreign substance, called an *antigen* (Figure 19.4.) An antigen can be a protein or large molecule on the surface of viruses, bacteria, parasites, mold spores, plant pollen, pet hair, insect parts, transfused blood cells, skin grafts, transplanted organs, etc. Problem: a human cell makes perhaps only 30,000 different kinds of structural and functional proteins — yet it can make more than a million different antibodies, each type with its own unique shape, amino acid sequence, and DNA code. How is that possible? The answer is *plan, purpose, and special acts of creation put into action.*

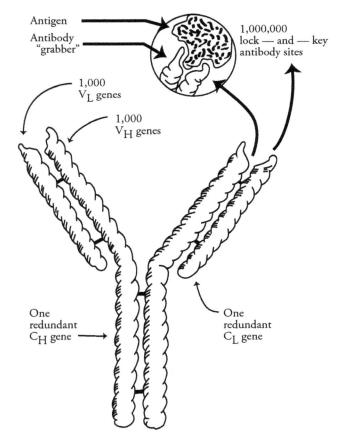

Figure 19.4. Antibody structure and interlocking antigen and antibody "grabber"

147

The base of an antibody Y consists of two protein chains that are essentially the same for all antibodies. Each Y branch also includes two protein chains, but the tips of each are "variable," different in each type of antibody. Here's the brilliantly creative part: the variation in one protein chain can be different from the variation in the other. The antibody's specific, interlocking shape, or "grabber," is formed by a combination of amino acids from each of the two protein chains. Hold your two hands in front of you as if you were holding a basketball. Now change the shape of your left hand as if to hold something else. Then change the shape of your right hand so your two hands are now shaped to hold (interlock with) a third object. Now imagine you can twist your left hand into a thousand different shapes and your right hand into a thousand. How many different shapes could your two hands form? Since each left-hand shape could go with 1,000 right-hand shapes, and each right with 1,000 left-hand shapes, the answer is 1,000 x 1,000 = 1,000,000 — a cool million!

The "hands shape analogy" illustrates how God designed a DNA mechanism to make far more antibodies than all other proteins put together. A thousand DNA genes would make 1,000 variations of the left protein chain at an antibody's Y-tip, and another 1,000 DNA genes could make 1,000 variations of the right chain at each Y-tip. So "mixing and matching" protein chains from 2,000 DNA genes (1,000 "left" and 1,000 "right") could produce 1,000,000 antibodies — sufficient to interlock with and neutralize all foreign substances, past, present, and future! Wow! The best news — and clear evidence of creative planning ahead — is that some human antibodies already exist to conquer every imaginable human disease or foreign invader, including germs produced by future mutations and chemicals human beings haven't even invented yet.

Before DNA and protein production were understood, evolutionists believed antibodies were produced by trial and error, random mutations that only increased in the population after unlucky losers died off. Some even thought antibodies were somehow "molded" around offending antigens to get their interlocking shapes. We now know proteins and their shapes can only be produced by pre-existing DNA with the proper code — plan, purpose, and special acts of creation!

Before man's sin and Darwin's war of nature corrupted God's creation and led to mutational defects producing a host of "germs," the antibody system would just have cleaned the human body of dust, pollen, partly digested food, etc. But again knowing the future and planning ahead, God provided a *way of escape from diseases to come* — just as He provided *deliverance from death itself through the sacrifice of His Son*, our Savior, Jesus Christ.

Viruses. When people think of viruses, they think of the flu, smallpox, polio, and other dread diseases. Viruses are actually "obligate parasites"; they can only multiply inside a living cell, where they "pirate" the cell's food and energy supplies and complex enzyme systems, water, and membranes. Yet viruses use a series of bases (either DNA or RNA) to line up a series of amino acids to make viral proteins, and DNA-protein (or base-R sequence) translation was earlier described as clear and convincing evidence of plan, purpose, and special acts of creation.

Does that mean God created viruses for the purpose of causing disease? If not, how did viruses and their DNA or RNA codes come into being, and how does their origin fit into the 4C biblical theme of Creation, Corruption, Catastrophe, and Christ? The Bible doesn't mention viruses, of course, but as usual, God's Word provides the surest guide to understanding God's world. Let's put that principle into practice.

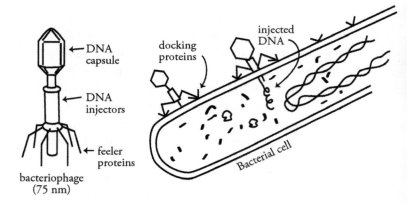

Figure 19.5. Bacteriophage virus

The most elaborate and elegantly designed viruses are *bacteriophages* (phages, for short), viruses that attack bacteria (so even bacteria can "get sick"!). A phage virus is designed somewhat like the syringe a doctor uses to give you a "shot." It has a geometrically sculptured head of interlocking proteins that hold the DNA "medicine." Below that is an injection tube with proteins that can contract, stabbing a needle-like tip right through the bacterial cell wall for injecting viral DNA into the living cell. The "feelers" around the injection tip interlock with "docking molecules" on the bacterial wall, meaning the phage will inject its DNA only into certain cells its feelers can recognize.

Once inside, the viral DNA can "take over" the living bacterial cell, "stealing" raw materials and energy, and "instructing" ribosomes, translases, and other enzyme systems to make viral proteins and more viral DNA. The bacterial cell may explode (lyse), releasing perhaps 200 virus to repeat the process, reproducing viruses (and destroying bacterial cells) at an astonishingly staggering rate (1 to 200 to 40,000 to 8 million to 1.6 billion in four short generations!). On the other hand, the injected viral DNA may simply splice itself into the bacterial DNA, multiplying along with the bacterium, causing no problem, perhaps even helping the bacterium by introducing DNA to make proteins the bacterium can use.

Note also that a phage, like virtually all *viruses, can only infect a cell that "invites it in."* The interlocking of phage feeler proteins with cell docking molecules acts like a key fitting into a lock, and it's so specific that certain phages can infect only certain strains of the common intestinal (colon) bacterium, *E. coli*. Similarly, various strains of the "flu/cold" virus can only enter certain cells, so we speak (loosely) of "stomach flu," upper or lower respiratory infections, etc.

To the author, observations about viruses like these suggest the following concept: viruses have the DNA-protein coding relationship and other properties of organization ("exherent" design) clearly pointing to their origin by deliberate acts of creation (science). Since God's original creation was complete and "all very good" (Scripture), viruses would have played a positive role in God's world before man's sin. Phages can carry genes from one bacterium to others and splice it into specific sites in the bacterial DNA, giving the bacteria additional properties useful in some environments, increasing their variability and adaptability without making other bacteria replicate DNA they don't need.

Feeler/docking recognition pairing keeps viral DNA from getting into the wrong cells and multiplying out of control. Viruses are excellent storehouses of specialized information, since, by themselves, they are actively neither living nor dying but persist without effort and little decay in dormancy or "suspended animation."

Man's sin changed all that, corrupting God's creation and bringing on struggle and death (Darwin's "war of nature") and random changes in DNA called mutations. Mutations in feeler/docking recognition would allow viruses to inject their DNA into the "wrong cells" where, in the absence of check-and-balance regulators in the "right cells" (designed target), the viruses multiply out of control and destroy their host. Blindly favoring the best survivors in each generation, *Darwinian selection would automatically reward explosive multipliers* with no thought to future destructive consequences. In our fallen world, half of all animal species are already parasitic exploiters, but a parasite that finally kills all its hosts also kills itself. *Praise God, before Darwin's war finally destroys all of life, Christ's return will conquer struggle and death and restore life, rich and abundant and eternal!*

Even today, God provides a way of escape from harmful viruses. Antibiotics don't work on viruses, because viruses "borrow life" from living cells to multiply, and antibiotics kill living cells. Antibodies, however, can block viral feeler/docking recognition so viruses can't even get into cells, and some antibodies disrupt viral DNA and RNA within cells, preventing them from taking over cell machinery. And God designed antibodies ahead of time, even preparing us to deal with viral mutations that haven't occurred yet. Unfortunately, it may take 7–10 days of feeling sick before enough antibodies are produced to wipe out an infection. Vaccination, pre-treatment with weakened antigen, can shorten the delay time to 0, and some people are naturally immune to some diseases.

The flu virus is a particular nuisance, because it mutates easily and often, sometimes making major changes by picking up parts of animal viruses (e.g., "swine flu" or "bird flu"). Antibodies are so specific that antibodies or a vaccine against last year's flu don't work so well against this year's form.

The flu virus is an *RNA virus*. Inside living cells, the viral RNA makes DNA; since that's the reverse of the more common sequence, RNA viruses are also called *retroviruses*. RNA retroviruses must bring in their own special enzyme, *reverse transcriptase*, to use RNA to make DNA. Successfully blocking this enzyme could effectively treat several serious diseases.

DNA and the Bible: Science and Scripture vs. Evolution

DNA is not mentioned specifically in the Bible, of course, but it's the "4C theme" in God's Word that helps us understand scientific discoveries in God's world, including DNA. The tools of science (logic and observation) applied to the way living cells convert DNA's "alphabet" into a code for making proteins provides clear and convincing evidence that all life is a gift of God's life, with the "exherent" kind of design and "transcendent simplicity" pointing to plan, purpose, and absolutely awesome acts of special creation (Gen. 1; John 1). That means the "Big Bang" theorists (from Hawking to Dawkins and down) have it exactly backward: **mind created matter**, *not* the other way around.

Since the interdependent parts and their interaction pattern were established by God's *completed, supernatural acts in the past*, living cells use DNA to make both proteins (for structure and function) and more DNA (for reproduction), *operating through continuing, "natural" (repeatable) processes in the present* that scientists have described in intricate detail, providing evidence that God the *Creator* is also God the *Sustainer*, the one who daily, faithfully continues to care for His creation (Col. 1:17).

Unfortunately, man's sin brought on God's judgment reflected in Darwin's "war of nature" (time, chance, struggle, and death — TCSD). These "gods of evolution" (TCSD) produced and rewarded DNA mistakes called mutations, a Corruption of God's creation (Rom. 8:20–21), explaining not the origin of species but the origin of defects, disease, disease organisms, decline, and disaster (Catastrophe).

But — PRAISE GOD! — Christ came to conquer sin and death and to restore life, rich and abundant forevermore. Being sure we are not "playing God" but are *following God's example in Christ*, we can use our growing knowledge of DNA and life science to *share in Jesus' marvelous ministry of healing and restoration!*

God's "eternal power and Godhead" are clearly seen in all "the things that are made" (Rom. 1:20; KJV), and DNA also reveals God as *Creator, Sustainer, Judge, and Redeemer* (CSJR). Christ, the Creator God, is both the first and the fourth of the 4Cs, "Alpha and Omega, the beginning and the end, the first and the last" (Rev. 22:13; KJV) in the 4C flow of history: **Creation, Corruption, Catastrophe, Christ.**

We now wait eagerly for Christ's return, ushering in a "new heavens and a new earth" (2 Pet. 3:13) in which Darwin's war is over, and once again:

> The wolf also shall dwell with the lamb . . .
> and the young lion and the fatling together.
> . . . They shall not hurt nor destroy in all my
> holy mountain: for the earth shall be full of the
> knowledge of the Lord, as the waters cover the
> sea (Isaiah 11:6–9).

Until He comes again, we can use our knowledge of DNA to overcome the effects of sin and Darwin's war, conquer defects and disease, and bring healing and restoration, following the lead of our Savior-Redeemer, the Great Healer, Jesus Christ.

It's not evolution's millions of years of struggle and death until death wins. LIFE WINS — NEW LIFE IN CHRIST! "Even so, come, Lord Jesus" (Rev. 22:20).

Form your foundation.

What we see in God's world agrees with what we read in God's Word, from evidence of Creation seen in transcendent design, Corruption seen in chance mutations and Darwin's "war of nature" that followed sin, Catastrophe in genetic bottlenecks and extinction, to the conquest of sin and death and restoration of new life, rich and abundant and eternal in our Lord and Savior, Jesus Christ!

Building Inspection

1. DNA's base pair replication is the basis for all "reproduction after kind." But is DNA truly a self-reproducing molecule? Explain.

   _____
   _____
   _____

Uv   nuclease   polymerase   ligase   DnA   cancer

2. Use the words above to fill in this account of DNA repair: Repair enzymes can prevent skin _____ in cells whose _____ has been damaged by _____ radiation. One enzyme, a _____, recognizes and cuts out the damaged DNA strand; the next, a _____, forms a new DNA polymer base-paired against the non-damaged DNA strand; then the final enzyme, a _____, ties or ligates the new strand into the main chain. PTL!

3. Use shapes formed by a pair of hands to help explain how God could use only 2,000 genes to make antibodies with 1,000,000 different "grabbers" to block poisons, germs, etc., to preserve life.

   _____
   _____

4. A phage virus keeps its (**DNA/protein**) _____ inside its geometric "head." When its (**feeler/injector**) _____ proteins lock into docking receptors on a bacterial cell wall, (**feeler/injector**) _____ proteins contract and "shoot" viral DNA into the cell. The viral DNA can "splice" itself into bacterial (**DNA/proteins**) _____, adding helpful genes, which may have been the virus's created purpose (**before/after**) _____ sin. After sin, random genetic changes called _____ alter feeler-docking proteins and otherwise (**improve/corrupt**) _____ viral-cell relationships, so injected viral DNA can cause a cell to (**explode/evolve**) _____. Mutations in other viruses could allow them to get into certain human cells, causing (**disease/evolution**) _____.

5. All life is a gift of God's life, and that means, contrary to popular opinion, that (mind/matter) _____ formed (**mind/matter**) _____, not the other way around.

Creation   Corruption   Catastrophe   Christ

6. Relate "4Cs" of biblical history to many different aspects of life science indicated below:

   _____ a. Darwin's "war of nature…famine and death"

   _____ b. Mutations

   _____ c. Using the many specific proteins in ribosomes and "translases" to establish DNA code for making specific proteins

   _____ d. Shuffling melanin control genes to produce all variations of human skin tone in one generation

   _____ e. Radically changed Earth's weather and soil conditions and mutations perhaps help explain why God allowed meat eating

   _____ f. Increased mutation rates and disease, possibly led to decreased life spans

   _____ g. Using "trained viruses" and other gene carriers to cure genetic diseases, setting right what once went wrong

   _____ h. Using research on adult stem cells to bring healing and restoration, following Jesus' example

7. "What we see in God's world agrees with what we read in God's Word." What's your favorite example from this book illustrating the principle above — the one you would most like to share with others?

Chapter

19

Index

Answers to Questions

Chapter 1 page 13

1. DNA, genes, alleles, hybrid, dominant, recessive, blending
2. ¼, ¼, ¼, ½ (as p. 7, using Tt in place of Rr or Pr)
3. one, one, melanin
4. medium, 5, one, little, lots
5. greater, universe
6. Sample answer (SA): Being able to relate God's world and God's Word is important in two ways: (a) it builds faith and trust in Scripture (the Bible), and (2) it helps believers use the wonders of science to introduce others to the wonders of new life in Christ revealed in God's Word.
7. plan, purpose, and special creation; time, chance, struggle and death; worse, Darwin, time, chance, struggle and death; better, death (wins), God, life (wins)
8. Catastrophe, Corruption, Creation, Christ (see pp. 3–5)

Chapter 2, page 19

1. less than, greater, constantly changing, always the same, always constant, ever new and unique, God
2. none, ¼, 16, ¼, exactly the same as, variation within, creation, equilibrium, inertia
3. a-genetic bottleneck, b-genetic drift or founder effect, c-specialization, d-reproductive isolation, e-mutations
4. very dark, very light, medium, any shade of
5. (only) ½, no, no!

Chapter 3, page 29

1. "multiply after kind"
2. genons, alleles, e, f
3. baramins; create(d); kind
4. morphotype, fertilotype, ecotype, fertilotype, ecotype, morphotype
5. (Carolus) Linnaeus or (Karl) von Linne; genus, species, genus, genus, genus, both (genus and species), genera, (still) species, *Homo sapiens*
6. unique, non-unique, unique, non-unique, unique, non-unique, unique, combination
7. creation, creation, creation

Chapter 4, page 35

1. See page 30, from first full paragraph in right column to its end at top left page 31—plus chart bottom left of page 31.
2. See page 31, begin with first full paragraph, then stop at new subhead on page 32 right column.
3. See page 30, first two full paragraphs and answer to #6 below
4. SA: The Bible teaches that God is the author of variety and that man's sin brought struggle and death into the world, and creation scientists rightly use those concepts to explain how and where varieties survive as they multiply and fill a fallen world. Darwin's followers, however, want to change a given kind of life into others — but they can explain neither where new kinds of variety (genons) come from nor why struggle and death make things better instead of worse, so their "survival of the fittest" becomes a silly circular argument, the "survival of the survivors." The famous peppered moth, for example, is recognized in several color forms dark to light as far back as records go (so not even one new trait "evolved"), and many moths moved to locations matching their color (habitat choice, or multiplying and filling) rather than waiting to be eaten (Darwinian struggle and death), and the light moths moved back into the original area after man cleaned up pollution.
5. SA: "Molecules to man" evolution absolutely requires a HUGE INCREASE IN BOTH THE QUANTITY and QUALITY OF GENETIC INFORMATION, and neither mutations nor Darwinian "selection" can provide either, since they only change or select existing varieties (pointing back to prior acts of creation).
6. SA: People who favor abortion-on-demand say they are "prochoice," most likely because it would be hard to "sell" the idea of abortion if you said you were in favor of "butchering babies before birth." Evolution's "salesmen" use the same logic. Darwin himself, summarizing his own theory, said that "the production of higher animals" (i.e., macroevolution) was caused "from the war of nature, from famine and death." Realizing that it might be hard to convince people the pathway to progress was paved with blood and dead bodies, Darwin's salesmen described evolution as a slow but ever upward and onward building process producing more and better forms of life one little step at a time. The idea of slow and steady progress as a "law of nature" even appealed to some Christian leaders, as well as to Lenin and Marx (the founders of communism). We definitely need to do a better job of teaching what evolution is really all about!

Chapter 5, page 43

1. See pages 36–37 and chart on page 37.
2. SA: "Fitness" is determined by counting surviving offspring. "Adaptation" is determined by seeing how well a feature is designed to accomplish its purpose in the "web of life." Engineering analysis may show a given woodpecker is exquisitely designed for drilling holes in wood, but the woodpecker's fitness (number of surviving offspring) may be low because, for example, lack of a soil nutrient (or presence of a pollutant) may make its egg shells weak. An opossum, on the other hand, with no obviously ingeniously designed adaptations has high fitness because it is very good at making baby opossums that survive!
3. See page 38, first full paragraph right column to (3) at lower left of page 39.
4. See page 39, first full paragraph at middle right, through top partial paragraph page 40.
5. See page 40, item (4) Intra- vs. interspecific competition.
6. See pages 40-41, item (5) Succession vs. evolution.
7. See page 41, item (6) Long term vs. short term advantage.
8. See page 42, item (7) to end of chapter.
9. SA: When "bears" got off the Ark, they looked like bears in general and could survive in a variety of new habitats (i.e., they were generalized and adaptable, like mongrel dogs). But as they multiplied and filled the earth, they broke up into groups with distinctly different appearances that survived best in more limited environments (i.e., subgroups became specialized and adapted). Each specialized, adapted subgroup had less variability to meet changes in its own environment or to explore new ones *so rates and amounts of change slowed or stopped*, but the varieties that developed within a few centuries after "bears" in general got off

the Ark revealed the creative ingenuity and variability God had built into the created kinds He brought to Noah.

Chapter 6, page 53

1. T
2. See page 44 through left column of page 49 (with your answer "condensed").
3. evolution; corruption (mutational defects following sin)
4. See page 49, right column through first full paragraph on page 50.
5. See page 50, first full paragraph through first two full paragraphs on page 51.
6. mutations

Chapter 7, page 61

1. species; defects, disease, decline, death (or equivalent)
2. See p. 57, especially summary top 2 full paragraphs in right column.
3. SA: Sometimes Christians glibly say "God created everything," but Genesis 1 tells us all the things God created were only "good." The bad things around us were not created by God, but brought on by man's sin, and sin allowed mutations to corrupt the things God had first created good. The bad is our fault, not God's — but God in Christ will remove the "bondage to corruption" (Romans 8) and restore goodness again!
4. e
5. genetic burden; extinction
6. faster; cannot; recessive; cannot; more
7. See p. 58, last full paragraph in left column to top two sentences on right.
8. e
9. do; don't

Chapter 8, page 67

1. nothing — he couldn't think of a single example (if you left this space blank, you got the answer right!)
2. less
3. SA: (a) people with one sickle cell gene and one normal (Ss) don't die of malaria and, though weakened from poor oxygen transport, they don't die of sickle cell anemia (ss).
   (b) HB^S is "good" for "fitness" — IN AND ONLY IN AREAS WHERE MALARIA CAUSES MANY DEATHS — because more children of carriers (Ss) survive to have children (fitness) than children of normal parents (SS) who die more readily than carrier children. HB^S is NOT good adaptation because sickle cell hemoglobin carries oxygen far less well than normal hemoglobin (HB^A), and oxygen transport is the purpose (design function) of hemoglobin. Because HB^S is poorly adapted for oxygen transport, carriers (Ss) survive less well (have lower fitness as well as poorer adaptation) in areas where malaria is not a problem—e.g., among people of central African descent in America.
   (c) The price for carriers of the sickle cell mutant is high! Half their children can still die of either sickle cell anemia or of malaria where malaria is a problem, and ¾ of their children suffer from reduced oxygen transport.
   (d) Your opinion here (but even when the author was an evolutionist he didn't use sickle cell hemoglobin to support evolution!).
4. See page 63 from subhead Mutations: Evidence… through subhead upper left page 65.
5. alleles; already exist; corruption (decline after sin)
6. pre-existing information; God — the Word in Christ

7. Creation — no; Corruption — yes; Catastrophe — yes (in part); Christ — no.
8. a-many; large; few; small b-better; new species; increase; after sin; worse; defects and disease; decrease
9. generalized; specialized; creation; variation within

Chapter 9, page 75

1. homology; evolutionists; creationists
2. See page 71, from second full paragraph through top four lines on page 72.
3. See page 72, first two full paragraphs.
4. mosaic; creation
5. a, b, c, d, e (i.e., all, although e was not in the text)
6. contradict each other; mosaic (or matrix or modular); creation

Chapter 10, page 83

1. taxonomy; systematics
2. taxonomy; systematics
3. color; no
4. a, b, c, d, (i.e., all)
5. sequential; hierarchical; creation; does
6. Carolus Linnaeus (or Karl von Linne)
7. kingdom, phylum (division), class, order, family, genus, species;
8. genus and species; genus; genus
9. both (at least potentially!)

Chapter 11, page 91

1. 46 (23 pairs); 23
2. XX; XY; father's sperm (½ are X, ½ are Y)
3. is; does; is not; does not
4. conception
5. No. Cloning requires DNA plus the instructions in the right kind of egg cell (and often a mother for the egg cell) to "read" the DNA instructions in the right order for proper development.
6. cleavage; differentiation; stem; adult; embryonic
7. notochord; neural ridges; neural tube; somites; backbones and muscle (either order)
8. metamorphosis; nothing like; entelechy
9. bud-bend-paddle-toes; people; frogs
10. T
11. fearfully (awesomely) and wonderfully

Chapter 12, page 103

1. Haeckel; are
2. fish; reptile; monkey; plan in God's mind—unformed substance — knit together
3. fertilized egg cell (or zygote); 1000/0
4. SA: All the genes for making both the tadpole (water-breathing plant-eater) and adult frog (air-breathing insect eater) are present from the start in the egg cell — as well as all the genes for making the complex, multi-step change (metamorphosis) between the two stages — which provides evidence of creation. Yet in nature only about 500/0 of tadpoles make the transition to land even with all genes already present, yet evolutionists want us to believe some fish with no "frog genes" made the transition to land with chance mutations adding the hundreds of genes needed one at a time, each mutated step winning the struggle for survival to produce a large population for the next lucky accident.
5. vestigial organs (or vestiges); all 180

6. a-D, b-E, c-F, d-G, e-H, f-A, g-B, h-C
7. See p. 99, beginning at second full paragraph, stopping at "Junk DNA" on p. 100.
8. The yolk is not needed (since the baby is nourished by his or her mother), but the baby needs blood and blood vessels to form the bone marrow and other organs that later make blood. The yolk sac (or "blood forming sac") is already designed for that purpose in reptiles and birds, and it's also designed to disappear after it serves its vital function, so it makes good sense to use it for the same purpose in mammals and man — where it also testifies to One Creator behind all these life forms!
9. evolutionists; scientists; had many important functions
10. caecum; human; only plants
11. vestigial, nascent; none

Chapter 13, page 111

1. H, O, N, C, P
2. H-1, O-2, N-3, C-4, P-5; double; triple; N ≡ (or − C ≡); or equivalent: $O-H$ $H-N-H$ $O=C=O$
   with H below O and H below N
3. –OH hydroxyl; -COH alcohol; -NH2 amine; -COOH (carboxylic) acid
4. isomers; left- and right-handed (either order); iso-mers; left-; right-; death
5. polymers; monomers; polymers (chains); amino acid; polymers (chains); sugar; monomers; water; water
6. water; evaporation; Brownian; hot; death; are destroyed
7. diffusion (and osmosis also); packed to scattered; high to low; warm; smaller; ends; never ceases
8. osmosis; swell; firm; exploding

Chapter 14, page 117

1. cells; nucleus; wall
2. a-membranes, b-enzymes, c-DNA, d-membranes, E-DNA, f-ATP, g-enzymes, h-water, i-water
3. SA: Enzymes need the energy supplied by ATP to put molecules together, and ATP needs enzymes to select the molecules that get a "dose" of energy.
4. SA: DNA "tells" the cell how to make specific proteins, but it takes specific proteins to make and implement the DNA code (alphabet) for making specific proteins.
5. creative design and organization
6. Pasteur; SA: Darwin's followers simply said that spontaneous generation (chemical evolution) occurred so far back in time and/or so far out in space that scientists could never disprove it or even test the idea; i.e., they made chemical evolution an article of absolute faith beyond the reach of science.
7. God; before; by

Chapter 15, page 123

1. materialistic philosophy; good story telling; except scientific evidence
2. without any; (a), (b), (c)—See p. 119 from "Miller's Spark Chamber" to "Fox's Proteinoids and Microspheres" p. 120
3. did not; prevent
4. a-(2); b-NO; c-NO
5. a-F, b-F, c-F, d-T, e-T
6. an orderly mechanism; organization; creation; death

Chapter 16, page 131

1. nearly exactly opposite of the truth; stop
2. See p. 124 through last full paragraph on p. 125.
3. DNA (or RNA); proteins; amino acids; bases; destroy; prevent
4. three; the same; R; absolutely no; 13; absolutely 0; still absolutely 0; imposed on; plan, purpose, and special acts of creation
5. neither; are NOT; ribosomes; plan, purpose and God
6. tRNA; translases (or activating enzymes); absolutely destroying; preventing; R-group; triplet codon (or "anti-codon"); never; destroy
7. b; was created

Chapter 17, page 137

1. evolutionists; creationists
2. GGACTTCTT; pro-val-glu
3. A-T; A-U; CCUGAAGAA; CCUGUAGAA
4. does NOT; ribosomes; proteins; proteins; creationists
5. tRNA; base pairing; cannot; TRANSLASES (or activating enzymes)
6. (2); (1); (3);
7. the same; destroy; (5); (4); never touch; destroy; unlike; absolutely no; a different; at least 20; goal-oriented plan and purpose; God; creation; God's (life)
8. Creator; Sustainer

Chapter 18, page 143

1. imposed on; plan, purpose, and acts of creation — PPC; everybody; logic and observation; c (any creation except God's!)
2. a, b, c-lots of, continuously
3. a-T, b-T, c-T, d-T, e-T (in author's opinion), f-T
4. a-Lipson, b-Crick, c-Dawkins, d-Hoyle, e-Denton

Chapter 19, page 151

1. See page 146, beginning at highlighted question
2. cancer; DNA; UV; nuclease; polymerase; ligase
3. See page 147, beginning near upper right, and continue through first three paragraphs on page 148.
4. DNA; feeler; injector; DNA; before; mutations; corrupt; explode; disease
5. mind; matter
6. a-Corruption, b-Corruption, c-Creation, d-Creation, e-Catastrophe, f-Catastrophe or Corruption, g-Christ, h-Christ
7. Your favorite illustration that "What we see in God's world (science) agrees with what we read in God's Word (the Bible)."